D1879713

CONTEMPORARY EDUCATION

CONTEMPORARY EDUCATION

Editor
V.C. PANDEY

KALPAZ PUBLICATIONS

DELHI-110052

Contemporary Education
(Education)

ISBN: 978-81-7835-057-8

Price: ₹ 270

Reprinted 2014 in India by
Kalpaz Publications,
C-30, Satyawati Nagar,
Delhi-110 052
E-mail: kalpaz@hotmail.com

Printed at: G. Print Process, Delhi

Preface

The 21st century striving for the development of the highest technological and informative skills in order to convert the entire world into a global village which may fail to produce a real man along with his deep-rooted human values and emotional blending. Education must move towards the fulfilment of social needs and manpower requirements and not only towards the attainment of advanced technological skills. With the advancement of educational technologies such as computerisation, satellite communication, internet, teleconferencing and audiovisual aids there can be a shift in setting the preferential goals of education.

The current systems of education was originally meant for white-collar jobs and perceptible and impressive. Unless education is made relevant to the life, needs and aspirations, it cannot be effective and successful. A large percentage of the present students in schools and colleges are first generation learners. In order to make education attractive and meaningful to them, new methods, materials and media are to be utilised. The composition of the intelligentsia must also change and now it should consist of competent persons, both men and women drawn from all strata of the society. The educated people must also represent from all vocations and disciplines like technical, scientific, skilled, artistic and so on.

Educational reform must be radical and continuous, from our inner concepts outwards through our institutions and practices—not just for reasons of social amelioration and so forth, though these are integral to our continuing civilisation, but also for reasons of technological necessity.

In the field of information technologies and computer networking, adequate policy and action plan are to be made; the preferential position given to education in planning along with the raised level of motivation and dedication will be needed. Until and unless the parents, administrators, politicians, reformers, planners and the educationists become fully involved in the development of education ranging from primary level to higher level, simple discussion over the challenges of higher education will not be of any use and would serve no purpose.

The contemporary situation of educational developments is well-portrayed in the present book. Students, scholars and teachers besides academicians, administrators and policy-planners will be benefited immensely by the contents of this work.

Editor

Contents

1

Introduction

The most distinctive feature of a modern society, in contrast with a traditional one, is its adoption of a modernisation. In all fields production has increased spectacularly with the utilisation of all modern means, materials and methods. This applied technology has also many other significant effects on and implications for social and cultural life and it involves fundamental, social and cultural changes which are broadly described as modernisation.

In a traditional society the quantum of knowledge is very limited gradually increases so that one of the main aims of education i.e., preservation and maintenance of existing culture, is achieved. But in a modern society, the quantum of knowledge is too vast and the rate of its growth is too fast. One of the important tasks of education is to keep pace with this progress of knowledge and teach the student to acquire such knowledge how rather than what. So process is found more important than product and critical as well as creative powers are encouraged.

In a modern society change is so rapid that the educational system has to keep itself abreast with the latest developments. Therefore, it is imperative to adopt a dynamic policy and infrastructure of education which can continually renovate itself. Otherwise, it will not only hamper progress, but also tend to create a lag between national aspirations and realities. So education is to be a dynamic process, not only for imparting knowledge as a finished material but also to generate interests and curiosity, inculcate attitudes and values and teach essential skills for independent study and judgment.

Any change in the society upsets various factors and thereby brings about many difficulties and problems. The old equilibrium gives way to a new one. Thus to change the society for setting up a new social order means in its trail a large number of problems—social, economic, cultural and political which demand immediate solution. Half-hearted solutions of faltering steps to solve these problems cannot bring about improvement, rather setback and harmful effects. That is why, a new equilibrium is to be set up with full knowledge and implications of globalisation. For this, political leadership is significant but education has to play an important role and technological preparedness is also necessary.

Education works as the potential instrument of globalisation. The progress of globalisation concept is closely related to the pace of educational development. The spread of education, the preparation of educated and skilled citizens and training of intelligents' promote modernisation. The Indian society is the succession of a hoary heritage and inherits a rich culture. But unless it becomes alerty education, industrious, it cannot be modernised. In order to meet the challenges of national and international needs and conditions, education has to be geared and engineered accordingly.

The current systems of education was originally meant for white-collar jobs and perceptible and impressive. Above fifty per cent of people belong to Scheduled Castes and Scheduled Tribes and about seventy per cent of people are below the poverty line. Unless education is made relevant to the life, needs and aspirations, it cannot be effective and successful. A large percentage of the present students in schools and colleges are first generation learners. In order to make education attractive and meaningful to them, new methods, materials and media are to be utilised. The composition of the intelligentsia must also change and now it should consist of competent persons, both men and women drawn from all strata of the society. The educated people must also represent from all vocations and disciplines like technical, scientific, skilled, artistic and so on.

Modernised society must develop with the contributions from all concerned, particularly must also be of high standard. So, for maintaining adequate standard of education, research and science, a good number of major universities and centres of advanced learning should be developed in our country. Modernisation does not mean complete isolation or segregation from the past traditions. It must be built on the past reflecting the needs of the present and vision of the future social order. India's prosperity and modernisation must be based on the moral and spiritual values enshrined in its culture.

Modernisation, if it is to be a living force, must derive its strength from the spirit. Modernisation aims, amongst other things at creating an economy of plenty which will offer, to every individual, a large of life and a wider variety of choices". Freedom of choices is very advantageous, but it depends on one's value system and motivation. The social, moral and spiritual values will greatly influence one's decisions for common good for selfish ends. Expansion of knowledge must be strengthened with these values.

Weakening of moral and spiritual values in the modern youths is creating many serious social problems and ethical as well as psychological conflicts. Therefore social workers and thinkers have suggested that knowledge and skills contributed by science and technology should be supplemented by values and insights associated with ethics and religion at its best. Inter-human and so on, should influence many of our decisions and choices. In short, value-judgment should orient our educational system. Right values are to be inculcated in the students at all stages of education. For inculcation of values through education, we should draw freely from the confidently upon our own heritage as well as the traditions of other countries and the world culture as a whole.

In India the entire educational machinery has to be geared to the solution of various problems. Now it has to operate on two fronts (i) children and (ii) adults. Although the constitutional Directive for providing compulsory primary education to all children in the age-group 6-14 years had not yet been realised, all attempts are being made to achieve this end during the 6th Five-Year Plan. Since India is known as the land of youths, it has rightly been observed that her "destiny is being shaped in her classrooms". That is why, universalisation of education within the shortest possible time is of utmost importance for effective modernisation.

Adult or nonformal education is of crucial importance. Adults are directly involved in the national reconstruction and developmental works. The urgent need of educating the adults without waiting for school children to complete their education and participate in the developmental activities of the country has been laid stress by various international as well as national education authorities and experts.

Need of reforms in educational context

Today's educational context—especially since the multiple crises of the early 1970—surrounds and pervades the perceptions of every teacher, student, and researcher. For the comparative educator this altered context not merely means that there is a wider span of countries, systems and populations engaged in formal education and indeed its evolution or reform to be studied but it has also introduced a quite different horizon of concerns and a reordering of priorities within any study. The experience and insights of far more people on far more occasions over a whole life-span are now recognised as the proper test-bed of theories and experiments once expounded with priestly assurance.

Comparative studies of education naturally share and are affected by the circumstances which constrain and condition us all materially—not just in resources or in the data before us but more in our appreciation of what can, and must be done because comparative studies are studies of education, concerned with ameliorative activity. Whereas the study of philosophy of even of animal species and communities still keeps us "outside" the object of our research even when our study requires some empathy with the behaviour we investigate, an effective study of education does not allow us the luxury of distant detachment.

Of course we try to obtain objective data, to categorise them "scientifically" and to process or compute them in a way that makes them universally relevant or at least intelligible; but there are two special pitfalls for the student of education which do not beset students in other areas of inquiry. The first is that involvement of the observer in the process of observation has been preconditioned by his own idiomatic upbringing and educational expectations—

quite apart from his academic preoccupations. The second is that everyone's expectations of education have undergone a marked change over the past two or three decades.

Most of us really need better management in our professional services; but until the end of the 1960s or even into the early 1970s it was not realised that management in education was special to education, or that management was not enough. It is no use "transmitting" culture or "delivering the goods" if they are left on the doorstep.

At least as early as the Berkeley remonstrances of 1964, the "flower power" phenomenon and other symptoms of rejection made it clear in highly schooled countries like Sweden and Denmark, with their respective problems of truancy and free school(s), that educational endeavour fails unless the learner accepts and identifies himself with what is offered - and, indeed, takes it further in his own idiom.

During the past decade that same message has come back to us repeatedly from Third World countries. We are just beginning, too, to recognise its full relevance to the case of our own "lower orders", to most young adults, and to the unemployed. So the early post-1945 comparative studies of structural reforms with their "juxtapositions" and tabulations and confident predictions that this or that "model" would prevail in retrospect look like preliminary classifications before an effective study could take place of what really went on both within and without school systems. "Competency" training of teachers and "efficient" training of heads and administrators were both, no doubt, pre-requisities to something; but to what? Obviously, to the effective self-education of the student, particularly in the later secondary stages and in life afterwards.

During international researches and many discussions in the early 1970s it was difficult to secure appreciation of what "effective" education meant - at least among teachers and administrators. In several languages there is no separate word for "effective", to distinguish it from the notion of "efficiency"; and in international statistics the word "effective" was used simply to denote a body enrolled in a classroom nothing to do with a mind engaged and a real-life commitment afterwards. But students themselves knew only too well what "effective" education meant for them; and the majority of the age-group not enrolled, or "failing" within or dropping out of the system, knew even more acutely what was "effective" in formal education and what was not. Hence it was deeply important to investigate not what was supposed to go on, or what providers intended to lay before the populace, but what actually was perceived as going on at the receiving end.

Several international investigations of "the view from inside" began in the early 1960s, including the 3-year, 5-nation, study of Post-Compulsory Education undertaken by the Comparative Research Unit at King's College in the University of London. In most instances it was the very first time that teachers - let alone students - had ever been asked for their opinion and insights. Though the LEA investigation of Achievement in Mathematics, directed and edited by Torsten Husen, in many ways blazed a trail for empirical research in comparative studies, it was marred in so far as it emphasised the aspects of manipulation and control by providers. So were many of the ideas then current in OECD and the International Institute for Educational Planning. Elsewhere, "computable models" of school systems were proposed.

The big turnabout followed consumer reaction, which was sometimes disastrous for education in the short term as parents and electors took issue with providers, although in the long run comparative studies of students' reactions may help us to a far truer understanding of education's need and feasibilities today. In Sweden, France, and many other countries with centralised administrations, there was no nonsense about "partnership" in determining educational policy and content. In Britain the tradition to "partnership" was exemplified in the sharing of provision, expense, and day-to-day responsibility for ultimate satisfactoriness. But until 1977 and the Taylor Report there was little official recognition that the "partnership" included parents, though of course some local authorities did so. The notion that school students might also share in school government had an even tougher passage, despite the fact that at 18 they can help to elect the country's government, or, if employed, participate in works' councils' affairs from the age of 16.

The "partnership" envisaged was therefore one of managing the provision, as though from on high, or externally. The related word "participation" is also worth examination. In many publications from OECD, the Council of Europe, and other international agencies, the word was used as a synonym for "enrolment". The only sharing considered was that of taking up whatever was set out by others, at least in education. That seems odd, especially when participation in a game or similar activity implies interlocking and relevant activities, perhaps even teamwork. That notion of really countries for something within the entire system was certainly taken up by countless American school boards during the 1970s.

The United States system of administration has long devolved responsibility for most educational decisions, including costs, on to such local boards, where parents may be the boards' direct electors. But the "grass rots" rebellion against superintendents, management and teachers' practices during the 1970s introduced demands for "accountability", cuts in school taxes, and some growing preference for private high schools—especially as a result of nationwide comparisons with other districts or other states of the Union.

International comparisons by Husen et. al. in the LEA surveys had prepared the ground but had not directly occasioned such parental distress or legislative onslaught on the entire state system. All of these and related phenomena exemplify a public demand for real participation in the process of education which is beginning to be worldwide.

At the present stage of international comparative study, it is vital to recognise the experiential dimension in our investigations and teaching. It means that the element of profiting from experience not only in order to understand better, but also in order to teach theorists and paper reformers what actually goes on when educational reforms are embarked upon. It is not simply that the world as a whole has moved on in its general experience, though that is tellingly true, but it is even more important to recognise that education in particular has moved on and to acknowledge two things:

(a) education essentially is a matter of organising experience into a personal system;

(b) this occurs within an idiomatic but evolving "educational system" —part of a wider cultural pattern, and within a larger social/economic/ technological system which "makes sense" according to the perceptions of that place, population, or occasion.

It is our business as comparative students of education to know the realities of characteristic systems and subsystems of education, to feel within the occasions and crises of judgement as experienced by the protagonists, and of course to adduce from one situation to another what may be helpful parallels or interpretations. In short, we must "teach" in the sense of offering aids to judgement, to more effective participation, and to reform. Thus our function is distinct from, though complementary to, that of students of politics whose concern is to show and classify examples of the interplay of power, or of sociologists demonstrating that in all societies there are particular groups and pressures. Pressure groups may use or frustrate education in order to exercise power or to re-order society; but the human beings involved in the process can accept or reject these manipulations in ways which we should know from an educational angle.

Educational systems formally set up, or the more diffuse folk-ways and local or topical "inside view", positively teach their populations to react in particular ways. These are part of our stock-in-trade, as foreign languages and comparative linguistic studies are the stock-in-trade of the comparative philologist. We know them with some precision; we teach about them; we know characteristic situations and present trends. Some generalisations are permissible—as hypotheses only, to be substantiated or refuted with reference to precise situations. Not for us the "ideal types" of the sociologist. People do not react that way, even in the mass—and least of all in the inevitably intimate encounter which education constitutes by its very nature. It has been said with some truth that any given curriculum is 100 different curricula for 100 different people. So much for what we might call "lateral" comparisons within a tiny bit of a system. Still more, continually over time and in a series of evolving contexts, we all re-engage ourselves and whatever we have learned.

To some extent that evolution is personal; in other respects it depends on our group contacts, each one of which obviously form part of a great complex of connections and communications. The point of repeating this truism is that many standard studies of education pay far too little attention to the dimensions:

(a) the general ecological dynamics surrounding "the process" at any time or place; and

(b) the long-term completion or frustration of the formal educational process. Perhaps more telling in the long run is the study of what that formal process omits, or fails to take account of in the formative context surrounding it.

The feeding into our study of fresh perceptions, unanswered questions, perhaps even questions unasked hitherto, presents a potent challenge to comparative specialists. In this matter as well as in more traditional ways we can make reform attempts more realistic. Nor should it be supposed simplistically that the reactions and questions just referred to occur with spontaneous clarity to individuals and groups, or that because of our common humanity there are universal responses and needs in education at any one time.

Thoughts and preferences in education clothe our minds idiomatically like language. Language is learned and taught unconsciously and consciously by parents, peer groups, and day-to-day communications, long before formal instruction in a language takes place. In that sense, educational expectation and preference are taught too. It is very hard to un-think ourselves from our schooling, and still more to dissociate educational essentials from the apparatus, traditions, and intentions of the schooling industry.

That technological metamorphosis of our time is of urgent concern to comparative students of education, and above all to those endeavouring to assist reform. The interface between national systems and internationally comparative considerations is more contentious than it has ever been. Moreover, the shifts in technological and educational emphasis between the era of heavy industrialisation and its associated commerce on the one hand and the microprocessor world of communications on the other are full of profound challenges for comparative study, both of educational responses as it actually happens and of projections for the future.

Projections and planning in considerable detail are now part of the data before us. Altered expectations of young adults—in school or college, in "the transition from school to work", in unemployment, and in returning to education and/or training—open up vistas of comparative investigation without previous example. Furthermore, associated changes have brought about huge migrations of underprivileged workers into hitherto well-settled systems, with resulting problems of multicultural education —even for previously self-satisfied monocultures—and numerous internal problems of urban decay, flight to the suburbs, and so forth. Hardly any of these problems were recognised as even contingent fields of comparative study a generation ago, when the foundation studies of our discipline were established.

Our comparative commitment must therefore be not simply lateral in some contemporary sense, but developmental and prospective too. Since, as teachers no less than as scholars, we care so much for effective education, we must now pay far more attention to the receiving end—indeed, we must think of it not as a "receiving end" but as a situation where education begins. That is particularly so when we examine in the industrialised countries all those frontier situations where a new educational style is demanded.

These manifestly include: the huge and varied increase in the enrolled over-16s in many countries, latterly accentuated by unemployment; the intermittent experience of paid employment and unemployment which now characterises the entire 16-25 population in the OECD countries of Western Europe generally, and in urban centres around the world in particular; the need to "catch up" with education and/or training at this level, though not at the usual age; and the case of new demand from hitherto neglected social categories such as migrants, girls, country people, and the old.

In Third World countries educational needs are now expressed in terms alien to those familiar in the formal education industry of the industrialised "West" and North. No longer is it sufficient to think in terms of "feedback" from these frontier regions of education. Our study must now be based upon the "view from inside", shared even for academic purposes with the local participants, and shared still more if we are to help in educational development and reform.

There are important ways in which all systems of schooling have become frontier areas in industrialised countries too. Reform must be radical and continuous, from our inner concepts outwards through our institutions and practices - not just for reasons of social amelioration and so forth, though these are integral to our continuing civilisation, but also for reasons of technological necessity. School systems as we know them are largely by-products of industrialisation. Following systematisation by Horace Mann and others in the United States, with mass availability of high schools and higher education in due course, the expansion of most forms of education throughout the industrialised world has been based on assumptions of assimilating people into the cultural and occupational mainstream of the host society, according to the ability and readiness of those being assimilated as well as in processing people as described earlier.

The big reorientation is necessitated by the "third technological/educational phase". Others, like Daniel Bell, have spoken of a "post-industrial" or a "communications" society. Whatever the name, today's society and industries call for a much wider range of aptitudes and qualities, varied fields of interest and knowledge, differently developed and constantly re-adapted skills. In place of much compliant convergence, adaptive divergence and judgement are continually needed.

Furthermore, this continuum of re-learning and recreating is spread over a lifetime. This idiom or phase of education recognises the provisional or conditional status of the present state of knowledge or understanding. Obviously, too, microprocessors and computer-assisted diffusion and analysis of knowledge, almost incalculably accelerated in little more than a decade, both demand and facilitate the participation and relevance of many people and activities not so far considered as partners in the educational process. The crumbling of industrial/occupational structures since the early 1970s, combined with the redistribution of much of the world's industry to new locations, had brought unemployment and job-changes into near-normal expectation in all the heavily industrialised countries of the Western World. At the same time, the "communications society" has thrust new concepts of learning relationships and feasibilities right down into the primary school stage—with, of course, a perspective of electronically supported learning and relearning throughout life.

More than any change since formal education became a major state commitment, this challenge demands complete rethinking of educational aims and practice. For comparative studies of education this metamorphosis challenges our supply of data, our analysis of aims, and our skills in reassessing all learning relationships—not just once for all time, but in a commitment of unforeseeable duration and complexity. By the same token, it puts our studies at the very centre of any reform plans. All effective education now must be a preparation for uncertainty, for responsible participation rather than indifferentism.

Educational development and planning too must take the same stance, in preparation for varied and flexible response to ever-changing "crises". "Predictions", "laws" and expectations of convergent assimilation have no place in our study—if they ever had. We need careful study of what is, what is moving by way of response and experiment, what is planned for, and how the implementation proceeds in the world's national and cultural workshops. The microprocessor revolution and the advent of a "communications society" mean that the world shares technological apparatus and opportunities as never before; but by the same token a plurality of responses is as evident as the plurality of fashions on our streets, indeed more so because cultural individuality is not only prized but persistently taught and identified with.

2

Educational Technologies in Digital Age

The impact of technology on society may be useful as a lever to bring about substantial change of university teaching and learning. The problems caused by the use of new technologies, come up again and again. These are mainly problems of automation and of introducing information networks. Besides the effects of rationalization we often observe negative consequences like problems caused by working with screens, the constraint of adaptation of human work to computer conditions, and the increasing possibilities of control of workers.

Audi-visual technologies

Role of radio and audiocasttets

Education authorities have set up an audio-visual unit in one of their local teachers' centres. Radio, and increasingly television programmes, are recorded off-air by a full-time technician in each centre. Schools are sent a catalogue of programmes from which they request the programmes that they need. The service is relatively cheap to run and there is virtually no failure rate in recording, with all programmes available to all schools. Indeed, there is no real need to broadcast radio at all, since all programmes could be mailed on tape at very low cost to the local centres.

Indeed, there is no real need to broadcast radio at all, since all programmes could be mailed on tape at very low cost to the local centres. Cassettes can be used for a variety of educational purposes for which radio is less suitable or convenient: practice leading to mastery of a technique; commenting on diagrams, charts, tables or text; talking students through a home experiment; backing up or commenting on the television programmes; recordings of conversa-tions, interviews, language use and discussions, which can be replayed several times for the purpose of analysis; and many other uses. Durbridge has designed an audio-cassette package which demonstrates various ways in which audio-cassettes can be used in a home-learning situation.

Audio-cassettes can easily integrate them with the texts as they design their courses. They can take a recorder home and rough out ideas as they develop the text, whereas with a radio programme, with its continuous and uninterrupted flow, it is impossible to develop such close integration between sound and print. The final cassette tape still benefits from being 'produced' to ensure good sound quality and to avoid mistakes or ambiguity in the script, but academics generally feel that they have much more control over the cassette script than with radio.

Role of video-cassette players

As with audio recorders, a video-cassette player in a school gives more flexibility to the teachers in their use of broadcast materials. However, there are far fewer video-cassette machines in schools, although the numbers are rapidly increasing. While the proportion of primary schools with video-cassette machines in Britain doubled from 1980 to 1981, this brought the number up to only 25 per cent, and few schools had more than one, which meant that they could not play back and record at the same time. Nearly every secondary school had a video recorder in 1981, but the average number per school was only two, not really enough to give the ease of access and flexibility required in secondary schools. Hayter concluded that an increase in video recording and playback equipment would do more than anything to increase the effectiveness of schools television.

It is significant that the increase in equipment over the last five years has been paralleled by an increase in the overall use of television, particularly in secondary schools. Nevertheless, there is still not enough equipment yet in schools to justify the transfer of schools television to night-time transission although, technically, it is easier to record television than radio off-air because of the in-built clock on most video-cassette machines. The Inner London Education Authority used to distribute its own programmes, and those of the broadcasting organisations, via a cable system at all the schools in its areas. Because of the high cost of renting the lines from the Post Office it closed down its cable service in 1979, since when it has distributed its programmes on video-cassettes.

By 1981 over 75 per cent of the primary schools in the ILEA area had bought video-cassette machines, largely due to a deal worked out between ILEA and a commercial rental company which gave the schools large discount prices. Nothing is more volatile at the time of writing than the expansion of home ownership of video-cassette machines. At the end of 1983, nearly 30% of all households in Britain had video-cassette machines in their homes, and sales are roughly doubling each year. Furthermore, according to the BBC Audience Research Department figures video-cassette machines are just as likely to be found in lower income as in more wealthy households. The rate of growth of video-cassette access is greater in Britain than in any other country. By 1986 it is expected that half the homes in Britain will have a video-cassette machine. This rapid growth is due to several reasons.

Machines can be rented for as little as 10 per month, and there are many High Street shops and back-street dealers from which video-cassette programmes, including feature films, can be hired at little cost. Because many of the broadcast programmes are still of high quality, it is also worth while recording these at home, especially since the range of choice at any one time is limited to four channels in the current absence of a widespread cable TV system. While video-cassette programmes require different production formats from broadcasts, the design features of audio-cassettes will not always be appropriate for video production. The production requirements of a video programme are much more demanding technically and in terms of manpower. This means that recording of material, and its editing, is separate from the preparation of the texts to which it relates, and makes it more difficult at the design stage to develop the very close integration between text and programme that is possible with audio-cassettes, although careful advance planning and editing of both programme and text can go some way towards this.

Nor can students so easily integrated video programmes and text simultaneously, because they cannot watch video and read the text at the same time. Taking notes during a video sequence is much more difficult than during an audio sequence and tends to lead to concentration on detail rather than on principles or general points. In practice, this means that video sequences will tend to run for longer without interruption, with interrogation of the material taking place segments, with some replay to assist. Particularly where students are having to share equipment-either a machine at a study centre, with other students waiting to use it, or at home, with the television set wanted by the rest of the family—it will be more difficult for students to spend a great deal of time working repeatedly through the cassette. This is less of a problem with audio-cassettes.

In the next few years there will be scope for a great deal of experiment and innovation to identify suitable video-cassette formats for education. Television is particularly rich in the quantity and variety of information it conveys. It uses a wide variety of symbol systems-sounds, pictures, colour, movement. Television is also highly ambiguous in the way it conveys meaning. This results from the techniques used in production-camera angles and movement, editing procedures, manipulation of structure-and from the richness of the information television conveys. Because of its ambiguity, television material lends itself to a wide variety of interpretations from each individual viewer, many different interpretations being equally valid. This means that each viewer will abstract different meanings from the same programme.

Television should therefore be valuable for developing creative or 'open-ended' thinking because it forces learners to impose their own construction of meaning from the programme material. If such a hypothesis is correct, it makes it all the more important that learners have the opportunity to explore television material more fully than is possible with a single, unbroken transmission. Broadcasts thus appear to be much weaker instructionally than cassettes in terms of integration with other material, ease of recall, mastery learning, deep thinking and possibly creative thinking. By their very nature, broadcasts tend towards stimulating more superficial levels of response compared with cassettes or books.

Cassettes could free educators from the dominance that broadcasters have exerted over the design and distribution of educational audio-visual materials. Until recently, distributing audio-visual material widely through formats other than broadcasting has been unrealistic because of the high costs of distribution on alternative formats, such as film or open-reel vide tape, and because of the lack of playback equipment in schools or homes. On the other hand, the distribution of broadcasts has been largely seen as a 'free' service from the user's point of view. The increasing accessibility of video-cassettes, are changing that situation. With broadcasting, the broadcasting organisations set the priorities, select content, determine style and decide production and technical standards for what they broadcast.

It is now realistic for other agencies-universities, colleges, local authorities, voluntary organisations, even schools-to commission, reduce and distribute effective video material for the specialized audiences that broadcasters have been unable to serve adequately in the past. Costs will depend very much on what kind of programme is required and on whether full or marginal costs are charged. There is, however, a good deal of spare production capacity, particularly in the public education sector, so marginal costing is often realistic. Highly effective, professionally-make half-hour educational vide-cassettes can be produced for between £8,000 and £20,000, depending on the nature of the material.

Implications of lower production costs and relatively low-cost non-broadcast distribution are far-reaching. Because wide distribution costs are related to the number of assets to be distributed, video programmes for very small minority audiences become a real economic possibility, provided that there is a framework through which they can be marketed. Secondly, educators can make programmes in the style, pace and format which they believe to the important. There are obvious dangers that the full potential of television will not be developed. by people who are not professional broadcasters. On the other hand, there are many able and trained production staff outside broadcasting organisations willing to work to a clear educational brief. Also, those who regularly deal with specialist groups are likely to be better judges of their needs than professional broadcasters.

There will still probably be a shortage of educators with the talent to exploit the advantages of television on cassette, but the technology does open up the market to those who want to try. Broadcasters still have two strong advantages: their programmes are available to schools and the general public at no extra direct cost; and they have a wealth of resources, experience and a powerful reputation behind them. Non-broadcast video is likely to serve rather different needs from those of broadcasters. Nevertheless, there will be areas of overlap, and where the broadcasters do not meet the needs of their target groups, they are likely to lose audiences to enterprising video producers. A number of agencies are now gearing themselves up for production and distribution of non-broadcast educational video.

The commercial television companies will move into producing their own non-broadcast educational video material, but the BBC might, through BBC

Enterprises. More likely is that educational broadcasting will be moved to night-time transmission for off-air recording, or be abolished completely, to free the air-waves for extended morning television in order to compete with cable and satellite competition. If the broadcasting organisations do start extensively producing non-broadcast material for education, it will raise some interesting legal and financial issues.

Video-discs

There are different manufacturers' formats for video-discs and a variety of models within each format but, nevertheless, the principle of video-disc technology is relatively simple to grasp. The more advanced systems using laser technology allow up to 54,000 single still-frames, with full colour, to be stored on side of a disc. Each frame can be individually identified and accessed almost instantaneously. The rate at which these frames can be played can be varied across a wide range of speeds, from stepping through single frames, through slow motion, up to normal or even fast speeds. Two high-quality independent sound tracks capable of synchronisation with the pictures when played at normal motion speed are also available.

These features allow a combination of moving and still pictures to be played linked to stereo or two independent sound-tracks. The systems allow for slow-motion, frame-by-frame presentation, fast motion, fast or slow forward or reverse search, or still-frame presentation, with no picture jitter at all on still-frame, each feature under the direct control of the viewer. More significantly, full computer control over the video-disc player is possible, either using an 'in-board' computer or an 'out-board' microcomputer linked to the video-disc player through an 'interface', i.e. a processor or computer programme that allows the microcomputer electronic assess to the video-disc player's controls. With the right interface, it is possible to link up low-cost domestic video-disc players with low-cost micro-computers, and to combine graphics or keyboard symbols from the computer with sound and pictures from the vide-disc, on the same television set, with pictures from both sources either overlaid, or presented in sequence.

Because the laser-based systems use light to read the disc, there is no mechanical contact. Therefore disc life and quality are not likely to be affected by constant use. Picture and sound quality, even on the cheaper players, is better than on video-cassette machines, although as yet commercial vide-disc machines cannot record, only play back. The low-cost and simpler domestic models retail at around £400, with the more advanced commercial machines costing £1,200.

Video-discs certainly provide more sophisticated and better quality video and audio facilities than video-cassettes, but it would be a mistake to think of video-disc systems as merely a more advanced form of video-cassettes in terms of educational functions. We shall see that video-disc technology is a distinct teaching medium in its own right, with a unique potential for education, and its own unique requirements for design and production.

Because access, control of speed and search facilities are more refined on video-disc machines, they allow learners even grater control over video materials. Furthermore, by linking video-discs to microcomputers, learners can interact with the video-disc and the computer. This means that the computer can provide feedback to learners on what they have learned from the disc and can guide learners through appropriate 'routes', so that the learning experience is more individualized and suited to each learner's needs.

Video-cassettes can also be linked to computers in this way, but less efficiently than video-discs. Video-cassettes do not have individual frames like video-discs, so on all but the highest-cost machines, it is difficult to get completely still pictures. While it is possible to lay electronic pulses as markers along a videocassette tape, thus enabling each point on the tape to be identified and accessed, this cannot be done so accurately and cleanly as with a video-disc. It also takes time for video-cassettes to wind backwards and forwards to the point to be accessed, whereas video-disc access is virtually instantaneous.

Nevertheless, a microcomputer linked to a video-cassette machine can do many of the things that a video-disc can do, if less elegantly. At the time of writing, very few educational video-discs have been made, so the educational potential of interactive video is still to be explored. The reason for the interest is that interactive video combines two well-established learning media, video and computer-assisted learning, in the hope that it will bring together the advantages and overcome the deficiencies of both. So far, three rather different ways of using video-discs in education seem to be emerging. The first is to use video-discs to provide a superior form of control and access. Thus a 'normal' television programme can be made available on disc format, with perhaps a second sound-track added. The learner can then use the still-frame, slow motion on fast search facilities as required. A refinement would be the provision of an index at the start of the disc so that the learner can go immediately to the section of most interest. Such discs can be useful for showing model procedures, such as the correct positions or movements for gymnasts or golfers and the correct procedure for striping down a car engine, or for showing animals operating in their natural habitat.

The BBC has produced a video-disc of this kind on British garden birds, with linked bird song on one track, and a commentary by David Attenborough on the other. No computer control is needed for this kind of programme but it is possible for those who purchase such a disc to add their own computer control relatively easily. In this way, tests, feedback and suitable routing through the disc dependent on test responses, can all be added through a linked computer. Alternatively, vide-disc and computer control can be designed together as the video-disc is being planned. The resulting package can be extremely complex, both to design and to work through as a student. Student responses via the computer need not be limited to selecting from an array of multiple-choice answers, but can involve feeding in data, or more complex problem solving. Very sophisticated programmes are possible in this form.

For instance, a video disc made at the University of Nerbraska provided training on instrument reading for flying light aircraft. After a short period of instruction, the learner is given a set of instrument readings, then has to make decisions about operation of the plane's controls in order to bring the plane in to land. Dependent on the action chosen, the disc shows the position of the plane relative to the earth. This is done by the computer processing the student's answer and selecting the appropriate part of the disc for such an action. Learners can in this way be provided with very realistic simulation exercises with the consequences of their decisions becoming painfully clear.

The computer programme that accompanies such a disc can either be physically separate, on cassette or on a computer disc, or it could be contained on the video-disc itself and 'dumped' from there into the computer when played. Computer programmes stored on vide-discs, though, can be used only on the type of computer for which the programme was designed. The first commercial interactive educational video-disc, on teaching physics, was made at the University of Nebraska and marketed in 1982 by John Wiley. There is a third way of using video-discs which is just beginning to be explored in an educational context.

Video-discs can provide an efficient and substantial data-base, with information stored in a variety of ways: as computer data, still-colour pictures, moving pictures, or text. Video-discs could therefore be used as a resource base, which the learner searches or used for a particular purpose. For instance, in training historians, or archaeologists, a whole set of materials could be archived on disc-pictures of archaeological sites and are facts, historical documents, short, dramatised extracts from historical events, archive film and so on.

Students could be asked to work through this material, drawing conclusions and testing hypotheses, with students to some extent imposing their own structure on the organisation of the data. A teacher could use the video-disc material to show a sequence of pictures as desired to students. The first such 'archival' video-disc commercially marketed featured the satellite photographs of Jupiter and Saturn. These are merely glimpses of the potential for education of video-discs. But what are their implications for educational broadcasting?

Although the cost of making the master for discs from the final edited tape is not expensive given the cost of production, video-disc production seems to require broadcast which, unlike video-cassette production are likely to be found mainly in production centres concerned with broadcasting. Secondly, to exploit the advantages of video-disc, programme production costs are likely to be towards the more expensive end of the scale. Broadcasting organisations thus are well placed to exploit video-disc technology, at least technically. The design requirements of interactive video-discs and their implications for broadcasting organisations, through, are critical. Where programmes are to be designed from the outset to be used in an integrated way with computer control, difficulties are likely to arise.

The structure of the video-disc, the choice of responses required from learners, the extent to which learners will be free to choose their own paths, through the material, what paths are permissible or desirable, the number of difficulty levels to be built into the disc, the balance between computer and video graphics, and the design of the computer programme, all have major educational implications and go far beyond the normal brief of an educational television producer. It would be a fundamental mistake to the normal television production is merely a mild extension of the normal television production process, with the computer programming contracted out as an afterthought almost.

This kind of disc requires a team approach, involving teacher, television producer, computer programmer and instructional designer/evaluator, working as equals from conception to final credits. This inevitably slows up the production process, limits the producer's freedom and increases the cost of production. It will be interesting to see whether broadcasters will be willing to enter into this more complex from of video-disc design and, if so, under what conditions; or whether they will prefer to stick to the safer form of video-disc design, where the disc can stand alone without being tied to pre-determined computer control.

Video-discs have only just come on the market and their commercial viability as a consumer product has yet to be proved. There are at the time of writing few commercial discs available for sale in Britain and it is not yet possible to record off-air on the disc. Video-cassettes are in the process of becoming well-established, at least in Britain, as a consumer product in direct competition with discs. It may be many years before home wonder ship of video-discs is a more realistic possibility.

The cost of a video-disc machine is not out of the question, but given the slow growth of video-cassette machines with far greater amounts of suitable programme material, we do not see schools rushing to get disc technology. Even more of a problem will be the cost of discs if they have to cover their full production costs. It is difficult to imagine a well-designed interactive video-disc costing less than £25,000 to produce. To retail at £10 a disc, at least 3,000 discs would need to be sold to recoup costs, and this is a high target for the school market given that there are less than, 6.000 secondary schools in Britain. It is likely therefore that video-discs will have a more specialised and restricted use than video-discs will have a more specialise and restricted use than video-cassettes, at leas over the next ten years, but where they are used and well designed they could prove to be extremely valuable.

Cable and satellites

Cable and satellite could have major implications for education, but given the slowness with which they are likely to develop in the United Kingdom. There are four basic characteristics of cable television that are significant for education: the ability to provide a large number of channels-from thirty to a hundred, dependent on the technology thereby theoretically increasing choice of service; the possibility of two-way communications through the cable system; the possibility of local programming; and the ability to 'filter' or 'select' viewers electronically. Satellite television can provide national coverage but, due to international regulations, Britain is limited to only five channels.

The following potential advantages of cable for education: better transmission times, more time available for educational television: channels dedicated solely to educational use; access to more potential students; more specifically targeted programming; increased interaction and student participations; more choice of educational programming; easier access to television for teachers; more scope for experiment; multiple sound-tracks or radio channels. These are all possible, but whether they are likely depends very much on political and financial decisions yet to be finalised. At the time of writing, though, it seems most unlikely that these benefits will be realised in Britain, and, in fact, cable developments are more likely to have negative educational effects.

For instance, even the most optimistic forecasts predict that less than 50 per cent of the United Kingdom population will be on the cable by the end of the century. Given the current unbridled commercial basis on which cable is to expand, the first and most profitable areas to be cabled up will be the outer suburban areas and commercial centres of large cities. Rural communities and the poorer inner city areas are less likely to be cabled up quickly, yet this is where the educational need and lack of provision is the greatest. Currently it seems that there will be no statutory obligation for British cable operators to carry educational or community programmes, unlike practically every other major developed country with cable systems. Nor are there plans yet to ensure the establishment of a nationally linked cable network.

Current proposals are based on the establishment of independent local systems. This does not guarantee local programming, though. At least one commentator, John Howkins, of the International Institute of Communications, predicts that London-based communications companies will make up 'packages' of programming which will then be sold to local stations.

The major attractions of cable for education frequently claimed by politicians is its potential for two-way communication, allowing the viewer to interact, respond or participate in the viewing event. This is the sort of claim that needs to be taken with a good pinch of salt. There are major financial and technical obstinacies that limit the likelihood of cable being a truly two-way communication system for some time. There are two types of cable that can be laid. Co-axial cable is the basis of virtually all current systems but, for practical purposes, co-axial systems tend to be limited to a maximum of thirty to forty channels in one direction. Co-axial cable is not really suitable as a two-way communication system. Fibre-optic cable has much greater capacity and is a realistic proposition for two-way communication.

Two-way communication will depend crucially on the configuration or design of the cable system. Co-axial cable uses a 'trunk and branch' system, i.e. a central 'trunk' cable running down a street with 'branch' off to each house. The street cable itself is probably a branch of a more central trunk running through the town. Even with fibre-optic cable laid in a trunk and branch configuration, 'backward' communication from the home could only follow the same route as the downward signal, i.e. back to the 'head-end', the local station.

It would not be possible to communicate across branches. i.e. with neighbours in the street, or the local college on the other side of town, unless this communication was relayed from the head-end. If all communications have to go thorough the head-end, this obviously limits the amount of communications that can be handled, even with a hundred channels. The alternative, only possible with fibre-optic cable, is a configuration similar to that of the public service telephone system. This has been named a 'star' system since each house would be linked directly to a central switchboard, which in turn would also be linked up with other switchboards. This would allow any one point to communicate directly with any of the others, as with the current telephone system but using much wider band-widths, including even television transmission 'outwards' as well as inwards. Fibre-optic cable would be essential for such a system.

A national grid or satellite-linked system would also be necessary for cross-connections between different cable also be necessary for cross-connections between different cable systems. Unfortunately, because of the amount of switching gear required, a 'star' system would be much more expensive to introduce. For these reasons, interaction is most likely to be limited to user typing, i.e. keying-in instructions along the lines of PRESTEL responses, enabling home banking and possibly some computer-assisted learning responses, through a local viewdata system. In other words, it would give little more than is currently available through PRESTEL. Until a national fibre-optic 'star' system is established, it will still probably be more practical to use the public telephone network for voice interaction or even telewriting. These technical considerations indicate quite clearly the kind of framework required for education from any national policy for cable development: statutory obligation on cable operators to carry at least one educational and community channel; a policy which will encourage cable operators to provide services in areas of greatest educational need—i.e. inner city and rural areas-as well as in commercially attractive areas; cable systems based on fibre-optics technology; 'star' cable configurations; and a national grid or a satellite-linked system for cable allowing inter-communication between all cable users.

The use of cable for educational purposes, therefore, is likely to develop very slowly and to be very piecemeal, as indeed will cable be generally. The original reason for setting up cable systems in North America was to provide decent signals for the many areas not covered by adequate off-air transmission, but in Britain most homes can receive high quality, off-air broadcast transmissions. Secondly, there is no guarantee that an increase in channels will lead to an increase in the range of quality of programmes available. Anyone who has switched from channels to channel on cable system in America cannot fail to have noticed the similarity of programming on each cannel. It is significant that the BBC plans to use one of the new statellite channels merely for repeating old BBC programmes. Leaps in technology are not necessarily accompanied by leaps in imagination.

The growth of video-cassette machine ownership, the ease of hiring video-cassettes for a small fee from the local corner shop and the opportunity to record high-quality broadcast programmes, are all real threats to the competitiveness of cable television. Most of all, laying the cables, connecting up homes, providing extra programming and linking cable systems together, will be extremely expensive and financially risky. There is likely to be a great deal of caution exercised, therefore, before there is a major expansion of cable services. The main danger of cable developments is that, despite their slow growth, they will put yet more pressure on channel controllers in the broadcasting organisations to remove educational programmes from transmission. Only the national broadcasting organisations are in a position during the 1980s and 90s to provide a national educational television services.

Teletext systems

Teletext systems are broadcast 'frames' or 'pages' of information that can be called up at any time by the viewer, have at the moment only two real educational advantages; they are useful for up-dating informations, such as news headlines and weather forecasts; and the services is free. Their educational limitations though are considerable. The number of pages that can be accessed is limited, in 1983 to around eight hundred, and since each teletext page holds far less information than a printed page, the total amount of information that can be accessed is very small indeed. Because of the inherent nature of the technology, teletext information tends to be geared to maximum audiences with common interests, and to deal primarily with information that can be easily condensed and up-dated. Thee is no possibility of two-way communication, and a viewer can have irritating time delays while waiting for pages called up.

Viewdata systems

Viewdata systems are based on the telephone have a much wider range of features which may prove more useful in education, but not to the extent of having much impact on broadcasting. Viewdata systems also have major educational limitations. In theory, the number of pages that can be accessed is limited only by the size of the computers that store the pages. However, like teletext systems, the technology limits the amount of information that can be displayed per page. Also, because of the cost of creating and accessing viewdata pages, information again tends to be presented in a condensed and simplified form. Viewdata systems, also like teletext, have no sound. The lack of synchronised sound and pictures is a major disadvantage, as too is the lack of movement, compared with broadcasting.

The way viewdata systems structure information is still unsatisfactory, searching through the branching structure for the information one needs is a tedious business-especially if it was never there in the first place. This technology structures knowledge in a way that is unhelpful for learning. Attempts to base systems on keywords may improve access and structuring, but it is hard to see how the system can ever have the flexibility and richness of an educational television programmes. There have been some experiments, particularly in Canada, to create teaching materials for use on viewdata systems. TV Ontario located Telidon terminals in 120 primary schools throughout the province, and asked teachers to create their own programmes by sending in specifications to TV Ontario where skilled Telidon advisers created the frames and stored them on the mainframe computer. Teachers could then call up on the mainframe computer. Teachers could then all upon the telephone not only their own programmes but also all the other programmes so created.

It may be too early yet to judge but it seems there are inherent problem with using systems such as teletext or viewdata extensively in education for teaching purposes, although they may have their use as a data-base or for general informational purposes. If they do have their values, they are more likely to complement than compete with educational broadcasts. It is the microcomputer which is likely to have the greatest long-term impact on educational broadcasting, as on many other aspects of out lives.

Microcomputers will enable individual teachers to create their own audio-visual teaching materials quickly, easily and economically, and will enable the individual learner to interact in a wide variety of was with such audio-visual materials, which can be tailor-made to the individual's needs. This material is likely to be highly motivating both for the teacher and the learner. To do this, teachers will not need to be highly skilled in using computers, and the learner need not have any programming expertise to study in this way.

Designing computer-assisted learning programmes is at the moment extremely time-consuming, requires a good deal of computer power, and needs a sensitive combination of high-level computing and teaching skills. Effective CAL programmes tend to be expensive to produce in terms of the actual use made of them. The learner is generally limited to responses via the keyboard, and the range of responses in this mode is also limiting. Another very real limitation of CAL is the lack of adequate sound, particularly the teacher's voice. This means that CAL programmes have a heavy reliance on textual and simple graphical presentation, although animation is also available at a price.

Creating good quality, effective graphics and animation requires a lot of programming time and can be difficult to achieve on the lower-priced microcomputers. The major limitations, however, at present is the need for teachers to become skilled programmes. Many have neither the time nor the inclination to do this, and in terms of what CAL can currently offer on microcomputers, they are probably correct in assuming that the results are not worth the effort. Those who have proved skilful in this areas have tended to produce packages which are used by other teachers-resulting in a degree of centralisation of teaching which in practice limits the use of such materials.

By the late 1980s 'peripherals' to standard microcomputers, and special packages of programming which can be loaded into a microcomputer so that it can be operated easily in certain way, will allow teachers to create their own sophisticated audio-visual materials very simply and without needing computer programming skills. Similar developments will also allow audio-visual material to be sent down a telephone line and for learners at home to communicate back with a teacher and other learners, both with voice and visually. It is possible to predict fairly accurately what a low-cost micro-computer-based audio-visual teaching system will look like, partly as a result of experience gained from using a prototype system called CYCLOPS at the universities and in schools.

CYCLOPS digitally converts simple colour-video graphics-handwriting, text, diagrams and very simple animation-into sound codes. These graphics can be very easily generated using a combination of a standard computer keyboard and an electronic writing-pad which also displays graphics on the TV screen. Still images from a video-camera can be similarly coded. Because the video signals are converted into a sound code, they can be stored on audio-cassette or transmitted down standard telephone lines, then decoded back into a video signal. Using either standard stereo audio-cassettes or two telephone lines, full sound can be synchronised with the visuals. The crucial point is that audio-visual materials can be created very simply and quickly this way without any need for computer programming skills.

CYCLOPS is basically a 'peripheral' system for a standard microcomputer since its 'core' can be made available as a cartridge or a ROM to be added to a standard microcomputer. While it may not be the

CYCLOPS system that eventually gets used, by the late 1980s microcomputer-based audio-visual teaching systems will be common in schools. A probable configuration will consist of a standard television receiver, a stereo-cassette player and microphone, a light-pen or an electronic writing-pad, and a standard microcomputer. This will incorporate a CYCLOPS-type facility, either built into the microcomputer itself, or as an add-on accessory, and a connection to the public telephone system. Most of this equipment is already available in schools in Britain at the time of writing. For instance, in 1983-98 per cent of british secondary schools were equipped with a microcomputer. The additional components-the light-pen and the CYCLOPS-type cartridge-will cost approximately 50 each, and in the future, facilities similar to CYCLOPS are likely to be built into a microcomputer as a standard feature.

Microcomputers will also increase in power and reduce in price over the next few years. With such a facility, teachers can create their own teaching materials. They can draw on the screen and add text via the keyboard. They can also use standard graphics facilities in the cartridge or the microcomputer itself, to create shapes such as triangles, squares and circles, and to 'fill-in' these shapes with different colours. They can also create certain forms of animation. The facility enables a teacher to build up pictures or frames which are then transferred to a standard audio-cassette. Each picture or frame can be coded and stored, enabling editing to be carried out simply and easily by the microcomputer.

When all the pictures have been assembled, edited and correctly ordered, the teacher can add the sound-track using the microphone and the audio-cassette player. As well as the teacher's or the pupils' voices, music or special effects can be added. The computer controls the length of time each frame is displayed to enable sound-track and picture to be synchronised. The programmes can be exchanged with other schools, ordered from a central bank or used for distance teaching. Teachers can learn how to use the system either by following a simple manual or by loading on a cassette containing a training programmes.

It is likely to take teachers two or three hours to learn how to use the system, after which time they will have no difficulty in creating their own materials. Learners will load the audio-cassette and work through the programme very much in the same way they would work through an audio-cassette or video-cassette. In addition, though, they can use the light-pen or keyboards or microphone to give answers to questions on the tape, and their responses can be recorded together with the original programmes, for later inspection by the teacher if so desired.

CAL features can also be added, with feedback given on keyboards responses, and the tape can be directed to appropriate sections according to the learner's responses. The technology to so this is already here and will be introduced to schools and colleges in the mid 1980s. We will have to wait and see whether teachers will want to create their own materials in this way or whether they will prefer to use materials prepared more professionally by others, probably marketed by publishers. Such developments, however, have obvious implications for broadcasters since microcomputer programmes of this kind will have a number of advantages over video materials. They will be much cheaper and easier to produce and distribute than video-cassettes. They will be much more interactive and specific to the needs of individual teachers and learners, especially if created by teachers themselves. But there will also be disadvantages.

It is likely that a majority of teachers will prefer high-quality, off-the-shelf material that is readily and easily available. The 'cottage-industry', teacher-generated computer materials cannot currently match the quality of professionally produced broadcasts, or even non-broadcast video-cassettes. Even with the advanced CYCLOPS-type facilities, computer-generated materials will still lack many of the features of video, no matter how professional the computer design. There will still be need for film or tape of overseas situations, for portraying human interactions, for presenting the world in a fully representational manner, for the more personal aspects of seeing a human face, for seeing things as they happen.

Microcomputer-based programmes will not eliminate the need for video. They will, however, provide teachers with a convenient and cheaper alternative. Video programmes will therefore have to compete against other highly effective media for the limited time of teacher and learners. If video is to compete successfully, broadcasters and video producers will need to identify and exploit to the full the unique advantages of their medium. The main developments likely to impact directly on educational broadcasting are cassettes and micro-computers.

Cable and satellite may have a further negative effect, increasing pressure on broadcasting organisations either to transfer educational programmes to inconvenient or impossible times or, for financial reasons, to drop educational programmes altogether. Cable is unlikely though to offer an effective alternative for education. The main overall effect on broadcasters will be the need to identify and exploit the unique educational advantages of broadcasting, since a range of highly effective audio-visual alternatives are now becoming available to teachers and learners.

Computers in education

Computers software for the schools is similar to other instructional material in its focus on imparting factual information and on low-level algorithmic skills. There is evidence that students can learn factual information effectively by using computers in academic subject areas. For instance, the effectiveness of computer-aided instruction has been consistently demonstrated in foreign language and in science. Across subject areas, computerized instruction is associated with greater or equal gains in learning when compared with traditional instruction. Furthermore, this achievement is obtained in equal or less time than is needed for regular classroom learning.

However, there is little evidences that computer software stimulates higher-level thinking. This lack of evidence is one of the reasons that software to promote higher-order thinking is used in schools only to a very limited degree. Another reason is that few programs are available, even though the quality of such programs is beginning to improve. It should also be noted that software programs which attempt to provide challenges to solve complex problems are

(a) apt to require a longer a longer time for the student to complete.

(b) difficult to integrate with the curriculum,

(c) difficult for the teacher to master, and

(d) difficult to evaluate.

Nonetheless, there are computer programs and programming languages that, according to authors' claims, can improve problem-solving skills. Programming languages that allow the student to control the computer and provide an inherently rich problem-solving environment have attracted much attention. One such programming language is Logo, developed explicitly for young children. It includes an interactive component that allows students to give directions to the computer by informing a "turtle" what to draw. The computer draws what the child has directed. This process allows for immediate feedback. Part of the advocacy for teaching even young children how to direct or program a computer results from a belief that learning to think like a computer makes a better thinker. The argument is not that thinking like a computer is somehow better than human thought, but that the consideration of thinking makes humans more thoughtful. Researchers have compared the problem- solving performance of subjects who used such programs with the performance of those who did not, but no conclusive results have emerged.

Some data suggest tat learning th Logo programming language is significantly different from learning other languages because of its interactive nature. Scattered and sparse evidence indicates that Logo instruction may have a positive influence on much things as fluency, originality, and divergent thinking. Some have hypothesized that increased facility with Logo provides the potential for improved thinking to the extent that it acts as a tool for expressing powerful ideas. By using Logo, children have the opportunity to gain a personal understanding of abstract ideas they are unlikely to encounter until a much higher level of schooling, if at all. Evaluating claims about computer programs or language designed to improve higher-order thinking skills is a more complex process than evaluating knowledge-building programs. Definitions are not as precise and, as we have indicated, there are no agreed upon outcome measures. It is only recently that researchers have begun to prove the claims of developers for programs to improve higher-order thinking.

One of the ways in which computer programs may possible help in developing the skills of higher-order thinking is through instruction in the use of heuristics, that is, instruction in particular strategies of problem solving. Before considering this matter, we found it useful to look into such questions as (a) Can heuristic strategies be taught and do they actually help students solve problems? an (b) Does training in such strategies transfer across various domains of content?

Feuerstein's instructional techniques to improve problem-solving skills include such activities as classifying and comparing attributes, recognizing relationships, planing, synthesizing, and logical reasoning. Lipman emphasized that it is important for students to monitor their own thinking by suing such strategies as identifying underlying assumptions, grasping whole-part and part-whole relationships, and applying principles to real-life situations. Newell, Shaw, and Simon argued in 1960 that "heuristics are...things that aid discovery. Heuristics seldom provide infallible guidance.... Often they `work', but the results are variable and success is seldom guaranteed." Suydam, on the other hand, found that "research evidence strongly concurs that problem-solving performance is strongly enhanced by teaching students to use a wide variety of strategies of heuristics, both general and specific." The twenty years that separate these assessments account in part for the disagreement, but good data are still sparse, and the methods advocated for teaching heuristics are mainly based on common sense and intuitive understandings.

Researchers explored the hypothesis that students who use explicit problem-solving strategies are better problem solvers than those who do not and that such strategies can be taught so that skills are improved. Bloom and Broder investigated the problem-solving skills of college students across a variety of subject areas. They found that bright students who were poor problem solvers could be trained to improve their problem-solving skills using the strategies employed by peers who were successful problem solvers. These who participated in the training tended to score. 49 to.68 grade levels higher than matched groups with no training. They also expressed confidence and optimism about their newly learned problem-solving abilities. More recently, Ptt found that specific instruction that followed the four-step heuristics of Polya's model was effective in improving fifth graders' use of the strategies, but he did not find significant differences in success in solving problems between the experimental group and a control group that had no training. Since the period of treatment was only four weeks, it is nt surprising that problsm-solving outcomes were not dramatically influenced.

In another study, fourth graders who were taught to develop pictorial aids, such as tables and diagrams, could solve more problems than others who did not receive such instruction. Within the area of mathematics, instruction in problem solving heuristics is generaly spplied to clearly structured problems. schoenfeld successfully trained college-level students to use specific techniques to improve their strategie for solving work problems in algebra. In a follow-up project, Schoenfeld reported that not only did college level students increase their use of particular strategies, but those who used the heuristics effectively wer also more successful at solving algebra problems. Perhaps as a result of this success, the students' self-reprts of their problem-solving skills were more favorable.

Some researchers believe that effective problem-solving strategies are specific to particular domains. The argument is that a student gets deeper into a content domain the problem solving skills become more and more specific to that modain and therefore may not transfer to other domains Studies of expert and novice problem solvers are particularly salient here. These studies have found that when novices and experts are faced with a problem in the experts' domain, they pproach the problem in different ways. Novices tend to focus on the litral objects defined in th statement of the problem. The possible strategies for solution seen by experts are expanded by their uderstanding of the relationships among concepts and procedures specific to that domain. How are we to reconcile the findings of these expert-novice studies with the views of those who see the value of generalized problem-solving heuristics across different subject matters? One line of argument is simply that increased knowledge of a content domain makes possible a more efficient and precise application of general heuristic procedures.

Greater knowledge of a domain should increase the chances fora person to define a problem accurately, allow on to decide more easily among possible strategies for solution and facilitate resting the validity of possible solutions. In this argument, procedural problem-solving skills interact with the knowledge base to increase the abilities of the student to solve the problem. We might imagine a model with three significant effects: two main effects and an interaction effect of the two. Drawing from observational studies of students, recent researchers have considered this issue. In a detailed analysis of problem solving in geometry, Greeno argued that three kinds of knowledge are critical for success:

(a) heuristic knowledge necessary for carrying out proofs, such as setting goals, forming plans, and generally organizing the problem-solving process;

(b) knowledge of specific geometiric facts, such as the definition of lines and angles;

(c) geometric concepts essential to making inferences and proving theorems.

Similarly, Glaser and Pellegrino concluded that two critical and interreleated components are necessary for higher-order thinking to occur:

(a) thoughtful consideration of 'procedural constraints of a particular problem area, such as inductive or analogical reasoning," as problem-solvig tools and

(b) subject area knowledge.

Recent rheoretical work in cognitive sciences has used the notion of knowledge structure or schemata to help explain the way people remember, comprehend, and solve problems. Schema theory attempts to describe the relationships between knowledge previously acquired, the way it is organized in the mind, and the ease with which new knowledge is acquired and used.

Experts reviewed as having rich and complex schema that facilitate the acquisition of new information and the rapid solution of many problems. The prior knowledge base and schema of the expert in physics is sufficiently rich so that many high school physics problems can be solved algorithmically. The expert "knows" the way to define the problem, "knows" the right strategy to solve it, and "knows" how to evaluate the solution. He may apply Polya's steps but he will do so unconsciously and rapidly; for him this is rotine processing, not higher-order thinking. To a high school student with a less complete knowledge schema in physics, however, the same problem may pose a complex task requiring higher-order thinking.

Although the student may have a solid base of facts and an understanding of the basic rules of physics, the probvlem may require combining the facts and rule in novel ways. The student may have to examine multiple ways of representing the problem and explorea variety of possible will be engaged in higher-order thinking ony when they are stretched beyond situations where tey already know how to find the solution. It also implies that constant deepenig of a subject area to include increasingly complex material is critical for either students of experts as they deal with tasks that require higher-order thinking. Psychologists investigating metacognition suggest that students who self-consciously consider their own cognitive procssing can enhance their thinking. Much recent research indicates that the student is very active in selecting, interpreting, and even altering the content of instruction.

The key processes seen as integral to effective monitoring of cognition are

(a) planning activities prior to undertaking a problem and

(b) monitoring activities during learning and checking outcomes.

These activities are remarkably similar to Polya's heuristics and they also reflect Papert's argument for teaching children to program computer. Controlled use of Polya's heuristic strategies may be viewed as an example of the regulation of cognition. Brown postulated that individuals have a centrl processing unit, much like a computer, that controls heuristic routines for problem solving, planning and scheduling appropriate strategies, and monitoring and evaluating the effects of strategies. The complex operations performed by the executive control component take one of two approaches automativ or controlled.

Automatic strategies are quickly retrived, make little demand on the cognitive system, require minimal conscious learner control, and are not dependent on short-term memory. controlled strategies are more slowly retrieved, executed in a deliberate, purposeful way, and thus require a great deal of lerner effort and control. Controlled strategies can evolve into automatic operations. For example, if Polya's heuristics are practiced in a controlled, conscious way across a number of problem areas, there is reason to believe that their application will become automatic. This discussion has implications for school curricula intended to encourage higher-order thinking. First, for students to find new ways of interrelating knowledge and algorithms they must have a firm grasp of the knowledge needed to solve the problem. If they cannot retrieve this information automatically, they will be distracted from the problem-solving task. Second, if students are to be challenge with higher-order problems at various stages of their knowledge development in a field, then the curriculum should not be organized hierarchycally to focus initialy only on learning facts and formulas. Instead, students should be challenged to solve problems earlky in their exposure to a field-problems based on the knowledge they have already acquired.

Considerable attention should be given early in the curriculum to the interrelatinship among facts and rules in order to develop schema that are sufficiently rich to enable students to deal with problems that require organizing informatin in ways new to them. The selection of content for early problem-solving activities is therefore particularly important. In addition to depth in a single content area, repeated successful experience in using problem-solving strategies across a variety of content ares reinforces learners' use of them in new situations they recognize as resembling the ones in which they succeeded. Psychologists endorse training in multiple contexts because it "decreases the likelihood that a particular piece of information will be wedded to a particular context."

If students assume that solving a problem requires the use of a formula or algorithm applicable only in a single subject area, then they will use these strategies only within that domain. But, if they see problems requiring heuristic strategies and other substrative concepts across a number of domains, it is likely that they will become more fluid thinkers and, ultimately, more successful in solving problems. Our brief literature review suggests the importance of teaching heuristic strategies, that using these strategies in a rich context enhances their effectiveness, and that there is some evidence that strategies may be transferable across content domains. The analysis indicates that students can learn problems-solving heuristics and that, if they use these strategies, they are more effective problem solvers. The instructional emphasis should be on the process of solving problems and not on the problem solution.

One implication of this focus on process is the need for students to practice using heuristic strategies across a variety of content domains and with different types of problems. The depth of the content appears to be a critical component in improving higher-order thought. Research on expert and novice problem solvers show the importance of a solid information base that is easily retrieved in a problem-solving environment. The problem solver should be able to retrieve facts and algorithms automatically, but should also be able to perceive the interrelationships among various concepts within a domain.

There are conflicting opinions about the use in schools of computer programs which "only" provided drill and practice or tutorial instruction.

One view is that these activities can be carried out by teachers or aids effectively and cheaply and that we use of such programs limits students' and teachers' various on the power of computers and reinforces the already strong emphasis in schools on knowledge development to the exclusion of problem-solving activities. Another view is that such programs can be easily integrated into the curriculum, that they can free the teacher for more demanding activities, that they have been shown to be effective, that they often command the attention of some students more than does conventional teaching and that they offer a convenient way to introduce computers into the classroom. We favor the latter view, though we quickly concede that many existing programs in these categories are not worth students' time and effort.

Drill and practice software focuses on previously learned factual knowledge and skills, in contrast, the other two types of knowledge development software focus on learning new knowledge or skills. Drill and practice software is used with greater frequency in schools than any other types of program, other than programming languages.

Over the past few years the aesthetic quality and the motivational attributes of these programs have improved greatly as program developers have acquired sophistication in the use of graphics and have learned something about how to design programs that sustain the attention of young people. Properly constructed drill and practice programs should enhance cognitive processing by requiring students to increase speed in retrieving information and in carrying out skill activities to the point where these activities become automatic. This automatic processing, in turn, should assist higher-order thinking by reducing certain cognitive demands on students when they are faced with a problem- solving situation. The goal is to get students to the point where they can focus on the dimensions of the problem rather than on the heuristics to solve it. One approach is to have the software deliberately focused on increasing student's speed in processing information. Unlike drill and practice activities that require only paper and pencil, a computer program can record the time it takes a student to carry out a problem or to remember or recognize certain information. In addition, it can adjust the amount of time required to present a problem, based on its record of how quickly similar tasks were complete. A second approach would be to design programs to increase the student's capacity to chunk: together related pieces of information. The ability to solve problems is partially constrained bay the amount of information a person can manipulate in short-term or immediate memory.

The capacity of human short-term memory is limited to a small and finite number of independent pieces of information-in the neighborhood of seven. If students could automatically chunk together pieces of information so that the pieces are no longer independent, they might be able to increase their ability to solve complicated problems. Based on some assumption about the structure and extent of students' knowledge schema, drill and practice programs might be designed to help them bring together or "chunk" related information.

Content tutorial programs differ from drill and practice programs by focusing on new facts and skills rather than on going over material already learned or partially learned. Typical software resembles some of the early teaching maching programs with dry presentation of desecrate information and only a limited branching capacity. Many of the early tutorial programs developed by the Minnesota Education Computing Consortium are of this sort. More interesting tutorial performance could challenge the student to become involved through game-like situations. The tole of these programs in enhancing problem solving is to provide sufficient grounding in content and skill areas so that complex problems can be presented. The ETS-LAUSD study and other reports indicate that programs in this category can be very successful in teaching information and skills.

The quality and sophistication of this type of program have also increased dramatically over the years. Their demonstrated ability to engage students, particularly low-achieving students, is a good reason to make them available in more schools. Nonetheless, or earlier review of the literature suggests a variety of ways to improve the usefulness of content tutorial programs for preparing a student to solve complex problems. As in the case of drill and practice programs, the concept of chunking has been neglected and might be used to enhance effectiveness.

Two strategies that could aid in chunking are (a) the use of mnemonic devices, and (b) semantic mapping. The first strategy is often used to facilitate the learning of lists of apparently unrelated objects. Pictures as well as key words can be useful. Semantic mapping is closer theoretically to the notions of cognitive scientists who perceive the ability to chunk as characteristic of "expert" thinking. It is designed to aid the individual to develop cognitive structures, or schema, to organize new knowledge. In semantic mapping, new concepts are systematically related to already known concepts in order to place the new information into a familiar structure or context. Using semantic mapping as a model for teaching new content would require that the computer program acquire information about the prior knowledge of students in order to relate new information to familiar concepts. Here the computer new information to familiar concepts. Here the computer is at a distance disadvantage when compared to a human teacher; not even the most powerful electronic brains comes close to the capacity of the human brain to make judgments about students' previous experience and to tailor information to meet special group and individual needs.

Nonetheless, we can imagine tutorial programs that initially interrogate a student to determine a general level of prior knowledge and then use the results of the interrogation to tailor the tutorial to student needs. Where schools knowledge is ordinarily learned in a hierarchical manner as in mathematics, the computer could pretest and then use responses to place students at the appropriate level in the tutorial. In areas where knowledge is not clearly hierarchical, the initial assessment would be complicated and require greater teacher involvement. A related way to improve tutorial programs is through the use of diagnostic routines that identify the type of errors that students make and then coach or instruct them in ways to avoid making such errors. This strategy appears to be particularly useful for learning skills such as arithmetic operations.

The classing example of such a program is BUGGY, a diagnostic program to detect the nature of errors made by students doing subtraction problems. In its original form it identified a very large number of possible independent error patterns, though the actual errors that students made tended to cluster in far fewer patterns. This software was initially written for a large computer but it being modified for microcomputers. The small amount of quickly accessed memory is still a general problem for developing effective instructional software for microcomputers. But the BUGGY experience suggests that programs containing a diagnostic and coaching component may need to include only the most frequently occurring errors.

Ideally, the program would instruct a student to request teacher assistance if it could not determine the student's error. This would free teachers to focus on the most complex instructional problems. Cognitive scientists have recently observed the phenomenon of systematic misconceptions in the areas of science and mathematics. In the early grades these misconception have only minor consequences for "getting the answer right" and therefore persist into later education, where they could have considerable influence on the problem-solving abilities of students. It should be possible to design computer programs that systematically test for prevalent misconceptions and then provide coaching routines to heop overcome them.

Heuristic tutorial programs are specifically designed to teach problem-solving strategies. These computer programs use a well-structured and circumscribed, often game-lime environment for training and practice in the use of specific heuristics. The classic computer programs in this area is the game of "Wumpus", which was designed to teach basic knowledge of logic, probability, decision analysis, and geometry to a wide range of learners, from young children to adults. The game logic resolves around a set of five basic rules of reasoning. The player is placed randomly in a connected web of vaves and is told the neighbors of his current location. The goal is to locate the horrible wumpus and kill it by shooting an arrow into its lair. Moving from one cave to another produces information on the new neighbors.

Players can minimize dangers and make progress in finding the Wumpus by using the warning signals to make appropriate ligistc and probalistics inferences. If the players exhaust their supply of five arrows before killing the Wumpus, the game is lost. We believe schools and most programs developers are missing major opportunity by not developing and using programs like "Wumpus" Properly developed programs could be used on a regular basis in schools with students of widely varying background to provide them with systematic exposure to problem-solving situations. For instance, the Sunburst Corporation has published a problem-solving skill matrix that is included with software packages designed to teach complex thinging skills such as discrimination, looking for a pattern, and information gathering. Generally, these computer programs are open-ended and create a fantasy environment.

For instance, in "Memory Castle." students learn mnemonic systems by playing an adventure game that leads them through a castle, and they must use a special code to find the way out. in another program, "The pond", a small green fraog, lost in a pond of lily pads, teaches students to recognize an articulate patterns and generalize from raw data. The student chooses from six ponds, or levels of difficulty, in which lily pads are displayed in increasingly complex patterns. The objective is to determine which pattern can get the frog across the pond. A second level of the game encourages students to collect points by directing frogs through as many points as possible in the fewest number of moves. There is little question in our minds that these programs ares successful in teaching students to use specific problem-solving heuristics within the limited program environments, but we know of no quantitative evaluations.

Whether the strategies learned from these programs have effects that generalize to other settings, particularly those where the problems are more complex or less well-structured, in another matter. Improvements in these programs might proceed along some of the same lines that we have suggested for content tutorial and drill and practice programs. The use of error diagnosis and coaching routines seems especially promising. Burton and Brown used this strategy in a modification of a well-known arithmetic game programs, "WEST", originally developed for the PLATO system. They included routines which contrast the player's moves with optional strategies and which occasionally suggest alternative moves to the player.

The task of problem-solving simulation programs is to pose complex problems for solution. Unlike knowledge-building programs, which provide practice in sing knowledge and skills and which teach students facts and how to use certain heuristics, simulation programs present situations where the problem itself needs to be identified, where there may be a large variety of possible heuristics to use, and where there may indeed be a number of acceptable solutions.

To present such a situation, the computer simulation must assume or create an environment with a sufficiently rich knowledge base and structure so that complex problems can be posed. Paper has labelled this idea "microworld" and defended it as a subset of reality or constructed reality that allows learners to exercise powerful ideas and intellectual skills. The use off a microworld is based on a learning theory that promotes active exploration in an environment that is sufficiently limited and thus conductive to constructure exploration and at the same time rich enough for discovery. We pointed out earlier that such a requirement creates a very difficult problem for computer programs because of the difficulties in assessing sufficient levels of students' prior knowledge and the limited memory of the microcomputer.

The limitation on memory, for example, reduces the computer's capacity to communicate easily with students, for only a small vocabulary and a simplified syntax can be stored in a microcomputer. One approach is for the program to build an environment based directly on the curriculum or the common real-life experiences of students, thereby reducing the effects of difference in prior knowledge. A second option is a computer-created artificial environment where the effects of the prior knowledge of the student are minimized. Both of these approaches are described here. Content simulation programs are designed to provide environments as lifelike as possible for students to use in problem-solving activities. A substantial number of existing computer programs do this in a sophisticated way. Programs that pose diagnostic problems in medicine, automobile care, or business management are widely used outside precollegiate education.

Unfortunately, much of the content would be inappropriate for elementary and secondary schools, and many of these programs are on large computers rather than on microcomputers and therefore not generally accessible to schools. But they can serve as a vision of what is possible. One prototype is the "MYCIN" system, an interactive program that simulates a medical consultant who specializes in infectious diseases. For approximately twenty minutes, the program questions and responds to doctors seeking the help of a specialist. They may ask "MYCIN" for advice on identifying organisms and prescribing drugs and, further, to explain that advice.

This program strikes us as particularly salient in at least three ways. First, it allows the physicians to lean more about the complexities of diseases and treatments outside their specialities. Second, the encyclopedic function embedded in explaining treatments in an option and not a necessary step in using the program. Third, it allows for improvements in the system as new information becomes available- it can always be current. It is not difficult to see how this model might be followed in training students in a variety of content domains. There are, however, few good examples in education and little use of content simulation programs in schools.

Two classic simulations for use in elementary schools have been developed by MECC: "Lemonade", where the students manage a lemonade stand and earn or lose money based on their decisions; and "Oregon Trail," where a student acts as the head of a wagon train in the middle 1800s. These simulations are popular as demonstration devices but typically are not integrated into the curriculum. At the high school level there have been some interesting new programs, but they only scratch the surface. For instance, "Revolutions: Past, Present and Future," developed by Focus Media, was designed to teach high school students a model for understanding the development of revolutionary movements. Students build their own model of events leading to a revolution following a computer comparison of the American, French, and Russian revolutions. This program is particularly appealing because the objectives include both process and content variables.

The limitation on memory is one reason for the lack of useful software in this area. the program needs to be fast and rich enough in content to overcome major differences in the prior knowledge of different students in the classroom. One approach to the memory limitation problem would be to build into the simulation itself tutorial software that could be interrogated by students seeking data or other information, such as the technical terms needed to solve some of the problems posed in the simulation. Similarly, drill and practice programs could be embedded in the simulation program. Error detection and coaching routines could be part of the simulation programs and could, in face, trigger the programs to indicate to the student the need for a tutorial or for a drill and practice experience. These "helping" programs could be designed as part of the simulation game" though every student need not use them. Desi ned in this way, they would not have to be carried permanently in immediate memory. Other strategies to overcome school-based problems seem plausible. It is not entirely possible to control time demands, for the very task of solving a complex problem may require considerable time, but it is possible for the computer to save a simulation until later, and advantage that could help fit higher-order thinking tasks into fifty-minutes time slots.

The biggest problem is to integrate simulations into the curriculum; it solution would require the acceptance and use of both the computer and problem-solving activities in the classroom. We actually feel quite pessimistic about whether this will occur to a substantial degree in the next ten to twenty years; the conservative nature of the major textbook publishers and the tremendous inertia inside classroom work directly against it. Nonetheless we have a number of suggestions about approaches that might be taken. One strategy would be to create first-class simulations that focus on content in areas outside the mainstream of academic life in schools. The vocational education are is a prime example; programs that pose problems in aircraft and automobile mechanics, in structural design, and in business management already exist and could be used in many schools. Art, music, health, and the chess club are other areas for which simulation programs are either already developed and used or easily could be. These areas may be able to respond to the new technology more creatively than academic areas in part because their knowledge domains are better defined and in part because they are less bound by tradition.

If we continue the logic about well-defined knowledge domains, the first academic areas to tackle would be mathematics and science. In both of these areas the national concern over the quality of the curriculum, pedagogy, and the teachers could work infavor of using some high-quality programs. Mathematics, for example, will be a fertile field for simulation programs that pose problems in statistics, probability, and data analysis, if the recommendation of a number of the national mathematics groups are adopted. In science, the potentially useful simulation situations seem limitless. Artificial environment simulations generate a make-believe world with a sufficiently rich knowledge base and set of rules of that complex problems can be poosed by the programs. Their capacity both to tutor and to pose problems in an integrated fashion allow them to control the influence of prior knowledge; this control enables the computer to provide successively deeper information and more complex problems.

A wide variety of types of programs fits out general conception of this category. These include fantasy adventure games such as the "ZORK" series, science fiction games such as "World Builders", and complex artificial problem steeings such as "Rocky's Boots". One such program, "Robot Odyssey I" is both a simulation and an adventure game. Students can either construct a simulated robot or work through and adventure game that teaches the basic of digital electronic. Players design, build, and test robotes in a parts laboratory and tutorials assist students in all stages of the game. The problems posed by these programs, in our view, often are of equal or greater complexity and take more ingenuity and preservenacne to solve than the most difficult problems posed in schools. Programs like these could present problems of varying complexity, designed to build on themselves in a regular fashion, and include systematic tutorial, diagnostic, and coaching systems to help students.

The task of designing effective programs, however, is probably minor compared to the challenge of concinving schools and the general public that problem-solving activities in artificial domains have merit and that time could be allocated for student use of these programs. The best of these programs are immensely popular in the home computing market and used almost not at all in schools. The reasons for the lack of use in schools are clear-they do not fit into the curriculum, they take a long time to run, and they seem frivolous since they are not based on real-life circumstances and are often advertised as games. In particular, adventure games seem most likely to be overlooked. We have observed student pursuing these programs and we have little doubt that such games motivate students and engage them in sustained cognitive activity, whether they are working individually or cooperatively. We have seen students with serious reading difficulties. Who rarely read printed material, spend extended periods working on adventure games that interact with users only in a narrative format. We know of no research on the effects of these games, but the motivation, the opportunity to control the environment, and the objectivity of the feedback appear to make them powerful teaching devices.

Problem-solving aids contain programs that require the student to use them in ways and will help solve problems which may be either self-defined or externally assigned. These programs, moreover, can be embedded in problem-simulation programs to help students to obtain information or to analyze data. We have included a large variety of programs in this category and have divided them into two general types:

(a) tools for obtaining information or structural problems situations, and

(b) programming languages.

Problem-solving aids are widely used in homes and schools, often for obtaining and structuring information for presentation or for aiding gin solving relatively well-structured problems.

In our experience it is rare that tools are used in schools to aid in solving ill-defined problems. Thus, for example, a data management system will be used in a school setting to display some data on a chart rather analysis. Or students will be given very highly structured problems in a programming course rather than be asked to design and program solutions to problems of their own choosing or that ar deliberately ill-defined. The exception may be when the aids are used deliberately to facilitate complex problem solving in advanced placement course for high school mathematics and computer programming.

Tools for aiding problem solving include some of the most imaginative, interesting, and well-developed programs now available for the microcomputer. One reason is that many of them are simply elegant extensions on the microcomputer of tools that already exist in many schools, homes, and businesses; for example, world processing programs function as sophisticated typewriters. Another reason is that these programs are usable over and over by the same person and therefore are cost-effective. In contrast, an adventure program, upon being solved, loses its usefulness to the solver.

In terms of frequency of use in schools and homes, word processing programs, such as "Bank Street Writer", outstrip just about all other classes of programs. The growing group of ideas or outline processors is also becoming very popular; they contain a variety of routines to help a writer organize and reorganize textual information. The use of these programs in schools parallels both the emerging literature on the close relationship between writing and higher-order thinking and the recent emphasis on the need to improve writing in the schools. As these programs become familiar to classroom teachers as writing aids, additional features can be added. For example, it should be possible in the future to combine the organizational aids of idea processes with routines which prompt students with question and information on topics related to he curriculum to encourage their writing. Other tools in this category include dictionaries, information retrieval systems, and data management systems.

In the context of out general discussion of software for problem solving, each of these tools could be viewed as standing along to provide information or assistance in carrying our analysis or could be embedded into problem-solving simulation programs. We might imagine a workstation of the future simila to "Dynabank" developed at Xerox Parc several years ago. As student would sit at a computer terminal and have control over an information retrieval system containing a s much information as the Library of Congress and the data-analysis power of any modern mainframe computer. It would included capabilities for music composition and graphic arts. The computer could pose a variety of types of problems for the student, provide diagnosis and coaching, encourage the student to enter into a drill and practice or tutorial mode, and keep continuous track of student progress.

Programming languages are essential programs that require their operators to define and solve their own problems within the specific constraints of the language and the general constraints of a computer. Although we have classified programming languages as an aid for solving problems, learning to use the programming language is itself a form of problem solving. Without question, the act of solving programming problem often meets our definition of higher-programming problem often meets our definition of higher-order thinking. But whether learning to program enhances a child's general facility in solving problems in another issues. Perhaps the view which links learning to programming with the development of higher-order thinking will wither away in the same way that the theories linking the leaning of Latin with complex reasoning have not survived.

Computer programming languages, like playing chess, may be too highly stylized and structured to provide training that can be generalized to very different domains, especially those domains with more complex and ambiguous rules. On the other hand, programming provides the opportunity for combining discrete elements to equal a whole concept, a gestalt. And this is a necessary skills for solving some problems. We indicated earlier that this literature is very thin and inconclusive. The most widespread use of programming languages in the content areas in in mathematics, where languages such as FORTRAN aid students in leaning how to formulate and solve problems. This is just the beginning of content-based programming languages. There are already sophisticated programming languages and enable students to concentrate on the form and content of subject matter as they composes music and design aesthetically pleasing and structurally sound buildings.

Role of communications satellites

Communications satellites are one of many technologies of current or potential interest to educational technologists and planners. The extent to which satellites will be used depends upon the extent to which educational and communications technology proves responsive to educational needs, the extent to which "cost-effectiveness" can be demonstrated, and the extent to which technology in general finds future use in education.

In particular, satellites have the potential for providing relatively low cost educational services-computer-aided instruction, radio, one-way and talk-back television, library and computer resource sharing, etc.-to large numbers of people and institutions, provided that economies of scale can be achieved. Such services may prove to be responsive to calls for greater access, individualization, and productivity in U.S. education, as well the need to extend education and literacy to greater numbers of individuals in developing countries.

However, to achieve this potential suitable organizational arrangements and structures must be devised which respond to the particular educational setting of the country or regions. Use of satellites for communications was first outlined by the radio engineer and science fiction writer Arthur C. Clarke in 1945. Just 18 years later, after a series of experiments with low and medium altitude satellites which required large and complex earth-stations, the stationary satellite Syncom-II was successfully placed in geo-synchronous orbit. In such an orbit the satellite is some 23,000 miles over the equator, and stays in one fixed position relative to points on earth.

Three of these satellites in the proper position could beam signals which cover almost the entire surface of the earth. The demonstration of the feasibility of using a stationary satellite in geo-synchronous orbit for communications paved the way for commercial communications satellites. Since the orbiting of the Early Bird satellite, launched for the International Telecommunications Satellite Consortium in 1965, communications satellite technology has come a long way and has acquired a high degrees of sophistication.

Satellites in use for international telecommunications today, and the present generation of domestic satellites coming into being, have relatively low power transmitters which provide "fixed-satellite services," to connect relatively large and expensive earth stations. However, the satellite technology has reached a point where relatively inexpensive, roof-top type receivers for receiving radio and television programs or broadcasts over a wide area from relatively high-power satellites will be feasible shortly. In recognition of this possibility, the 1971 World Administrative Radio Conference, held in Geneva, defined and allocated radio frequencies for a "broadcasting satellite service" in which signals transmitted or retransmitted by satellites are intended for direct reception by the general public.

Two distinct categories exist in this service; systems that allow individual reception by simple receiving units in homes, and systems that are designed for community reception, either by a group of the general public at one location or through a distribution system covering a limited area. However, it should be pointed out that WARC regulations for broadcasting satellite service do not permit direct reception by unaugmented conventional TV receivers of the type in use today. The applications currently contemplated for communications satellites in education are indeed diverse, reflecting the differences in educational systems and needs of the nations or regions where uses of communications satellites have been proposed.

In the U.S., formal systems of education have been serving large portions of the school-age population, and higher education is becoming more widespread with the inception of the community college. According to Koerner, three current educational demands center on greater access to education by those not served, greater individualization of education, and greater economy.

There is also current emphasis on nontraditional forms of study. These movements may provide clues as to opportunities for satellite utilization in the U.S. In a developing nation like India, higher priority may be given to building a system of basic education and an infrastructure, almost from scratch, to communication skills and attitudes necessary for the economic and social development of the nation, with particular emphasis on rural areas. In the U.S., with its relatively well developed telecommunications infrastructure, including considerable investment in educational telecommunications facilities, the rationale for utilizing satellites for educational communications differs from that in countries which may not have well developed telecommunications plants.

The key to satellite utilization, as opposed to other communications technologies, lies in provision of significantly new services that existing terrestrial facilities are unable to accommodate or provide, and provision of services similar to those provided by existing technologies but at significantly reduced cost. Educational satellite planners are emphasizing educational networking for sharing of library, computer, and human resources, educational services which are not adequately provided by the existing formal system; direct delivery of high-quality educational material and resources to small and remote institutions; and educational television and ratio networking. In developing nations like India, the emphasis is on taking advantages of the wide-area coverage and broadcast capabilities of the satellite to provide a quantum jump in the, ass-communication capabilities of those nations, and to expand and improve their basic education system quickly.

Brazil's extensive satellite planning effort emphasizes educational radio and television programming, to be used in formal education in the remote, less developed areas of the Northeast.

The use of satellites for direct delivery of services to rooftops of schools and learning centers is of interest in areas where tropical and/or demographic conditions make local distribution and interconnection stems less attractive economically-areas such as Alaska, the Rocky Mountains, and parts of Appalachia. Satellites look promising for delivery of educational services to wide but sparsely populated areas, and for interconnection of cable systems, but the cable-television headend interconnection is not necessarily promising unless educational interests can make greater inroads into local cable systems.

Telecommunications technologies

A national effort is underway by both private and public sectors to build and expand electronic-based information highways. These information highways provide the infrastructure to change the nature of educational delivery from a traditional classroom to a "virtual" classroom that is more geographically distributed.

While these electronic approaches to improving the education dilemma in rural areas seemed the long-awaited "magic pill," a review of literature uncovered some serious issues with EDE (Electronic Distance Education). These concerns included questions regarding the instructional effect-iveness, methodology, and design of some previous EDE courses. During several studies, researchers have reported poor cognitive performance and increased attrition. Electronically Mediated Instruction (EMI) through distance learning technology is still a rather new domain. Initially, distance educators simply duplicated the teacher -centered formats typically found in the traditional classroom. This resulted in disastrous "talking head" presentations.

The computer-based distance learning machines offered a barrage of electronic attributes, such as sounds, colors, lights, animations, and video sequences, the learner became enamored of this awesome technology and missed the intended instructional message. Some educators felt that students using electronic technologies frequently were subjected to fast-moving entertainment-type experiential experiences possibly at the expense of the reflection necessary to complete the mental processes of learning. This so-called "edutainment" process adversely hampered student cognitive achievement and reduced student motivation to continue, thereby increasing attrition.

Most students were accustomed to having instructors present in the classroom to provide extrinsic motivation. Studies have shown that without visible classroom leaders, some students felt isolated, unmotivated, and cognitively disoriented. This ultimately increased attrition at higher rates than for those students who participated in conventional classroom courses. Because of the above mentioned deficiencies that seemed common in EDE studies, Cyrus and Smith, Hannafin, and Terrell suggested that a paradigm shift was necessary in the way in which EDE was delivered. Terrell warned that without making instructional changes, institutions offering EDE faced the same failures. One possible new paradigm mentioned in the literature involved using learner-centered approaches for EDE.

Payne and Stoddard suggested that there were wide-open possibilities for research into the benefits of such designs, especially in the area of EDE-based technical training such as found in EMS courses. While emerging EDE technologies may deliver onsite education, there seemed be justifiable concerns that the resulting "virtual" instructional environment may be woefully inadequate. It appeared that EDE instructional designers needed to develop new learning strategies, such as those found in the emerging constructivist learning models. The purpose of this study was to determine if students who take instruction delivered by EDE incorporating constructivist models could have scores and attrition rates equal to those students who take the same instruction delivered in the traditional classroom. The study also sought to determine if there was a difference in scores and attrition between those students in the two EDE courses which were taught using different distance education technologies.

The Texas Bureau of Emergency Management, mandated by state law to certify EMS courses, readily approved traditional class, but seemed hesitant to approve EDE courses. The two-year study conducted in rural central Texas communities involved volunteer EMS students who attended one of three types of emergency medical technician - intermediate courses. Students in the control group (n = 25) took the instruction in a traditional classroom setting. The other two groups received training via two separate EDE systems (n = 18) The first was a two way audio/ graphic network incorporating standard telephone communications, and the second was a two-way audio/video system linked by a NASA satellite (n= 14). The type of course was assigned randomly to each community involved in the study. Students from the same communities were placed in the same study group. An analysis of the student demographics showed no significant difference (p =.07) in gender, age, or level of education between the groups. All students took a standardized 174-question multiple choice posttest. Attrition rates were based upon the number of those who qualified for EMT-I certification testing at the conclusion of the courses.

The students in the control group received the typical teacher-centered instruction found in the traditional classroom. The instructor chiefly delivered lectures to the students with some audiovisual support. For the students in the two EDE courses, the study sought to overcome the previously mentioned problems with EDE using two corrective approaches. The first involved developing an appropriate instructional model, and the other provided additional extrinsic support to the learners so they would want to complete the courses. The instructional strategies selected for the two EDE courses followed the recommendations of Williams and Paprock. In their constructivist-based model, the responsibility of learning shifted to the student, and the instructor became a facilitator. The students became proactive, rather then reactive. To accomplish this shift, instruction delivered at the distance sites progressed through three well-structured stages. This allowed the locus of control to transition gradually from teacher

-centered to learner centered as each lesson progressed.

These three stages include: (1) teacher-directed teacher -centered (objectivism), teacher -directed learner -centered (constructivism), and (3) learner -directed / learner-centered (collaborativism, a form of constructivism). Before teaching the two distance education courses, the instructor participated in a 12-hour Telecourse. When presenting the lessons in the EDE treatments, the instructor opened each lesson with a brief lecture on a specific medical topic. This information supplied the students with the cognitive base for them to move into the constructivist sections of the instruction later.

After the initial lecture, the instructor directed interactive exercises in which individual students responded to questions or interacted with the material displayed on the computer screen or videoconferencing monitor. When this activity ended, students separated into small groups. The instructor then presented a videotaped emergency care scenario or introduced a detailed case study. Each group proceeded at its own pace and sought its own resources to derive unique solutions. At the close of these collaborative sessions, each group explained its solutions to the other groups. Group members interacted with their peers in defending their solutions and arriving at a consensus. The instructor facilitated the discussion and provided feedback. The electronic attributes of the EDE delivery systems cued or enhanced the instructional message, not detracted from it.

There were three specific ways in which this study attempted to reduce the increased attrition previously reported during distance learning studies.

The first was to include constructivist models when designing lesson plans. These approaches gave students a sense of power and ownership of the course, thereby increasing intrinsic motivation and reducing attrition.

Secondly, in light of studies that indicated providing supplementary materials and additional feedback decreased attrition during EDE programs, the investigators installed computer-based training (CBT) workstations in the rural ambulance stations. CBT seemed to best complement the personality profiles of emergency workers. The interactive CBT software modeled an instructional design adapted from Gagne, Wagner, and Rojas. Their model progressed learners through nine external "events of instruction" that complemented the internal cognitive processes of learners. The design included appropriate, immediate feedback throughout the tutorials and drill and practice sessions. As with the distance education technologies, attributes such as color, sound, graphic, images, animations, and text, purposely delivered intended cues or specific messages.

Thirdly, the instructor used telephone communications during and after the course to help students who needed clarification, elaboration, remediation, or feedback as dictated by academic performance. These procedures enhanced rapport between the instructor and those individual students who were falling behind in the courses and discouraged attrition.

Trends in educational broadcasting

Broadcasting as a profession has its own standards and criteria for judging success, and these criteria have been developed as a result of organisational and institutional pressures unique to broadcasting. Professionalism in broadcasting allows the potential or richness of the medium to be fully exploited, but at a price. Producers have a different approach to teachers. Educators see viewers and listeners as students for whom a broadcast is only one, relatively minor event in a much broader learning context; for a producer, the programme is the centre of attention. This is not to argue that broadcasters' criteria and approaches are better or worse, more right or more wrong, than those of teachers.

However, educational broadcasters, many of whom started out as teachers, are to some extent caught between these different professional ideologies, and one will therefore find a spectrum of approaches in any educational broadcasting department. On balance, though, I believe that the technological pressures of creating broadcast programmes, the full-time commitment of educational producers to programme making, and the organisational milieu in which they work, clearly identify them as broadcasters rather than teachers.

There are several clear trends emerging in media development, each of which will have implications for educational broadcasting. Educators have more audio-visual media to choose from. Broadcasting is therefore facing increasing competition from other sources for teachers' and learners' time. Both broadcasters and teachers then will need to identify and fully exploit the unique teaching strengths of broadcasting if it is to continue to be used. Broadcasting can no longer be considered a comprehensive teaching medium in its own right.

Technological developments are bringing together print, the telephone, the computer and video, into integrated systems that combine the strengths of each medium. Such developments have major implications for professional boundaries. Broadcasting skills will not necessarily carry over to the design of computer-assisted learning programmes, not to overall instructional design. Indeed, computer programming and television production require very different approaches and ways of thinking, and tend to attract different kinds of people. Thus training and skills in one are may inhibit an individual's ability to work in another. Successful integrated teaching will require a genuine team approach, drawing on the separate skills of different professions and the expertise of the teacher. Currently, the existence of independent, professional broadcasting organisations, with their own career structure and methods of rewards separate from the educational system, is a major obstacle to a fully integrated team approach. Broadcasting is not a superior instructional medium to which others must pay obeisance. For this reason, we can see independent non-broadcast, multi-media production companies who contract consultant staff willing to work together as equals, becoming increasingly more influential in education during the 1980s and early 90s. It will be a measure of their flexibility if broadcasting organisations are willing to enter into such arrangements as one amongst equals.

Many attempts have been made in the past by academic to develop theories of media selection, based primarily on pedagogic considerations. All have failed miserable to come up with a theory that can be applied in practice. The difficulty is in finding a practical set of guidelines which can at the same time take account of all the different contextual factors found in education. Also, most previous attempts have concentrated almost entirely on pedagogic factors. Although these are important, so too are factors such as cost, accessibility, convenience for both learners and teachers, and academic control.

Further development of this issue is beyond the scope of this book; it is sufficient here to note that educators are now being forced to choose between a wide range of media, and this will require the unique characteristics of broadcasting to be clearly differentiated from those of other media if a rational choice is to be made. Current developments in media allow for alternatives very different from the mass media model of education fashionable in the 1960s and 1970s, a model which led to such radical but different innovations as the Open University and the El Salvador ETV school reform. More diverse, smaller and less centralised models are now possible. This could mean a move away from large national systems of audio-visual production and distribution for education, to more diversity of provision and more local initiatives. There will be much greater opportunities for 'do-it-yourself' production of audio-visual materials by teachers, or for buying audio-visual materials from sources other than broadcasting organisations.

New media allow local schools and colleges to develop their own on-campus, and, more significantly, off-campus multi-media course at reasonable cost. With enrolments of full-time students steadily dropping in a number of countries, local, off-campus teaching using low-cost audio-visual media will become increasingly important. This development will affect not only the use of educational broadcasting but even more so large centralised distance teaching systems, such as the Open University. The spread of technology, particularly to the home, is likely to increase educational differences within society. Not everyone will be able to afford to be connected to a cable system and to erect a dish aerial for satellite transmission and to buy or rent a video-cassette machine and a video-disc machine and a computer and a telephone, nor will everyone be able to afford the purchase of the software that will carry the educational material.

Broadcasting reaches the parts that other forms of education do not reach. In the United Kingdom and North America, 98 per cent of homes have television sets, and 97 per cent one radio set least. About 80 per cent of the United Kingdom population watch television at least some time during each day, and just over half listen at least once a day to the radio. The average time each adult spends watching television in Britain is between two to three hours per day.

In many developed countries, more than half the population will be watching television at the same time during some parts of an evening. Access to television and radio in developing countries is less universal, particularly regarding television. According to Katz and Wedell, there was less than one radio set for every ten people in fifty-four developing countries in 1976, despite a massive and continuing expansion of radio ownership over the previous twenty years in such countries. Nevertheless, there is now only a handful of countries without any form of broadcast television service. There is no country in the world without widespread geographical coverage by radio, and in all but the poorest countries, a high proportion of households have at least one radio receiver.

Broadcasting has the capacity to reach people who are uninterested in or disenchanted with conventional educational provision, even if local courses are available. There is a good deal of accidental or unplanned viewing and listening. At certain times-in particular early evening and weekend mornings in Britain-millions of people will be randomly accessing television; not switching on because they know a particular programmes is on at that time, but just waiting to see what comes on.

Broadcasting can therefore ply the role of recruiting agent for education, either attracting and holding the audience through the intrinsic interest of the programmes themselves, or leading viewers to pursue the subject further, through purchasing accompanying books, contacting agencies, or enrolling in local classes or correspondence schools.

Broadcasting clearly has the ability to make education interesting and enjoyable, when it is used well. It provides a break from the normal school routine. For adult learners, independent study, especially starting back to study for the first time, requires considerable motivation. Through the variety of techniques used to appeal to audience, broadcasting can provide a real stimulus to learning. Broadcasting can help to raise general awareness of problem or situations about which the general public were previously ignorant or apathetic. Thus,as well as the primary target group for a set of programmes, there is often a secondly target audience; the general public, local or national politicians, leaders of industry, whose awareness of a problem may be raised by the programmes.

Broadcasting can be the cheapest way to get large quantities of audio-visual learning materials to large numbers of people scattered throughout the country. This is particularly important for schools. Even if schools have an abundant provision of video-recording and playback equipment, broadcasting and local recording is the cheapest way to distribute large quantities of audio-visual material. This applies also to computer-based audio-visual media which can be broadcast within a radio bandwidth. Educational broadcasting can be multi-purpose, not only in raising awareness but also in presenting an alternative source of programming to that available on the general service, an alternative sometimes desperately needed. For those who otherwise would be left with a choice between Nationwide, Crossroads and a rock music programme, an Open University programme on the economics of oil-pricing can provide a welcome alternative.

The cultural argument for educational programmes only holds if the programmes are comprehensible to a general public and available at times when most people are able to watch them. Having set out some of the special advantages of broadcasting for education, there is still much that needs to be done to make it more effective. It should be permissible to record selected general broadcast programmes and series, so that they can be used in schools and colleges and for adult education courses. This means easing copyright and royalty agreements on general programmes for strictly non-profit, educational purposes, Support materials for schools and adults using pictures and materials from selected general programmes and other sources should also be prepared, either by the existing publication departments in broadcasting organisations, or by external agencies with particular interest in the series.

Broadcast announcements before and following the programmes should be made indicating the availability of support materials and permission to record for educational purposes. The value of such general programmes and series would be enhanced if there was liaison between the production team and appropriate educational agencies or voluntary organisations from an early stage. Easing copyright and royalty restrictions would not mean loss of income for artists and performers in general programmes since at the moment no income is generated by educational users, unless programmes are available for purchase, which many are not.

Serious considerations needs to be given to the appropriateness of current broadcast provision to schools. Continuous broadcast programmes of a set length are not necessarily the best way to use television or radio. Self-standing programmes, even when recorded on cassette, are difficult to integrate with other teaching activities. More useful to teachers will be integrated multi-media packages with varying combinations of print, video, microcomputer material and audio-cassettes. This requires broadcasters to join with other agencies in the design of such components, as equal members in a team.

Improved and extended training of teachers in the use of media is becoming desperately urgent. Saunders carried out a thorough study of training for use of broadcasting in schools provided by eleven initial teacher-training centres and a variety of in-service courses in five countries in the south of England. She found that training was on the whole inadequate and misdirected. Teachers after training frequently used broadcasting incompetently and unimaginatively, yet broadcast materials is if anything being used more than ever. Cassettes offer greater opportunities for more effective use as integrated components in a carefully planned curriculum. The range of media available is rapidly widening, and teachers will need to know not only how to use the different media available but when and why the should use each medium.

However, on balance, broadcasting has tended to be a marginal educational activity. For it to be used successfully very demanding conditions have to be met, and meeting these has often proved to be impossible. Within the formal education sector, more recording and playback equipment, improved training of teachers and major changes in the way lessons and curricula are designed, are all necessary if television and radio are to be used as effective learning resources rather than as a weak form of enrichment.

Broadcasting's real potential for meeting special needs in schools has been largely unexploited because the broadcasters are not expert in these areas and have not used their advisers to the full. In developing countries, while the introduction of direct teaching by broadcasting has led to improved educational provision, it has had little impact on their wider political, economic and social problems, which can really be resolved only by radical political, economic and social reforms. While broadcasting has helped a little then, it is no substitute for more radical action. In non-formal education the huge educational potential of general broadcasting is chained within the prison of copyright and royalty restrictions.

Furthermore the shunting of educational broadcasts to minority channels and unsocial hours limits their effectiveness. This is a particular difficulty for basic adult education which needs access to its target audience through the more popular channels. Broadcasting has generally proved ineffective educationally in non-formal education unless combined with substantial non-broadcast support services. Although i recent years thee has been an increase in truly co-operative projects between broadcasters and other agencies providing the support services, too often partnerships, where they have existed, have been unequal ones, with broadcasters setting the agenda and timing and the other agencies scrabbling in the wake.

Implementation of ISDN

Accelerating demand for communications services enabling real-time delivery of distance learning applications is sparking renewed interest in Integrated

Services Digital Network implementation in the school and university setting.

ISDN is distinguished by its support of end-to-end digital connectivity for reliable transmission of voice and nonvoice traffic over the same twisted-pair commu-nications lines in use for plain old telephone service (POTS). Initial work on the ISDN standard was completed by the ITU (International Telecommunications Union). Opinions on ISDN range from its consideration as a remarkable breakthrough to a belief that it is an interim solution in accommodating institutional bandwidth requirements until high speed broadband networks become more affordable. ISDN has yet to achieve its overall objective of serving as a unified global public telecommunications network. Nonetheless, ISDN is gaining in popularity as a facilitator of telelearning activities in the school, home, and community. Projects such as the following illustrate ISDN capabilities in facilitating distance education.

At Nova Southeastern University (NSU), ISDN supports deployment of such tele-instructional initiatives as videoconferencing so that working professionals can earn advanced degrees in education, public health, and pharmacy programs offered at their place of employment. At Appalachian State University, ISDN services enable telementoring activities, teleworkshops, and telecourse delivery to high school students at a network of North Carolina sites (http://www.acs.appstate.edu/). At the University of Ulster, ISDN technology provides learner access to the Internet and enables teachers in outlying areas in Northern Ireland to upgrade skills on site (http: / / www-iet. open. ac. uk/ ie/bt_awards /awards/ ulster. html).

Although ISDN promotes new ways of sharing knowledge and subject matter expertise, an analysis of my case study research demonstrates various concerns among those investigating ISDN implementation. Potential barriers include costs, insufficient geographic coverage in rural locales, inconsistent ISDN service offerings from communications carriers, and technical complexity in integrating ISDN into the telecommuni-cations infrastructure. ISDN products can be incompatible since ISDN standards are subject to interpretations (http:/ /www.niuf.nist.gov/misc/niuf.html). The basic building block for the ISDN paradigm is the 64 Kbps (kilobits per second) B (Bearer) channel. Through consolidation, B channels support dial-up data service for remote LAN (local area network) connections and Web exploration at 128 Kbps or more than four ties faster than the 28.8 Kbps modem.

With the addition of compression technology, this data rate is increased to 512 Kbps. Among the physical user-to-network interfaces supported by ISDN are BRI (Basic Rate Interface) and PRI (Primary Rate Interface). BRI features two 64 Kbps B (Bearer) channels for user information and one 16 Kbps D (delta) channel for call control and low speed data transfer. This 144 Kbps combination is known as 2B+D. A more sophisticated service for bandwidth intensive applications, the PRI features 23 B channels operating at 64 Kbps each and one D channel operating at 64 Kbps resulting in total bandwidth of 1.544 Mbps (megabits per second).

In sophisticated networks, multiple B channels are combined into H channels (hyperchannels) that enable gigabit speeds for broadcast quality video and audio transmissions. The size of the digital pipe for ISDN information transmission depends on the number of communications channels used, types of applications deployed, and budgetary constraints. A determination must also be made about the number of locations and devices that will be networked, wiring, and existence of an ISDN connection at the termination of the call. ISDN requires special equipment. A network termination (NT) device such as an ISDN modular plug facilitates a physical ISDN connection. Terminal equipment (TE) includes those devices that are ISDN enabled (TE- 1s) such as ISDN ready telephones and those devices that are not ISDN compatible such as workstations (TE-2s). Terminal adapters (TAs) such as routers or bridges for LAN connections and external stand-alone boxes or internal cards for workstations perform protocol conversion necessary to interface non-ISDN equipment (TE-2s) to the network.

ISDN development is controlled through various standards organizations such as the ITU. ISDN use with wireless technology is also being examined (http:/ /www. sms. co. uk/isdn /wireless. htm). ISDN's support of videoconferencing configurations contributes to its popularity in the distance learning community. Whether in room sized settings or at the desktop, ISDN enabled videoconferences enhance the quality and intensity of communications, engender a sense of responsibility and involvement among individuals who could not otherwise meet with each other, and transform ways in which students and faculty work together.

In an ISDN based videoconference, participants express understanding, consensus, dissension or irritation with a spoken word as well as the nod of a head, a grimace, a glance, or a shudder. Richer interactions facilitated by videoconferencing result in individual productivity and more constructive problem-solving at all organizational levels. Implementation of ISDN supported video-conferencing enables students to earn education credits and attend training sessions in their home or work environment and creates new options for bringing instructional applications to remote learners. ISDN enables us to provide tutorials for athletic teams on the road and educational services to private colleges, business, and industry throughout the state.

Benefits of ISDN enabled videoconferencing also include substantially reduced travel expenses, more effective use of time, and the ability to link dispersed groups to optimize collaboration. Richard Bazillion, Dean of Library and Information Services at Winona State University, indicated that plans are underway at his university for library professionals to use ISDN based videoconferences for providing reference services to distant learners and local residents. ISDN technology enables a wide range of options for student and faculty participation and involvement. ISDN connectivity permits students working at their own pace to submit coursework online to instructors at a variety of locations and electronically access multimedia materials and video-on-demand at their convenience." Students benefit from telementoring and gain experience in using computer-based tools as part of their training experience.

ISDN connectivity facilitates a variety of administrative functions in the learning environment as well. An ISDN network deployed by the school system is used for video surveillance. School administrators use ISDN links for monitoring data relating to student attendance, grades, immunization records, and class registration. ISDN's support of dialed service and reasonably fast speeds also provides new opportunities for information sharing and distribution. Brevard Community College and the Brevard Workforce Development Board plan to use ISDN based desktop videoconferences to facilitate job training and placement (http://www.brevard.cc.fl.us/ distlrn/ ISDN.HTM).

ISDN implementation typically involves purchasing terminal adapters and network terminal equipment and working with communications carriers in setting up the network and provisioning ISDN services for acco-mmodating institutional requirements. ISDN pricing is inconsistent and depends upon such factors as sophistication of the equipment, type of configuration supported, the communications carrier, and site locations. In commenting upon the price of ISDN usage, Jean Luker, Coordinator of Technology Services for the Washington County (VA) Schools, related: "Even at what is generally considered to be a premium rate, $75.00 a month per line, the total expense to our school division for ISDN use is $7,500 per year.

Since ISDN connectivity facilitates Internet access for 4,500 students, expenditures for this technology are viewed as remarkably cost effective. The quality of ISDN support for applications such as videoconferences depends upon the frame rate, bandwidth of the communications channel, and speed of the connection. Jones related: "At ETU, faster speeds are associated with higher rates." A major roadblock to ISDN deployment is the accelerating availability of optional solutions such as ATM (Asynchronous Transfer Mode) for achieving high speed network interconnectivity. Steven Zink,. Associate Vice President for Information Resources and Technology at the University of Nevada at Reno, noted: "ISDN is used on campus as a quick-fix until the FDDI (Fiber Data Distributed Interface) backbone is in place." Zink added: "Given the alternatives we do not see extensive usage of ISDN on our campus in the long term."

ISDN enables us to create a temporary higher bandwidth link to the Internet for those areas that do not have a high penetration of fiber but from our perspective it does not make sense to invest in ISDN. Our goal is to put a province wide ATM network in place that will interconnect high schools and post-secondary educational institutions." Despite present day technical difficulties, financial barriers, and competition from networking solutions such as ATM, ISDN creates new options for enriching the learning environment and deserves consideration in the planning process. Initially in planning for ISDN deployment, decision makers should determine the need for ISDN and prioritize this need with respect to other communications requirements. A feasibility study can establish with greater accuracy the potential of ISDN deployment and its likelihood of success.

On the basis of the feasibility study, a determination can be made to implement ISDN or discontinue the investigation. A report reflecting inputs from the feasibility study can be developed detailing such factors as resources needed, equipment required, anticipated benefits and limitations, and timetable for deployment. Effective ISDN use for distance learning also requires paying careful attention to instructional strategies. For instance, in terms of ISDN based videoconferencing, faculty should become skilled in using the equipment and work in practice sessions in order to gain experience in helping students adjust to the remote interactive process.

While a prepared agenda can facilitate the implementation of a successful videoconference, students' contributions and collaboration with peers and instructors can also greatly influence educational outcomes. ISDN accommodates basic and sophisticated applications such as file transfer, e-mail, desktop publishing, internet-working, fax transmission, and videoconferencing and promotes creation of a dynamic educational environment. The general area of communication technology has been of growing interest to students. Students are interested in new methods of communication and learning, since they are being exposed to the new media in the home.

From a very early age, they want access to various media so as to enable them to read critically, listen critically, and observe critically, and also be able to interact with the media. Media not only make learning more interesting but also accustom students to the reality and immediacy of media in their everyday lives. Over the past twenty years, research studies have constantly supported the view that, in most cases, well designed computer-based learning (CBL) materials provide both an effective instructional system and an efficient learning environment. With the advent of the multimedia personal computer (MPC), educators are finding new and exciting ways to educate their students. Using video, sound, animations, graphics, and text coupled with interactivity, educators found that their students learning curves are accelerated.

Studies have shown that the retention rate of students using an interactive multimedia (IMM) courseware is up to 30% greater than the rate achieved by students using other traditional methods. Not many research studies are available related to adults learning about IT. The few which were carried out focussed on employing a more direct instructional technique similar to how university courses are taught. Indeed, very few studies have also been conducted using newer instructional techniques particularly in training of adults about IT using CBL materials. From the literature search, it can be generalized that the education of adults, especially in IT related areas are still very much an emerging field of study.

Webster and Martocchio, for instance, employed the traditional computer training method on a group of clerical and administrative full-time employees to use a mail merge function within Word-perfect. Results from the study showed that adults trained in pairs and alone with supporting materials were more positive toward IT than the ones learning individually. This study has the support of Wolfson. Data gathered showed that students preferred to have someone nearby who would help them if they needed it. It was also interesting to note that even though students have the opportunity to work individually on a computer terminal, yet many preferred to work in a group of two or three at a terminal. Generally, studies have supported that acceptance of IT increased after much exposure to it. Zandri and Charnes and Morris found out that giving adults positive exposure to IT results in more positive attitudes toward IT. Czaja and Sharit also discovered that attitudes toward IT became more negative for adults who performed poorly on IT related task.

University Technology Malaysia (UTM), as one of the institutions of higher learning in Malaysia, plays a role in helping the country to develop IT literacy among adults, in particular Malaysian teachers. It is conducting a teacher education degree program in different areas of specialization-technical and vocational, computer science, science, and social science. The student population in the Faculty of Education ranges from adolescents to adults. UTM, in particular the Faculty of Education, not only has a curriculum that is IT-based in nature, but the methods of presenting materials to the students are also IT-based. Besides using the web as a mode of delivery, an attempt has also been made at UTM to develop an interactive Computer-based Educational Resource and Development in Information Technology series. "CERDIk IT" is a Malay word for "IT Intelligent."

The first CERDIk IT series is titled "IT in Education," with the main purpose of improving teachers' knowledge and attitudes regarding the use of IT in education. A prototype version of this IMM courseware is a screen delivered interactive computer-based learning application running under Microsoft Windows on a MPC. The courseware is written in Malay and will be translated to English in the future. This language is an appropriate choice as it is the medium of instruction in Malaysian schools. Efforts to integrate different learning styles into the design of the IMM courseware have been initiated. It is also hoped that the courseware will be as user-friendly as possible with the integration of commonly accepted user-interfaces and screen design by adults. Students are also expected to make use of a multimedia courseware that will involve a significant amount of reading and reflection.

The IMM courseware is designed and developed as a self-study and flexible learning aid. It is developed so as to allow individual students varying degrees of navigational freedom through the courseware. Even though advice is given as to the preferred initial route to follow, students can decide which sections they wish to explore and in what order. Students are able to control according to individual pacing as they travel through the courseware. They should be able to choose which material they are unfamiliar with and to skip material that they already know.

In conjunction with existing course material at UTM. This courseware will be the starting point for further study in a particular area of interest. It can present introductory information to define its area of interest. The end of each section is not the end of its educational offerings. By linking to the Internet, for instance, users will get access to further learning. The provision of computer loans to teachers and tax exemption upon purchase of a personal computer. Currently, some students are already IT-literate even without formal training. So, teachers need to keep abreast with the IT world. If not, they will lag behind their students.

Therefore, this courseware will not only give teachers the opportunity to learn about IT in Education but also they will be able to experience the process of self-paced learning using CBL materials. The successful use of IT, such as the use of IMM in schools, requires the teachers themselves to be familiar with—and competent in the use of such technology, both in their own teaching and in making flexible-learning opportunities available to their students.

The Ministry of Education demands educators who are also highly trained and competent in the use of IT. These IT experts must be capable of maintaining the equipment, developing educational courseware in a variety of subject areas, and developing IT training packages for staff development. With this background, this courseware is developed with an intention to help increase the quantity of training materials, particularly computer-based learning materials, about IT-related areas for staff development. Multimedia holds great promise in enhancing learning as well as in improving the quality of education.

Hofstetter strongly believes that multimedia is an effective medium for learning. Research studies have shown that the retention rate of students using interactive computer-based multimedia is up to 30 percent greater than the rate achieved by students using traditional methods. Multimedia can be used to develop active and mastery learning. In this learning situation, there is active participation on the part of the learner as opposed to passive learning listening to lectures and demonstrations. It can also stimulate the student's mind and encourage learning through all senses because multimedia can combine so many media together.

Furthermore, multimedia is nonlinear and interactive in nature. The interactivity nature is considered to be the most important feature. Interactivity describes the response to instructions and receiving feedback to users and requiring them to be active participants. Psychologists acknowledge the importance of interactive process for knowledge retention. IMM generates a lot of excitement as a learning tool.

Courseware is crossing traditional boundaries of school, work, and home, and enabling students of all ages to choose what they want to learn, in their own time and at their own pace. "Education and training applications are being developed for... computer education, and adult self-improvement. Interactive multimedia brings content to life in developing courseware for education, edutainment, and interactive training". Operating System - IBM-PC compatible; Platform - Window based; Processor - 200 MHz, Random Access Memory - 48 MB RAM: Internal storage - 4.0 GB hard drive; External storage - Removable Hard Drive, for example the Zip Drive; CD-ROM Drive - 16 X speed; Display unit - VGA 17-inch monitor with equivalent to 16 million colors display or true color video display for smoother and sharper display; 640x480 resolution; Sound Card - 16 bit sound card; MIDI playback and animation; Video capture and playback card; Authoring software; Graphics and animation software; Sound and video editing software; CD-RW -Recordable and/or Writable. The courseware is not a how-to CBL material. The information in the courseware does not tell you how to use a word-processor, spread-sheets, or databases for educational purposes.

Nor does it cover how to use the World Wide Web (WWW) or electronic mail (email). These kinds of CBL materials are already available in the market, even though they are in English. This courseware, however, is primarily designed to introduce teachers about the use of IT in education. It will not make individual teachers who use it become IT experts. Rather, it will be useful for teachers who lack specific knowledge and experiences about IT to become more knowledgeable and positive regarding the applications of IT in teaching-learning and administrationmanagement in their educational settings.

When determining the objectives and content of the IMM courseware, measures were taken so that both the objectives and content are suitable to teachers in terms of depth and degree of difficulty. A few methods were used to determine the objectives and content of the courseware. Interviews were conducted with a few experts in computer studies at UTM; information was accessed via the Internet, in particular the World Wide Web (WWW); and books on computer studies which were written in English and Malay. An needs analysis, using open-ended questions, was also done on practiscing teachers who are attending an in-service program. This analysis is important in order to determine their needs and goals relative to IT in Education. The content of the courseware is designed to help the user be actively involved when using the courseware by answering questions, completing activities, or selecting options based on their experiences.

Computer-based learning materials are often presented in an effective way for students learning, particularly for adults. These interactive materials offer a variety of presentation modalities and a high degree of control to learners in terms of the pace of learning and the use of self-assessment. Current learning theories emphasize the importance of accommodating students' different learning styles. Hence, teaching and learning methods that provide for a variety of learning styles will help towards achieving this goal. Students use various learning styles in studying various topics such as being an Activist, Theorist, Pragmatist, or a Reflector.

Knowledge of these learning styles needs to be determined to ensure the use of appropriate learning methods. Time, manpower and effort are among the requirements in producing and catering separate modules for each learning style, and they are the obstacles to good intentions. However, the development of the IMM courseware takes into account different learning styles. Instead of producing separate modules for each learning style, an initiative has been taken to produce modules with a distinct approach to fit a particular learning style. At the time of this writing, this IMM courseware is at the development stage. The adults will consist of practicing teachers who will be undergoing an in-service degree program for two years at UTM after satisfactorily completing one year of study at a Teacher Training College. The teachers represent schools from all over Malaysia and from different specialized areas.

3

Distance Mode of Education

Distance education is a system of rational actions for the imparting of knowledge, skills and attitudes, whereby the originally direct social relationships between teacher and students are substituted to a great extent by indirect relations which are characterized by technical rules and prescriptions, a context-free language, conditioned prognoses and conditioned instructions, goal attainment with the help of target-means relations, and the systematical increase of effectivity.

If we consider the context of the origin of distance education not in a concrete socioeconomic, but in a more general, far-teaching sense, then a new dimension emerges for the understanding of distance education. In order to achieve this it is, however, necessary to describe some structural elements of historical forms of instruction. In many countries educational politicians consider distance education as a means for equalizing educational opportunities. Such a way of thinking, it is true, overlooks the enormous sociocultural barriers on the way to education and surely underestimates the real difficulties. Nevertheless, it must be admitted that distance education provides at least necessary technical and organizational preconditions for a universal admission to continued and higher education. There are several reasons why distance education has developed structural approaches for forms of learning which are free from teacher dominance and the influence of the teacher's authority and why, hence, distance education would have its place at the end of this dimension:

— The increased availability and accessibility of distance education enables the learner for the first time to check through the learning material of a number of respective courses and make decisions himself when selecting one of them. The necessary qualification for doing so may still be lacking with most learners as, so far, usually other persons have decided what is to be studies and when and where the studying will take place. It can, however, be acquired with the help of systems of distance education and their counselling services.

— The teacher may not physically present when the student learns. He effects his learning only indirectly. In the same way as in the political sector the personal power of the king was objectified as soon as his personal exercising of power with the help of written documents which then led to bureaucracy, the personal interaction between teacher and student became objectified by the written word and the use of other media. Thus a scope of independence and freedom came into being, which, indeed, is used and appreciated by the students.

— The student takes over the control of the time, the frequency and the duration of his learning.

— Very often adults begin to study a course in distance education by their own free decision. In such cases, the relation between the teacher and the student is entirely different from the

> corresponding relationship in the traditional and institutionalized schools, where the teacher is usually the representative of the power which makes students attend the school and even controls their learning behaviour and school life.

If distance education is organized as a part of compulsory general education—as, for instance, in Australia, Canada and the United States, with the military services or in vocational training—repressive effects of those who have the power are not removed, but only distributed in another way and sublimated. Their power cannot be done away with simply by replacing face-to-face instruction by distance education. In spite of this, it must be stressed that the objectivation of learning processes offers more scope for independent learning than instruction tied to special teachers in special situations. Above all, it enables the critical cooperation of students when instruction is evaluated even if this happens only in a representative form.

When, for instance, selected students are members of the course team their influence upon the intended teaching-learning process can be increased. Here, dominance-free learning might, indeed, have more scope for its development in distance education than in face-to-face instruction. Obviously, face-to-face instruction is still far from this extreme point, as the learning process is often not only influenced by the teachers' dominance and predilections. Tausch have shown so impressively in their research on the language behaviour of teachers and students, but also by traditional and institutional constraints. Criteria of repressive teaching behaviour are: corporal punishment of pupils which is still preserved in many primary schools, various forms of disciplinary action at secondary schools, and sending down from universities. In these cases the teaching-learning process is still connected to the process of disciplining the students.

Distance education, especially in its form of integrated multimedia systems, will again have to be placed at the present end of this line of development. With regard to the decreased importance of the physical presence of the teacher it is surpassed only by programmed instruction. Traditional face-to-face instruction, however, must be classed with an earlier stage of this development, especially when the teacher and his spoken words dominate. In spite of the use of technical media such as paper, books, blackboards, pictures or even film, the basic communicative structure has not detached itself from the original oral form of instruction.

Distance education is a form of instruction which reached the final stages in each dimension only because it applied principles of industrialization. It can be egalitarian, as the application of technical media overcomes some of the traditional barriers to educational opportunity. These media enable schools and universities to extend their instructional systems in such a way that every capable citizen can profit from learning if they wish—even after their school or college years. In the present historical -economic situation of highly industrialized societies the increased availability and accessibility of education thus assumes a special importance, as the further democratizing of society will increase the educational needs of all citizens considerably. Distance education provides for instruction in which teaching and learning have been secularized to a high degree, as the relation between teacher and students has been isolated from its traditional social context and objectified. Teacher and students do not interact as persons in their totality, but as special teaching and learning functions which operate only in order to reach the defined goals.

Distance education would have been unthinkable in a tradition-directed society. Only the inner-directed society provided the necessary subjective preconditions for it. Every characteristic trait used by Riesman to describe the inner-directed person can also contribute to the explanation of the situation of distant students. Their strongest motivation is derived from vocational career prospects. When they study at a distance they dispose of their leisure time, make sacrifices, have many difficulties and are typically 'dissociated and sheltered from others'. Hence, it can be assumed that the phenomenon of the adult distant student is in accordance with an inner law of development of our culture in the era of industrialization.

It influenced the student's sociocultural and intellectual development in such a way that the motivation of millions of distant students became strong enough and their inner-directedness so stable that it caused them to stay outside of the institutions of traditional education and to commit themselves to an unorthodox way of teaching and learning. Furthermore, it can be postulate that the individual's consciousness is also influenced by life in an industrialized society itself.

Distance education is basically determined by technical rules. Most behaviour possibilities for the teachers and the students are carefully planned, calculated, formalized and standardized. Originally global and complex behaviour patterns are reduced to the setting and control of specific functions.

The students are informed about the rules of the teaching-learning system, and these rules must be followed. Instruction in the class room is a system of 'communicative acting' and uses intersubjective divided colloquial language. This language is characterized by the traits of special persons, groups of persons, places and times. Thus, in a special sense each communicative situation is experienced as being unique.

Distance education, however, uses a language which is taken out of its originally associated surroundings, and is thus free of its context. The technically mediated communication of necessity remains unaffected by particular circumstance, as it addresses students everywhere. In the classroom the communicative acting is determined by reciprocal expectations of behaviour. This means that the teacher who acts expects the students to react in a special way and vice versa.

The expected reactions take place with a higher degree of probability the more the interacting persons have internalized a role consensus and the more the expected behaviour has become ritualized by habit. In industrialized distance education the segments of interaction are constructed on the basis of conditioned prognoses and conditioned imperatives.

Types of distance education

Three different approaches to identifying the forms of distance education are presented: the medium on which the learning materials are based, institutional type and didactic model. The different forms of distance education can be identified by their use of technical media and as the basis for the learning materials.

Print-based distance education

By far the great majority of distance education programmes are print-based. The teaching basis of the Open University of the United Kingdom, for example, is approximately 80% print-based, 10% broadcasting (radio and television) and 10% face-to-face seminars and summer schools. A real disservice has been done to the field of distance education by overemphasis on terms like 'University of the Air'.

Educators, administrators and politicians, not only in developing countries but also in developed countries where finance for education is now being limited, should realise that the vast majority of distance education courses are print-based and will remain so. Exceptions to this in the foreseeable future will come only with populations for whom literacy is a problem and perhaps in those regions where there is traditional reticience about correspondence-type programmes.

Audio-based distance education

Audio-based distance education courses in which the educational content is carried by audio-cassettes or transmitted over radio and to which printed materials are peripheral, if used at all, have been used by distance educators. They are frequently cost-effective, can be used by people with literacy problems and may be a successful method of teaching languages. The University of Waterloo in Ontario is an extensive user of this method.

Video-based distance education

Distance education can be video-based when the basic educational content of the course is broadcast on television or contained on video-cassettes. Some printed materials containing background, further reading and assessment procedures often are supplementary, to the course. The development of cable television and the possibility of home ownership or rental of VCRs make this an area of interest in some cultures. Series of programmes for television have already been developed by a number of groupings in America and elsewhere and a series of programmes based on video-cassettes is offered for credit by the independent study division of the University of Minnesota. Such programmes are to be regarded as distance education when they satisfy the characteristics outlined in the first section of this article. A variant of both audio and video-based programmes is the educational use of satellites.

Computer-based distance education

A computer can be the medium on which educational programmes that fall within the definition of distance education are based. A number of institutions have developed computer-based distance education programmes and the Fall Education Company lists over 300 computer-based courses already developed for the ATO system. They range from Accounting Fundamentals to Zeiss—a model Planetarium. It is known that in America negotiations are in progress for the accreditation of some of these computer-based programmes for college and university credit. No evaluation of the relative merits of the media described nor of the possibility of developing a multi-media system by combinations of the various components is offered here. Nor can consideration be given to whether it is possible or desirable to combine distance education with on-campus education.

Institutional distance education

Private, proprietary correspondence schools have made valuable contributions to this field of education since the last century. In recent years standards have been set by affiliation to national accrediting bodies: the National Home Study Council of the U.S.A., the Association of Accredited Correspondence Colleges of the United Kingdom. Some of these institutions are non-profit making and a number receive some government support and they are found throughout the world.

Government sponsored schools, colleges and universities have played a role in distance education for the last seventy years. Many of these institutions are specially structured for distance education: Athabasca University, Edmonton; the Open College of Further Education, Adelaide; the Centre National de Tele-enseignement in France; the Fernuniversitat-Gesamthochschule in Hagen. Many other colleges and universities have a department which concentrates on the distance students : the independent study department of the University of Minnesota, Minneapolis; the external studies department of the University of Queensland, Brisbane. The Open University at Milton Keynes in the United Kingdom founded only ten years ago, has already made an impressive contribution to research, theory and practice in the field of distance education.

Wide range of institutional type distance education, incorporating both public and private operations, makes the defining of the limits of the educational field within which all lie a difficult task. It is felt, nevertheless, that all institutions in this area because of the separation of their students from their teachers are engaged in the planning or purchase of learning materials and possess or have access to an integrated range of technical media, by which the student is given the possibility of two-way communication, not only when beginning but throughout the course. These institutions are representatives of the most industrialised form of education.

Didactic model of distance education

There are three forms of didactic structure characterise distance education institutions, especially when considered under the headings: a) provision for two-way communication and b) possibility of occasional seminars. Variations of the three models presented here are to be found employed by the different institutional types considered above in their effort to link learning materials to learning. The correspondence schools send learning materials by post to the student, the student studies the materials and posts assignment back to the institution which marks and comments upon them and posts them back to the student. The correspondence element in distance education is here reduced to a minimum and once the learning materials have been developed and distributed to the students, the emphasis is placed on compulsory fortnightly two-to-three hour consultations. At these groups of students meet their tutor for evaluation of their home study and for explanation and preparation of the next stage of learning materials. In a system similar to that of the Open University of the United Kingdom the link between learning materials and learning is promoted by as coherent a structure as possible. The student is supported by a wide range of activities, most of them optional unless the course team has decided otherwise.

Open learning and extension programmes

There are certain forms of education which have some similarities to distance education but are not identical with it. Four of the most important are here presented for consideration: extension programmes, University Without Walls, experiential learning, the external degree. Three more general terms: 'non-traditional learning', 'off-campus studies' and 'open learning' are first considered briefly. One cannot define 'non-traditional learning' without first defining 'traditional learning' and that is clearly beyond the bounds of this article. It seems at times that in the United States any educational programme that is not a four-year, residential, university degree programme can be regarded as non-traditional learning, though there are clearly more restricted usages. "Non-traditional learning' is to be regarded as a vague, generalised term of which distance education is one example. 'Off-campus studies' is another general term for any programme which does not take place on the central university or college campus—distance education is one possibility.

It is difficult to find a common definition for the many experimental programmes that call themselves *open*. However, all open schools have one principle in common: they are to a greater or lesser extent efforts to expand the freedoms of learners. Some are open only in a spatial sense while others provide freedoms in more significant dimensions—in admissions, selection of courses, individual adaptation of the curriculum and time, goal selection and evaluation.

Extension programmes are ways of extending the expertise of a university or college to new populations. The terms can imply offering the same programmes as for full-time, day-time students by different means, at different locations or at different times. An extra-mural department usually has a similar function of extending the expertise of the university to a broader community. Some of these programmes are for credit, others not. The range or extension and extra-mural programmes is very extensive and distance education can be regarded as one grouping of a number of possibilities of providing education outside the normal lecture room.

Extension, especially as used in the United States, is a much broader term which can include part-time day or night, conventional lectures on campus. University without walls implies the design of an individualised programme based on a learning contract for students with clear learning objectives who cannot realise their whole educational aspirations through existing programmes. A University Without Walls programme can include experiential learning credits, ordinary lectures, distance education elements, learning from community sources or job-related activities, all of which can be evaluated towards a college or university degree.

Experiential learning programmes are those which give credit for prior learning which did not take place in a lecture room setting and was not sponsored by an educational institution, but was acquired through work experience including volunteer work, co-operative education or self-study. A degree programme which can be completed in the following manner: a student entering the programme with the minimum entrance qualifications can complete it with less than 25 percent of the required work taking the form of campus-based classroom instruction. In the attempt to place some conceptual order around the wide range of study programmes that are associated with non-traditional and distance education, the question of whether or not the external degree should be included within the concept of distance education is the one which poses the most precise definition and research problems.

Distance education in higher learning

There are four fundamental types of distance education in higher learning:

— *Type 1*: Distance education is accomplished by studying the printed material sent to the students by their university teachers, as well as by means of an exchange of letters between them, whereby the university teachers and their assistants correct the assignments and guide the further work of the students. This type was developed out of the traditional correspondence instruction and can be found especially in countries with long experiences in this field; for instance, England, France, the United States, Canada, Australia and South Africa.

— *Type 2*: Here distance education type 1 is supplemented by regular and obligatory teaching-learning activities which take place face-to-face. It was developed in the Soviet Union and later introduced in eastern Germany. Variations of this type can be found in Japan, Sweden, Cuba, Mexico and Costa Rica. In extreme cases the face-to-face periods become so important that it becomes doubtful whether one can still speak of distance education.

— *Type 3*: Distance education types 1 and 2 are supplanted by lectures and demonstrations on radio and television. This multimedia approach has been tested in the United States and England.

— *Type 4*: Distance education is organized in such a way that a programmed computer performs important teaching functions. The type has been tested by the US Air Force.

Distant students

As distance study differs from country to country in the same way as other forms of higher learning, it is difficult to describe the distant students in unified, general terms. However, it is possible to distinguish three types of them according to the goals and the duration of their studies. There are undergraduate, part-time and postgraduate distant students.

— *Undergraduate distant students* tale courses in order to prepare themselves for graduation. We find them, for instance, in England, South

African, the Soviet Union, Poland, Czechoslovakia, Hungary, Romania, Bulgaria and East Germany. As they usually have also to work for a living they must extend their study time considerably. Often they have to carry this double burden for five to seven years, and in many cases even longer.

— *Part-time distant student* are to be found among the regular students of a university. They enrol for recourses the contents of which are normally delivered by professors or lecturers in one semester. This type of student emerged especially in the United States, but also in Sweden, Norway and the Netherlands. It includes regular students who had to discontinue their studies for health, family of financial reasons or had to go into the armed forces but wish to use their free time for studying single course at a distance until they are able to resume their regular studies.

— *Post-graduate distant students* are graduate students employed in the professions who wish to enrol in distance education courses in order to continue their education. Up to now this group has been comparatively small. But there are signs that it will grow considerably in the years to come.

For undergraduate students, studying at a distance is a central life task which determines their way of living for a long time in specific way. If they drop out, their plans for a professional future have failed and they have to dispense with the vocational promotion they had in mind. For the regular students who enrol in only one or in several single course, the new learning experience might merely be an interesting episode. And for the professional employees who are continuing their education, distance study will be considered as an additional task which will not bind them very much, especially if they volunteered to study at a distance and think that they can postpone it for any length of time.

Most distant students belong to the age group up to thirty five years, but many of them are considerably older. In eastern countries there is an age limit. In western countries, however, it is possible to become a distant student if you are considerably older even that. At the University of Wisconsin, for instance, they have enrolled a seventy-year-old man and at the University of South Africa the oldest student was seventy-two years old. As distance students are generally older than day students greater portion of them are married and responsible for children. Experience has shown that married distant students are 'better' students. However, the years before and after their marriage are reported to be rather unfavourable for their studies. Female students often have to discontinue their studies for longer periods because they have had children. The disadvantages of higher age, however, are compensated for b higher motivation.

As distant students are more experienced in the world of work and in life, it is easier for them to judge the importance of graduation and continuing education for their professional development. Tutors, in particular, confirm that their maturity is obviously a favourable conditions for the learning process and the general progress of their studies. If their study programme is related to their vocational work, their motivation can be supported in a unique way. For universities and colleges the higher age of their distant students means that they are in the process of slowly becoming institutes of adult education as will, which will make considerable adjustments necessary.

Distant students are even more likely to be respected than scorned, although group life is highly regarded on the campus. The students and the university teachers hold that distance education is 'more difficult' and compels the distant students to deal with the subject matter longer and more intensely than is the case with day students. If they have successfully finished their course, their achievements are duly acknowledged - in spite of their special way of studying. The status of distant students is also different in East and West, as the respective societies judge the importance of vocational work quite differently—mainly for ideological reasons. Whereas the necessity of working for a living is considered to be rather an impediment to university studies in western countries, it is appreciated as a necessary precondition for successful university study in eastern countries.

Typical of the western attitude is the remark of a Canadian professor who said, 'Every encouragement should be given to all persons who desire to become better educated and more highly trained, particularly those who have sufficient zeal and ambition to learn while they earn.' Apart from the view that vocational work is such a great, but unavoidable, burden that it could be carried only by distant students with special qualities, these works convey an attitude towards distance students which still suggests a philanthropic benevolence. It would be worth examining whether this attitude is disappearing in western industrialized countries. In eastern European countries distant students are systematically made conscious of the fact that they have an obligation to society which they are expected to live up to, an din government and communist party reports they are called the 'pioneers of a new socialist intelligentsia'.

Distance teachers

Because distance education can take place only when special teaching functions are performed and because it is organized at regular universities as well as at special institutes, it is possible to subdivide teachers in distance education into five groups, each representing a special type.

— *Type 1*: University teachers who are responsible for their day students as well as for distant students. Their traditional field of activities, which is already very complex, is extended by the additional functions of being an author of teaching material and a tutor of distant students. Many of them like these new functions and endeavour to become excellent in performing them. Writing teaching material for distant students is new for them as it differs decisively from writing down their lectures. They no longer write for the day student in the class or the auditorium, but for the student who sits at home and tries to reach his goals by reading the texts. As it is necessary to use their limited time necessary to use their limited time economically, such teachers will have to calculate their approach very carefully and thereby realize the importance of new didactical perspectives which induce them to separate the two groups of students and deal with them to separate the two groups of students and deal with them in different ways. The function of a tutor of distant students is also new to such a teacher. It will call for developing further those guiding and counselling functions which are used when talking with the day students about their tests and seminar papers—a considerable educational task.

— *Type 2:* Teachers at distance teaching colleges and at departments for distance education in universities. They deal with distant students only, which changes the profile of their work. It consists mainly of writing teaching material and tutoring. As they can specialize in these activities, they are more likely to develop new concepts of distance teaching of their own.

— *Type 3:* University teachers who conduct seminars for distant students regularly. A typical representative of this type 1 the *Konsulent* in East Germany, where a considerable amount of distance education consists of obligatory face-to-face teaching. Generally, they are lecturers and readers working under the supervision of a professor. They perform a very demanding job as they have to combine and adjust principles of face-to-face teaching with those of distance teaching, which is difficult as there are no traditional patterns for this special teaching approach.

— *Type 4*: A professor who typically does not write any teaching material and does not correct assignments at all, but exchanges letters with a number of advanced students in order to guide and conduct their doctoral studies. There students usually live far away from the university and are working in the production process. At this level of university education the work of a student is already so specialized and individualized that regular courses will no longer do. Furthermore, these students are already so self-reliant and have become able to master the techniques of acquiring knowledge b methodical reading that they need professional advice which is given to them by their academic mentor. An experiment at the National Extension College in the United Kingdom shows that this type of distance duration can also be tried out and be successful at a lower level.

— *Type 5*: University teachers who assume responsibility for the management of distance teaching departments of institutions. They are confronted with tasks differing decisively from the corresponding tasks at conventional universities. Vice-chancellors and presidents, for instance, do not normally deal with teaching problems, as this task is dealt with by the individual professors or lecturers. The heads of distance teaching universities or departments, however, have to see to it that the contributions of all departments and sections can be guided and adapted in such a way that they fit together and elicit the intended learning effects. Furthermore, they have to keep complex technical systems going as the success of distance teaching relies on them entirely.

If we examine university-level distance education in various countries of the world we can see that the special educational traditions and socioeconomic conditions of these countries have led to individual models of distance education in each case. In spite of this, it is possible to identify two distinct, supranational models of distance education if we disregard some particular developments and minor exceptions: a western and an eastern one. They differ with regard to their rank in national educational policy, the competent and responsible persons for it in the hierarchy of the university, the degree of their organizational integration into the university, and the methods of teaching and learning employed.

The different goals of distance education have also led to different areas of responsibility. In the western model the establishment of distance education rests usually with the departments of university extension or adult education. These departments decide the contents and procedures of their distance education themselves. The result can be highly differentiated programmes, as, for instance, at the University of Wisconsin and the University of Nebraska. On the other hand, one can also find meagre programmes with a small number of accidental and unrelated correspondence courses often administered by only one secretary.

The way in which distance education is integrated into the hierarchy of the university sheds some light on its relative institutional importance. In western countries distance education is usually organized by a section of the department of university extension or adult education. As these departments lack the academic reputation and the weight and power of the classical faculties or departments, this organizational structure is bound to be detrimental to the healthy development of distance education. The same can be said about universities which cooperate with correspondence colleges outside the university by using their course material as, for instance, the University of Lund. There, distance education is even less integrated. An extreme form of this non-integration of distance education can be found when the university limits itself to conducting final examinations only and relies on private correspondence colleges for the teaching of the courses.

In Eastern European countries the organizational structure of distance education provides that most professors, deans and reactors of the universities have to be responsible for their distant students in the same way as for their day students. Quite often the universities even have special pro-rectors for distance study. In this way, distance education is fully integrated not only into the general teaching programme, but also into the hierarchy of the university. A total integration is achieved in seventeen higher educational institutions in the USSR and in

China. There, the entire faculty of the college caters exclusively for distant students. If we want to find out what a similar set-up would look like in a western county, we need only examine the University of South Africa, where there is a whole university which takes care of distant students only.

Teaching and learning methods

Over the last hundred years private correspondence colleges have accumulated special knowledge of how to teach at a distance, which could easily be systematized into a methodology of teaching by writing. However, the value of this methodology should not be assessed as being higher than that of traditional methodologies for face-to-face teaching based on common sense, pragmatic approaches and didactic recipes. Nevertheless, wherever western universities insist on a careful development of written special materials for distance study courses and on a regular correspondence between teacher and student, they profit by these early experiences.

Eastern European models of distance education, however, are not related to this tradition. Consequently, little or no attention is paid to the development of special teaching and learning material and to the regular, individual correction of test papers. Mostly, these elements are substituted by regular consultation periods at weekends, and b yearly seminars of several weeks' length. This may be considered as an adjustment of forms of traditional university study to the conditions of distant students. It was made under the unfortunate socioeconomic conditions of the time after World War II. Hence, many measures were dictated by sheer need. The students were urged to work in full-time employment and to study at the university at the same time.

The universities had to rely on the professors and the further teaching staff as well as on the infrastructure at hand. They used the same curricula and the same text-books which were provided for the say students. Hence, one could define the eastern model of distance education as a system of administrative measures which enable the universities to cater for considerable numbers of additional students who were expected to study mainly at home. This, of course, means that the eastern model is not derived from any elaborated concept in which the elements of self-study, regional consultation periods and yearly seminars at the university are carefully related to one another.

At present a model of distance education is becoming discernible. It is characterized by the calculated use of modern technical media—for instance, television, radio, computer and telephone, as well as audio and video tapes. This development changes the structure of the teaching and learning process to such a great extent that it seems to be justified to speak of new form of distance education, which we should like to call for the time being the 'technological model'. The structural change can be seen immediately if one realizes that the use of these technical media confronts the teachers with new and difficult problems, as the contents of teaching and the teaching functions have to be redistributed if they change from the use of predominantly one medium—the correspondence course—to bi-or multimedia teaching activities.

The new technical media force them to objectify longer sequences of their teaching. Careful, time-consuming and expensive preparations have now become inevitable. All the problems of planning the teaching-learning process, especially the division of labour between the teachers and media experts, and the organization and control of learning activities, assume a new importance. Fortunately, the new model of distance study can profit from the 'technological turn' in the methodology of teaching which can at present be identified—mainly as a consequence of experiments with programmed learning.

Today, it is easier to recognize the characteristic outlines of the emerging new model of distance education and to further its progressive elements than it would have been only a few years ago, because the newly developed 'educational technology' already provides us with a number of categories necessary for analysing and describing it. Such assistance, though, cannot be expected from an educational technology which regards itself as the technical or instrumental side of the teaching-learning process only and attempts to reinforce it. Rather, we will have to look out for an educational technology which concentrates on the use of scientific methods and procedures for the planning, development and evaluation of teaching-learning projects.

In short, the technological turn in the methodology of teaching and learning means that those process are to be explored and manipulated which can help to influence the learning situation. Flechsing has pointed out that the technological turn in the methodology of teaching is brought about in five phases. In the first phase, the technical medium is used to stimulate the teacher, in the second phase this approach is given up and teaching techniques are developed in a rational way, which are optimized in the third phase. In the fourth phase, teaching techniques are coordinated with the help of systems approach, and in the last phase the development work is based on curriculum research and the duplication of teaching techniques. If we analyse the relationship of distance education to the five phases of the technological development we can conclude that it had a remarkable affinity to some of these phases long before this concept was developed, and, on the other hand, we can identify several features which do not yet correspond to these phases.

Only ten years ago the improvement of projects of distance education took lace more or less arbitrarily at best based on conjectures or according to the principle of trail and error. Even if money was available, one could not really identify the critical factors in the system of distance education which needed purposeful changes. The real contribution of the new educational technology is that now things have changed. It provides us with a system of scientific instruments and procedures which enable us to improve distance education systematically and also verify the outcomes. Even more, if we match a given project of distance education with the five phases of the technological turn its structural advantages and deficits become clearly visible. This is very favourable precondition for slowly raising the development of distance education to higher levels of accomplishment. An additional advantage of the new technological model of distance education is that the techniques of planning, designing and optimizing projects in distance education can be favourable for the further development of distance study at university level.

Distance learning and industrialisation

Distance study represents facts new to education in several aspects. Compared with other forms of study it was novel in the form in which it made its first breakthrough over ninety years ago. With even greater justification it can be called novel in its present form in which it is currently spreading throughout the world, contributing towards the discovery of the educational opportunities provided by the modern media, such as radio and television. It is, above all, novel and pointing towards the future when it makes use of electronic data-processing equipment and wide-band.cable transmission techniques.

It is no coincidence that university study at a distance, in its early form of correspondence teaching, began its development only about 130 years ago, as it requires conditions that only existed from then on. One necessity, for example, is a relatively fast and regular postal and transport service. The first railway lines and the first correspondence schools were established around the same time. When one further realizes how much technical support distance teaching establishment need nowadays in order to cater effectively for large groups of students, it becomes clear that distance study is a form of study complementary to our industrial and technological age. Lectures, seminars and practice sessions, on the other hand, have developed from forms of teaching derived from ancient rhetoric and were practised at medieval universities; the colloquium originates from the dialogic teaching methods of the humanistic era.

Industrialization is the symbol of a new epoch in the development of man fundamentally different from all previous epochs. It is without example in history, above all, on account of the basic changes in most spheres of human existence. Academic teaching alone seems to have remained largely unscathed by industrialization - with the exception of distance study, for this form of study is remarkably consistent with the principles and tendencies of industrialization. For this reason, experimentally, structural elements, concepts and principles derived from the theories of industrial production are used here to interpret the distance study phenomenon. This does not mean that the teaching and learning processes occurring in distance study are equated with processes in industrial production.

In the sixties, experiments were carried out which tried to explain the teaching and learning processes using the technical model of the feedback control system, in order to find approaches to a 'cybernetic pedagogy'. Most impressive, however, was the achievement of Gottfried Hausmann who, in 1959, condensed the analogy between the dramatic arts and education into a 'dramaturgy of teaching'. In it he interprets the educational structure of teaching and learning processes in detail using the terms and principles of the dramatic are in the theatre. Paul Heimann saw the merit of this comprehensive and detailed comparison in the possibility that 'it might give rise to a complete revision of our teaching and learning models'. Furthermore, it may not be without significance for this planned interpretation that for another important aspect of university or college work, namely research, comparisons with the production process already exist.

In 1919, Max Weber defined structural similarities between research institutes and capitalistic organizations and, in 1924, Helmut Plessner pointed out that the 'mechanization, methodization and depersonalization of the manufacturing process equally dominate the production of economic as well as cultural goods'. The following comparison between distance study and the industrial production process will prove similar consistencies. From the start, distance study has a special relationship with the industrial production process in so far as the production of study materials in itself is an industrial process built into the whole teaching process as a constituent part, quite unlike the production of textbooks, for example.

In the case of commercial distance teaching establishments the further question of selling the printed or otherwise duplicated study units adds calculations of applied economics to the teaching process. Even the distance teaching departments of government-financed universities are not entirely free from these considerations. It would be interesting to examine how far these facts have already influenced the structure of distance teaching. In order to facilitate the discovery of further relationships between distance teaching and the production process, the following structural changes—essentially brought about by industrialization—in the development of the production of goods should be noted:

— According to the principle of rationalization, individual work as was traditional in the craftsmen's trades changes at an early stage to a production based on the division of labour (e.g., in factories), and this later leads to the development of assembly lines and mass production.

— Work processes initially characterized by the use of tools are increasingly restructured by mechanization and, later, automation.

These changes lead to the following results:

— The preparatory phase becomes increasingly important.

— Success depends, among other things, on systematic planning and organization. Scientific measures of control are needed.

— Work processes must be formalized and products standardized. The production process is objectified.

— Each developmental step towards increased

mechanization leads to changes in the function of those involved in the production process.

— Small concerns are no longer able to raise the investment needed for developmental work and technical equipment. A strong tendency towards concentration and centralization becomes noticeable.

Distance education and rationalization

In education, a rationalizing way of thinking is nothing new. In a general form, it influences the reasoning for numerous educational decisions. For example, the introduction of lectures to larger groups of students, the use of printed books and the specialization of university lecturers were considerable steps towards the rationalization of the academic teaching process. Every university teacher will, when planning a lecture, choose those subjects that will best help him or her to fulfil the purpose of that particular lecture.

In distance teaching, however, ways of thinking, attitudes and procedures can be found which only established themselves in the wake of an increased rationalization in the industrialization of production processes. The characteristic details are, among others, as follows:

— In distance study the teaching process is based on the division of labour and detached from the person of the university lecturer. It is therefore independent from a subjectively determined teaching situation, thus eliminating part of the earlier mentioned obstacles to rationalization. The division of labour and the objectification of the teaching process allow each work process to be planned in such a way that clearly formulated teaching objectives are achieved in the most effective manner. Specialists may be responsible for a limited area in each phase.

— The use of technical equipment (duplicating machines, organization systems, transporting devices) makes it possible to convey the knowledge, ability and teaching skills of a university lecturer, by means of the detached objectivity of a distance study course of constant quality, to a theoretically unlimited number of students. The rationalization effect of mass production becomes apparent here.

— The rigorous application of organizational principles and means saves teachers as well as students unnecessary effort.

— At some of the newer distance teaching establishments, modern means of technical support, such as film, television and electronic data-processing installations, have replaced teaching staff in certain areas of their work, in particular, in the fields of giving information and assessing performance.

— Student work through a course which has been tested prior to going to print. This prevents misunderstandings and stops students from going in the wrong direction.

— The quality of a distance study course can be improved, because its effectiveness can be monitored at any time by scientific methods.

If the number of students required in a society outgrows the number of university teachers available, rational thinking should be able to find ways and means of changing teaching methods in such a way that the teaching resources of the university teachers available are used to the best effect, quantitatively as well as qualitatively. Distances study can be regarded as a result of such endeavours.

Division of labour has played an important role in the sociological theories of the last 100 years. Applied to the production processes it means that the work is split in the sense of 'dividing one complete work process into a number of elementary procedures', as described by Adam Smith at an early stage. With an extensive division of labour training periods become shorter, more people are able to carry out the work and wages can be lowered. Just as the division of labour is a precondition for the mechanization of work processes and for industrialization as a whole, it has made university study at a distance possible. The division of labour is the main prerequisite for the advantages of this new form of teaching to become effective.

The principle of the division of labour is thus a constituent element of distance teaching. The 'complete work process', which is split in distance teaching, consists of the teaching activity of the university lecturer: namely, the entirety of the measures he takes in order to initiate and guide learning processes in students. Initially, the two basic functions of the university teacher, that of conveying information and that of counselling, were allocated as separate responsibilities in distance teaching departments of universities or colleges. Both functions, above all however that of transmitting information, are now even further divided. If, for example, the number of students enrolled on a distance study course is high, regular assessment of performance is not carried out by those academics who developed the course.

The recording of results is the responsibility of yet another unit; and the development of the course itself is divided into numerous phases, in each of which experts in particular fields are active. This specialization may bring the following advantages:

— Materials required for the development of the distance study course can be assembled by leading experts in the specialist fields concerned.

— Having completed the manuscript, the author can then be freed from the time-consuming processes of exact source references and of lecturing.

— Educationists and experienced practitioners of distance teaching are able to revise the manuscripts of study units in order to make the planned teaching process more effective.

— Colleagues from the 'academic middle tier' may be involved in the correction of exercises carried out by students. There are cases where even senior students have taken or such tasks especially where they are concentrating on marking the exercises from a limited number of correspondence units. As in the industrial manufacturing process, the level of previous training may be lower on account of the division of labour and, as there, 'more people are able to carry out the work'. Since with extensive specialization of this type the number of scripts one university teacher is able to mark may be much higher, this process is also cheaper.

Mechanization means the use of machines in a work process. These machines replace the work done by the muscles of men or animals. In part they even take over elements of brain work. There are varying degrees of mechanization. The pre-industrial stage is characterized mainly by craftwork making use of tools. The first level of industrialization was reached with the use of 'dependent machines'. The second level of industrialization led to mass production as a result of the use of 'semi-independent machines' and assembly lines. Finally, the third level of industrialization is characterized by the spread of automation. In order to stay with this analogy, distance study could be ascribed to be industrial levels, as it cannot take place without the use of machines. Duplicating machines and transport systems are prerequisites, and later forms of distance teaching have the additional facilities of modern means of communication and electronic data processing installations.

The production of distance study courses represents mass production. Apart from reasons of profitability, the large number of courses produced forces distance teaching organizations to analyse the requirements of potential distance learners far more carefully than in conventional teaching and to improve the quality of the courses. Most American distance study courses are revised and re-issued at regular intervals. As American universities charge fees to cover the greatest part of the budget allocated to distance teaching departments, the quality of distance study courses must not be allowed to deteriorate.

When, on account of mass production, the University of California has more distance study courses to offer than there is demand for them, it occasionally places advertisements for students in newspapers. Statistics prove that the number of graduates in areas without a university is lower than in areas near universities. It is possible that, according to the principle of mass production, distance teaching will one day equalize the opportunities to study, just as industrial mass production has assimilated consumer patterns in town and country.

In a production situation where a division of labour prevails, economy, quality and speed of the work process depend on the right type of preparation. This is necessary in industries producing a type of preparation. This is necessary in industries producing a variety of articles and needs to be carried out by senior specialist staff in special departments, as workers, foremen and masters involved in the production process lack the necessary knowledge and experience. During the preparatory stages one determines how workers, machines and materials can usefully relate to one another during each phase of the production process. In addition, there are developmental and constructional tasks. The more thorough the preparation, the less is a successful production process dependent on the particular abilities of the workers involved. Consequently, workers can easily be exchanged.

In distance teaching, success depends decisively on a 'preparatory phase'. It concerns the development of the distance study course involving experts in the various specialist fields with qualifications also often higher than those of other teachers involved in distance study. Here, too, each section of the course can be carefully planned. The use of technical support and a suitable combination of this with individual contributions from distance tutors and advisers play an important role here.

Compared to university teachers in conventional study, who are responsible for the entire teaching process, distance tutors and advisers are more easily exchangeable on account of the thorough preparatory work. Finally, the development of distance study courses also requires investment to an extent that has never before been considered at establishments of higher education. The separation of preparatory work and individual instruction and the distribution of these function among several persons is a particularly clear example of analogy with the production process.

An essential element of preparation is planning, which needs to be far more comprehensive and detailed in the industrial manufacturing process than in manual production, as it requires the coordination of many interacting factors. In the developmental phase of a distance study course planning plays an important role, as the contents of correspondence units, from the first to the last, must be determined in detail, adjusted in relation to each other and represented in a predetermined number of correspondence units.

Where instance study is supplemented by residential weeks on campus or weekend seminars, planning becomes even more important; these supplementary teaching events are not intended to repeat academic contents already offered, nor have an 'enrichment' function, but should be structurally integrated in the distances study course. When combining distance teaching with other media, one has to consider carefully which type of contents suits what medium. Finally, where computers are used in distance study, preparatory planning is most advanced and demands by far the greatest expenditure, as the teaching activity of the computers needs to be programmed. In all these efforts to predetermine and arrange the course of teaching processes as far as possible, we are dealing with effective planning.

As a consequence of the division of labour, the production process has to be rationally ordered according to organizational principles and with specially developed organizational means, since 'the continuous interacting of numerous people towards a specific purpose requires organization'. Furthermore, productivity depends on the type and degree of organization. In distance study, likewise, there is an immediate connection between the effectiveness of the teaching method and rational organization.

Organization, for example, makes it possible for students to receive exactly predetermined documents at appointed times, for an appropriate university teacher to be immediately available for each assignment sent in, for consultations to take place at fixed locations at fixed times, or for examinations to be held, or for counsellors to inform themselves at any time of the progress of a student or a group of students. Organization becomes easier in large distance teaching establishments, as trained personnel and modern means of organization are available.

Application of the principle of the division of labour and the use of machines, as well as the duplication of correspondence units in often large numbers, force distance teaching institutions likewise to adopt a greater degree of standardization than is required in conventional teaching. Not only is the format of the correspondence units standardized, so also is the stationery for written communication between student and lecturer, and the organizational support, as well as each single phase of the teaching process, and even the academic contents. Whereas the academic giving a conventional lecture may indulge in an interesting deviation, because he sees educational advantages in this at a particular time with a certain group of students, the distance study lecturer has to be aware that he is, when writing a correspondence unit, addressing such a large group of students that situation-dependent improvisation becomes impossible. Instead he has to find a standard adequate, as far as possible, for every student admitted to the distance study course in question. This is achieved by developing a model for the course, perfecting it through the involvement of several experts and then approximating it to the required standard by testing it on a representative group of students before printing large number of copies. Just as the production of a branded article can only remain economical if its quality is continuously adapted to the constant needs of a large group of consumers, a distance teaching institution has to standardize the academic contents of its courses in such a way that it can be sure they appeal to all distance learners as equally as possible.

The adaptation to any number of students, however large, forces the lecturer more strongly than in conventional study to consider the necessary standard that is, at the same time, realistic for as many students as possible. Consequently, the choice of contents of a distance study course is less likely to be a reflection of the particular interest of an academic giving conventional lectures, than of the objective requirements of the total course profile. On account of the division of labour and the use of various types of machines, the function of the worker in the production process has changed considerably. Whereas it was typical for the craftsman to plan the production of a piece of work as well as acquire the necessary materials, carry out the work and finally sell the finished piece of work himself, industrialization led to a more marked functional differentiation.

When preparatory work and selling became separate from production and, within these three phases, many individual functions were allocated to different individual, a loss of function naturally occurred for each single worker. On the other hand, new roles were created and new achievements became possible. For example, 'in jobs where, due to mechanization, the processing of the material has been taken out of the worker's hand, speed and energy of execution are no longer required: they have been replaced by accuracy and diligence; the work no longer shows quantitative but qualitative criteria'. As a result of the division of labour, the function of the lecturer teaching at a distance also changes.

The original role of provider of knowledge in the form of the lecturer is split into that of study unit author and that of marker; the role of counsellor is allocated to a particular person or position. Frequently, the original role of lecturer is reduced to that of a consultant whose involvement in distance teaching manifests itself in periodically recurrent contributions. In order to ensure the effectiveness of the four functions mentioned, numerous support functions of an operational-technical type are particularly important, as, without them, distance study could not take place. As tutors and consultants have largely been relieved of the task of conveying course matter, they are able to devote themselves to a considerable degree to more demanding tasks, such as aiding motivation, providing individual support, structuring course contents for students, identifying problems, establishing connections and so on.

The university lecturer who lectures from his chair or leads a seminar discussion has the freedom and the opportunity to allow his subjectivity to influence his way of teaching: he is free to decide how and how much to prepare, he determines his own academic aims and methods and is able to change them spontaneously during a lecture, whereby not all the changes in his teaching method need to be reflected. In distance teaching, however, most teaching functions are objectified as they are determined by the distance study courses as well as technical means. Only in written communications with the distance learner or possibly in a consultation or the brief additional face-to-face events on campus has the teacher some individual scope left for subjectively determined variants in his teaching method.

In cases where a computer is used in distance study, even this opportunity is limited further. The advantages of objectifying the teaching process in the form of a distance study course lie in the fact that the teaching process can then be reproduced, thus making it available at any time and, above all, that it can be manipulated. Without objectification distance study courses could not take place anywhere and at any time and be continuously improved. The objectification of teaching practice in distance study is of particular importance in societies where, on account of an hierarchic structure of universities and colleges, the function of the provider of knowledge is combined in many academic with that of a holder of very great authority. As a result of this the relationship between student and lecturer is similar to that of subordinate and superior.

As distance study has largely been freed from subjectivity, the process of providing knowledge is hardly affected by situations of this kind. In this context, distance study is particularly suitable for the further education of adults. The investment required for mechanized mass production involving the division of labour has led to large industrial concerns with a concentration of capital, a frequently Centralized administration, and a market that is not seldom monopolized. In this context it is significant that some distance teaching establishments cater for very large groups of students. The largest universities teaching at a distance in the Russia and in South Africa have over 40,000 students, and the Open University in England has more than 70,000. Each of these three establishments—as well as their Spanish equivalent — caters for the national demand. Obviously, a minimum number of students is necessary to make the technical installations and the establishment of an efficient organization feasible.

Economically, it is therefore more worthwhile to create a large central distance study establishment rather than ten or twenty small regional institutions. Just as the industrial markets for certain products have long expended beyond narrow regional frontiers, such centralized distance teaching establishments must cross the traditional areas of the responsibility of universities and the educational administration. If all the said principles of distance teaching are rigorously applied, monopoly-like prestige positions in teaching activity are created for leading experts in various disciplines.

4

Open Learning: Problems and Prospects

The use of the term Open Learning (OL) had emerged during mid-1970s. OL was concerned with equal opportunity, and preached the message that whatever training and education individuals required and wished for should be accessible to them. In other words, education should be designed to match more closely the aspirations of learners. Education was to become 'learner-centred'. OL came to imply any situation in which all those features and characteristics of learning programmes and systems which reduce opportunity and access are identified and modified to avoid closure.

Traditionally, the organization of Higher Education (HE) has been largely course-based, and as a consequence most educational activities have centred on the course. The past decade, however, has seen the introduction of a number of educational initiatives designed to enhance the accessibility and flexibility of HE, bringing with them a number of significant benefits for both students and employers. The main innovations include the following:

— *Modularization*: Students are no longer expected to commit themselves to entire courses that may last several years. Rather, they can enrol on individual modules and can shape their programme by selecting subsequent modules with the benefit of the experience gained.

— *Credit accumuation and transfer scheme (CATS)*: With modularization,it became necessary to develop a system that enabled academic credits to be 'banked' and recognized by other institutions, allowing students to transfer more easily between institutions than had traditionally been the case. Between 1986 and 1991, the Council for National Academic Awards spearheaded the development of CATS, thereby helping to change the culture of HE by enhancing flexible provision and structures. This scheme has now been adopted by many universities.

— *Accreditation of prior learning/prior experiential learning (APL/APEL)*: This increased student mobility between education institutions through CATS required, in its turn, the establishment of a formal system to assess and accredit prior leaning. Only thus could it be ensured that students received both full, formal academic recognition for previous learning, and appropriate guidance about what modules needed to be successfully completed in order to gain a particular award.

Adopting the flexible and open approach to teaching and learning can offer real rewards to any college brave enough to install the necessary management and develop or buy in the support required. OL and flexible learning, by eliminating barriers to access and applying the principles of OL provision, can:

— extend the geographical reach of courses in terms of the hinterland for recruitment

— increase the penetration and take-up rates within the local market area

— ensure higher success and retention rates among students once enrolled

— maximize the use of existing physical and human resources

— enable tutors to handle more students without appreciably increasing their workload

— improve the quality of the student learning experience, and thereby the reputation of the providing institution

— enrich and enhance the nature of the tutor's job through variation, open procedures and more creative approaches to assessment.

The overall promise is therefore to reduce student unit costs while, at the same time, improving the quality of the service and raising staff and student morale. Such an array of claims will undoubtedly be viewed with some scepticism by anyone who has sought to introduce innovatory practice at any but the most mundane level! There are certainly problems to overcome. Institutions consist of an uncomfortable truce between people and structures. Those who already occupy powerful or personally satisfying roles within the existing structure will undoubtedly wish to preserve the status quo.

Radical change always tends to increase workload before it eventually rationalizes and controls it. Individuals at all levels are made uncertain as time honoured skills and procedures are called into question. In addition, even those who support the changes know that it is always the new departures which receive the sharpest critical analysis, and they worry about the consequences of failure. Many teachers in FF and HE fear that the new methodologies being advanced will replace them and make them redundant. Such doubts and reservations cannot be ignored. It is a fact that relatively few manage to set then sights on the beneficial consequences of a shift towards more open approaches a different kind of job, more rewarding, more creative and more supportive of students.

The developments lead to an increase in accessibility an flexibility. They open up HE opportunities to a wider section of society including part-time and mature students, and remove many of the barriers of inflexible structures previously encountered by many students. Increasing numbers of institutions are realizing the need to explore new approaches to teaching and learning, and are beginning to explore how Open Learning (OL) materials might be incorporated into new and existing modules to enhance the flexibility afforded by modularization, CATS and APL/APEL.

The OL approach brings together a sound educational principles and an organizational framework which is practical and suited to the needs of our times. Its success depends on the provision of effective learning materials which have been specifically designed to enable students to take responsibility for their learning. It is characterized by the flexibility, adaptability and responsiveness of organizational structures and not least—by the reduced reliance on teacher availability at specific times and places.

In all these respects, OL provides a significant alternative to conventionally taught courses within traditional HE structures. Within a programme that uses OL materials, there can, of course, be substantial differences in the amount of openness and control offered to students. Students may be involved in decisions such as the kind and amount of support needed and who might provide it and whether the learning will be assessed and, if it is, how it will be assessed and when. At the other extreme, lecturers may wish to exert far more control over the learning process, determining what is studied, broadly when it is studied, and how and when learning will be assessed.

However, even when such parameters are defined at the outset, the use of learning materials which encourage active learner involvement and which can be studied away from an educational establishment may still allow students greater flexibility and control over learning than is usually possible in conventionally taught courses offered within traditional educational structures. Finally, the middle course between teacher control and student autonomy is readily achieved by the inherent flexibility of an approach in which OL is given a significant role. At present, despite the success of local schemes, the use of OL still appears to be somewhat marginal. It is largely confined to areas where access to conventional education provision is problematic, or where a student population tends to be scattered over a fairly wide geographical area. In order to examine the case for open/distance learning, it may be helpful to explore some of the potential advantages and disadvantages. To do this, we shall focus on two different pesrpectives: that of the lecturer and that of the student.

As we examine each of these in turn, the following list of key characteristics of education will provide a useful framework to evaluate the possible contribution of OL:

— accessibility
— availability throughout the lifespan
— responsiveness to widely differing individual life circumstances
— ability to cope with learner diversity
— affordability
— demonstrable effectiveness.

From a teacher's perspective, there would appear to be a number of potential advantages in using OL. First, the continuing move for providers of HE to widen access faces teachers with the challenge of meeting the learning needs of increasingly large, heterogeneous groups of students who may also be at different starting points in terms of background knowledge, needs and academic ability. The use of learning materials can help cope with larger student numbers while still maintaining the quality of educational provision. In addition to the use of OL materials to meet the needs of large numbers of students, OL can also enable lecturers to offer options to small groups that might otherwise not be regarded as economically viable when face-to-face teaching costs are calculated.

For those HE lecturers involved in delivering programmes of professional education, this is an important consideration. The benefits of OL do not, therefore, appear to be restricted solely to the cognitive domain. The application of theoretical and conceptual issues to work experiences is also of central importance for teaching groups such as social workers, nurses and midwives, teachers and managers. Lawrence et al. found that through the use of carefully designed activities, OL materials can provide an effective means of helping students to relate theory to practive, thereby bridging the theory-practice gap that dominates much of the literature on professional education. Perhaps not surprisingly, there are also some potential disadvantages.

The cost of the learning materials can be high, whether they are developed in-house or bought in from an external producer. This may require pump-priming funds, or some form of loan, since in HE fees follow student enrolments, and this can make it more difficult to fund any new development that is front-loaded in terms of costs. If money is borrowed to purchase learning materials or to develop them in-house, and has to be repaid from income derived from running the programme, a sound business-planning approach is vital. There may also be additional costs incurred in adapting or augmenting the materials so that they can be used within a particular programme to ensure that learning outcomes are full addressed. An even greater disadvantage in some areas is that suitable learning materials simply do not exist, forcing lecturers to consider whether they should become involved in developing them in-house. With just this reason in mind, the Open Learning Foundation was established in 1990, encouraging its 23 founder members to collaborate in the development of core learning materials that would meet their needs.

The change in role to 'facilitator of learning' may initially seem rather threatening to some lecturers in HE. This feeling is clearly reflected in one of the findings of the survey of OL undertaken by Lawrence *et al*: 'Teachers frequently expressed the need for training in the use of learning materials and for the development of the facilitator role. There is a sense of anxiety about the loss of control of the learning experience in many of the statements made by teachers, which may reflect their uncertainty about their own future roles.

Initially, the use of OL may involve a period of considerable uncertainty for some lecturers while they adjust to the shift in emphasis from the role of teacher to that of facilitator of learning and to a perceived loss of control over the learning process. To address this issue, some producers offer their learning materials on a computer disk to enable teachers to select particular sections, adapt the text and add local examples, case material, etc., prior to reproducing the material for use with their own students, the rationale being to increase the sense of ownership. Some teaching staff will, therefore, need additional preparation to develop the skills, attitudes and confidence required to facilitate learning and to encourage students to become more self-directed. They may initially require considerable help and support from more experienced OL tutors.

Initial staff development and institutional development needs can incur high start-up costs which need to be regarded as a long-term investment. Although, in the long run, effective, supported use of OL materials within an educational programme can enable students to become more self-directed, this can take time to develop. Teaching staff must realize that, initially, some students may need considerable time and support during their early exposure to OL until they have developed sufficient confidence to work with reduced teacher input, direction and control, and patterns of independent learning have been established. In addition, lecturers may need to adopt more flexible working hours to meet student' needs, particularly those of students studying part time.

OL can allow students to shape their own learning programme by defining their own learning outcomes and working through learning materials at their own pace. The use of individually negotiated learning contracts can help ensure that learning meets the specific needs of individual students, although this is essentially a two-way process. It aims to help students avoid repetitious learniing and build on existing knowledge and skills. A further benefit is that students can study in ways that are best suited to their individual circumstances, and make optimum use of available time to meet their own particular learning needs.

As a practical consequences, opportunities may be increased for those who, due to unsocial working hours and personal commitments, might otherwise be unable to attend a more traditional programme. In addition, there is also the important educational gain in the understanding of, and commitment to, the learning process. We have seen that OL offers flexibility and the scope for individuals to study different topics at different depths and different speeds according to specific interests and needs. The use of learning materials can allow learners to exert greater control over the pace, place and time of learning.

The use of good learning materials can help to ensure quality education provision that is not dependent on who is teaching, how the teacher is feeling and other factors that can affect the quality of face-to-face provision, such as unsuitable teaching accommodation and the like. If the quality and suitability of learning materials are carefully evaluated prior to their use, an OL programme can be of a very high quality. Not only may the use of such learning materials raise the morale of hard-pressed lecturers who are committed to the delivery of quality learning opportunities for their students, but they can also help to engage the understanding of students and thus motivate the learner. Among the advantages perceived by students is also the choice of working either alone or in small groups, depending on preference and on individual learning styles.

The use of learning materials need not, therefore, necessarily imply isolation. Moreover, learning materials are always available to the student for reference in a way that a teacher cannot be. As a further benefit, it can be easier to make up for lost study time if a student is absent due to illness or some other reason. Students can also become more self-directed and begin to acquire the habit of lifelong learning that is all-important when working in environments that may constantly be changing. It can help to empower students to take charge of their own learning through greater control and ownership of the learning will process. Students who are able to organize and structure their own learning will have developed the key skills of self-motivation, self-discipline and self-management that are now required in so many work contexts. Turning now to the major potential disadvantages, some students may experience isolation if they are not able to attend regular, scheduled face-to-face sessions during which ideas can be exchanged and the enthusiasms of others shared.

Mann argues that student support by teacher's is the key to motivating students to ensure that they successfully complete a programme of learning. Negotiated access to tutorial support at specified times/places is crucial, as is the installation of direct telephone lines with answerphones. A student whose interest and motivation may be failing is unlikely to persist in trying to get in touch with his or her totor if the swichboard is always slow to answer a call, or if an individual is constantly unavilable. Due to the problems associated with isolation, students will often welcome a mixed mode of delivery, whereby OL materials are integrated within a module that includes some scheduled face-to-face sessions that allow students to benefit from the advantages of both modes of delivery.

The creation to self-help groups can also provide a valuable source of peer support that can help to reduce the sense of isolation. Students need to feel a high level of commitment and internal motivation to succeed, since much more is left up to the learner. It has to be acknowledged, therefore, that OL may not suit all individuals at the outset: some students may need considerable support initially before they begin to feel comfortable and confident with a more self-directed mode of learning. This point is reflected in one of the findings reported by Lawrence *et al.* who state that 'not everyone responds to this learning approach, it may be that some degree of preparation is needed to cope successfully with this learning method'.

Industrial and commercial organizations are looking to OL to help meet the education and training needs of the workforce Those HE teachers who are offering education and training programmes for either the public or private sectors should be aware of the reasons why an increasing number of employers are finding that the use of OL materials can help meet their needs. The potential benefits include:

— a means of relocating some components of education into the workplace

— an educational resource that may be shared by colleagues in the workplace—such sharing can also encourage the creation of a subculture where continuing education is highly valued

— a means of implementing work-based learning that can help to bridge the gap between theory and practice, since learning occurs while the individual is actually doing his or her job

— access to materials by those, such as mentors and facilitators, responsible for supporting the student in the workplace, which can also assist the provision of more effective learner support than might otherwise be possible for students following a conventional teaching programme, where the mentor/facilitator may have considerably less understanding of course content

— not needing to release staff from the workplace at set times and on set days

— study time that can be programmed more flexibly around the needs of the organization, enabling times of peak workload and staff absences to be more readily accommodated, while meeting individuals' professional development needs

— possible reduction of travel time, travel costs and subsistence costs, although it is important to stress that OL should not be regarded as education/training on the cheap.

Cost effectiveness is often assumed to be one of the main benefits of open/distance learning and, indeed, it may turn out to be highly cost effective. At present, however, there is insufficient evidence either to support or to challenge this assumption. It can be difficult to measure in any meaningful way the full costs of providing an OL programme and compare these with the full costs of an equivalent conventionally taught course. When costing any education programme, it is necessary to calculate both the fixed costs and the variable costs, which will vary depending on the number of students. Fixed costs for OL include items such as the cost of accommodation, publicity material, scheme managers and administrators, institutional overheads, and developing or purchasing the learning materials. If the idea of using OL materials in your own teaching appealing, then you might find the following checklist useful, since it outlines the kind of environment in which OL might thrive:

— support from the top; management being seen to value OL
— learners and organization in agreement about the aims of learning
— provision of local support for open learners
— an education framework in which OL can fit together with other types of educational provision
— careful and efficient management of hardware, resources and support systems
— systems for evaluation and feedback
— skills in student and feedback
— skills in student support and counselling
— study-skills training
— teachers who regard OL as an opportunity rather than as a threat
— teachers who are ready to take on new roles in the support of learning
— time and resources to develop sound OL schemes
— skilled co-ordination of the many activities needed to develop OL materials and to set up OL schemes.

If OL is to become more widely used within HE, and if it is to offer a good educational experience for every open learner, we need to consider a number of key issues in relation to staff and institutional development. David Baume 'Staff Development for Open and Flexible Learning', also considers possible approaches to staff development for those using OL and the need for institutional development. Lecturers will need to develop the skills required to evaluate published learning materials prior to their use within specific education programmes. They will need to distinguish between 'experienced and competent providers of OL and those whose enthusiasm outruns their competence and whose ignorant or exploitative approach to OL might bring the whole idea into disrepute'.

Any systematic evaluation of learning materials will need to assess the extent to which they meet an agreed set of criteria, including the learning outcomes for a particular education programme. Robinson and Clark suggest that a minimum of 10 per cent of the total study hours may be required to evaluate a set of materials. If the evaluation suggests that the materials are not entirely appropriate either to student needs or to the desired learning outcomes, then additional time and resources will be required to adapt or supplement the materials. In addition, as we have seen, some teachers may need considerable support while adjusting to a shift in their role from teacher to facilitator of learning, as well as help in encouraging students to become more self-directed. Some may also want to acquire further skills in guidance and counselling in order to provide better student support, and to help students to formulate their own objectives and plan how these might best be met. Some teachers will also need specific preparation on the use of the learning materials, telephone tutorials and the management and administration of an OL system.

Thus, a programme of staff development will usually be required to develop a critical mass within the overall population of teaching staff with the necessary attitudes and commitment to implement OL successfully. And, even if there are already significant numbers of teaching staff who are experienced in using OL. They will need time to become thoroughly familiar with the learning materials that form the basis of a specific module or programme. Recognizing this, the OU pays a staff development fee to all tutorial staff who are new to a particular programme to cover the cost of this all important familiarization period. Once successful OL schemes have been established both within and beyond mainstream undergraduate provision, they can be set up as demonstration projects within an institution, or even within the HE sector as a whole, to help raise the level of awareness among colleagues.

The use of demonstration projects, coupled with work-shops and more widespread dissemination of ideas through publications such as the Times Higher Education Supplement and journals such as Open Learning, can go a considerable way to further the debate about the potential value of introducing more flexible patterns of teaching and learning. Internal debates may be needed within an institution about the proportion of the total number of study hours that can be dedicated to OL and still contribute towards an award previously based on fixed number of hours of classroom teaching. The concept of minimum course attendance requirements would obviously need to be reassessed. This in turn raises the question of whether it is necessary to specify minimum time periods for the achievement of particular learning outcomes.

Some students may be capable of achieving specific learning outcomes in a considerably shorter time than other students and should perhaps be allowed to complete summative assessments whenever they are ready, rather than at fixed points in a module or programme. The emphasis needs, therefore, to be shifted away from specifying numbers of study hours, module/programme duration and/or minimum attendance, and towards the development of more flexible means and timescales for students to demonstrate the achievement of specific learning outcomes at predefined academic levels.

In some institutions, there may be concerns about how to weight students who do not attend programmes in a traditional manner. Indeed, OL students may be weighted differenly in statistical returns, making it less beneficial for staff members wishing to incorporate OL materials into their programmes for sound educational reasons. If, under a modular scheme, one student full-time equivalent is regarded as equivalent to a student enrolled on six modules, then one student enrolled on one module equals one-sixth of an FTE. If the same criterion were to apply to OL students, then six OL module registrations would equal one FTE. Students need to be provided with clear information about the availability of tutorial support when undertaking any programme of self-directed learning: the use of OL should not be viewed simply as a means of reducing the amount of teacher contact or teaching hours. Students should also be encouraged to set up self-help groups or study pairs to help reduce the sense of isolation that some may feel.

Conventional teaching requires relatively little administrative support and, as a consequence, there is a tendency to underestimate the amount of administration time needed to establish and manage an effective OL system, and the cost of providing that support. Administrative support is needed to deal with enquiries, and to ensure the avialability of learning materials which need to be ordered, checked, logged in, stored and issued. If a loan scheme is in operation for the learning materials, returned items also need to be checked, and non-returned items nced to be chased to ensure their availability for future students.

The establishment and maintenance of accurate and up-to-date records is also essential, particularly if assessment does not occur at fixed points in the programme or at fixed points in the year, and if a large number of students have enrolled. A crucial aspect of any OL system is, therefore, an efficient administrative system. In my experience, many course/programme leaders have, at the outset, seriously under-estimated the amount of administration time needed to run a programme involving OL, and this element needs to be adequately costed.

As OL operations develop within a school, department or faculty, it may become necessary to appoint an administrator with special responsibility for OL. Moreover, this person may be required to work flexible hours to ensure that adequate administrative support is available to both students and staff during periods when OL students come into the institution. Existing institutional validation procedures may not readily accommodate the special needs of a programme with a substantial OL component, and may need to be adapted. Members of a validation panel for an OL programme must be familiar with the specific issues that would need to be addressed in both the supporting documentation and during the validation event, to ensure that sufficient attention is paid to all aspects to the OL system that could affect the overall quality of the student learning experience. This should include the provision of flexible student support and also adequate administrative support for both students and teachers.

Whenever published learning materials are to be used, evidence would be required that a systematic evaluation of the materials has been undertaken to establish their suitability for the proposed use. In a mixed-mode module/programme, validators must ensure that the various components are well integrated, and that a consistent educational philosophy is maintained throughout and is clearly understood by all members of the course planning team. Where learning materials are being developed in-house, it should be noted that it would be entirely inappropriate for validators to require to see all the learning materials prior to validating the course. They should, however, reassure themselves that sound procedures have been implemented, by requesting a clear description of the stages of materials development and the steps that have been taken to assure quality, together with a sample of the learning materials that have been developed.

5

Transformation of Contemporary Education System

In education this has meant that individuals are, in principle, treated according to ability rather than on the basis of described characteristics such as social class, gender, or race. This principle has given rise at the notion of equality of opportunity which, the context of the development of the nation ate, has three functions. It acts as an efficiency principle by by selecting and locating individuals for the labour market on the basis of ability; it acts as a moral principle by selecting students on the basis of a theory of justice; and it also acts as a tool of assimilation.

It provides the means by which the heterogeneous peoples of a nation, in terms of class and chnicity, could aspire to and achieve common prizes offered in industrial society. In going so, it helps to create a single measure of personal success in individualistic industrial societies: the attainment of wealth and status by promotion to professional and senior management positions within corporate and public bureaucracies. It is against the background of these economic, cultural, and social conditions that the role of education in the postwar period can be understood. For the first time in the postwar period education took a central position in the functioning of the advanced industrial societies, because it was seen as a key investment in the promotion of economic growth as well as a means of promoting social justice. This was premised on two widely held assumptions about the nature of education in advanced industrial societies which have both been confounded by empirical evidence.

Firstly, economic efficiency in advanced industrial societies depends on getting the most talented people into the most important and technically demanding jobs, regardless of their social circumstances. Hence, if individuals had the ability to succeed, the old barriers of social class were no more than gossamer threads to be brushed aside in the ascent up the social ladder. The key to this ascent lay in the notion of intelligence. It was assumed that in society there was elimited pool of individuals with high intelligence who were required to run the engines of industrial growth. This pool of talent needed to be selected and promoted through the education system because, as Halsey and Floud noted, education is a crucial type of investment for the exploitation of modern technology.

Secondly, educational opportunities needed to be extended, given that the vast majority of jobs were predicted to become increasingly skilled, requiring extensive periods of formal education. Hence everyone would eventually become middle-class, as semi-skilled and unskilled jobs were replaced by machines and workers became technicians, managers, or were appointed to positions in the expanding professions. During this period, education was also seen as contributing to the foundations of democracy.

The link between education and democracy has long been established in Western thought, and was given particular impetus in the twentieth century by the work of John Dewey in the United States and in Britain by R.H. Tawney, as well as during the 1950s and 1960s through the writings of Anthony Crosland, A.H. Halsey, and others. The focus of the link between education and democracy turned on a fundamental insight of Dewey's that 'a democracy is more than a form of government; it is primarily a mode of associated living, a conjoint communicated experience'.

The type of school which, it was argued, best contributed to this form of 'associated living' was the common or comprehensive school. Here students from all types of social background, ethnicity, gender, and ability could mix and develop tolerance and mutual respect for each others' point of view, dispositions considered essential in democracy.

The common school ideal embodied much of the spirit of the age. It was designed to provide greater equality of opportunity by deferring the selection of students into 'academic' and 'vocational' streams until later in a student's career, giving them the chance to manifest their academic potential. It also assumed that students of different genders and cultural backgrounds all learnt in much the same way: that they would all benefit from greater equality of treatment. And it assumed that from this common treatment and experience the essential foundations of democratic life could be taught.

From the democratic-socialist perspective of the time it could be seen and still can be defended as a major advance in breaking down the barriers of class, gender, and ethnicity. From a post-modernist perspective it could be seen as a continuation of the assimilationist spirit of the age, as we will go on to show. The optimism attached to education in the age of economic nationalism is reflected in government support for its expansion in the 1950s and 1960s. Indeed, it was common to hear politicians, journalists, and policy makers extol the virtue of 'keeping politics out of education', given all-party support for the expansion of education and its reorganization along 'comprehensive' lines as a way of achieving the dual objectives of economic efficiency and social justice.

Consequently, the education systems of the western world expanded to perform their new role of providing the human capital, as it came to be called in the mid-1950s, for the expanding middle-class occupations in industry.

In 1938 only 8.4 per cent of children in Britain attended state secondary schools between the ages of 11 and 18. By 1951 the figure had risen to 30 per cent, and by 1968 still further to 37 per cent. Higher education also expanded. In 1938 there were 69,000 students in full-time higher education. By 1963 the number had risen to 2 15,000, and by 1970 that figure had doubled.

Despite this expansion it should be noted that Britain, along with its European counterparts, started from a low base in terms of participation, especially in higher education. However, a start had been made, and expenditure on education rose substantially during this period, reflecting the increased participation in education and its newly found importance in advanced capitalist society. In 1940 2.1 per cent of national income in England and Wales was spent on education; by 1965 it had risen to 4.1 per cent.

However, despite the expansion in middle-class jobs and an increasingly educated workforce, the guiding idea that everyone would eventually get a middle-class job and that occupation and status would be determined according to merit were myths. The myths were understandable, given the accelerated expansion in middle-class jobs and educational opportunities; but working-class jobs already-privileged remained.

Universities were still dominated by those from professional and managerial backgrounds; and even when intelligence was taken into account, social background remained a significant factor in individuals' life chances. In effect, the expanding occupational structure had created more room at the top and in the middle of the occupation hierarchy for those originally from working-class backgrounds, but the reproduction of privilege remained.

The first 'oil shock' in the early 1970s marked the breakdown of economic nationalism as prosperity, security and opportunity were all called into question in what Schumpeter would have described as a 'gale of creative destruction'. The world recession which followed the escalation in fuel prices was accompanied by an increasing awareness that in a global economy the mass production of standardized goods and services which characterized Fordism was no longer able to support the economic livelihood of workers and their families.

The revolution in new technologies coupled with cheaper transportation costs have made it economically viable, if not essential, for multinational corporations to move production to whatever country has comparative advantage. If the work to be done is relatively low-skilled, such as in the mass production of standardized goods and services, a key factor will be labour costs, and multinational corporations are likely to move standardized mass production to the newly industrializing countries (NICs) where these are significantly cheaper than in North America or Western Europe. In the Philippines or in Vietnam, for instance, forty-seven workers can be employed for the cost of single worker in France.

As a consequence it is argued that Western nations must either reduce wage costs to compete with those in Asian or African economies, which will be extremely difficult to achieve, or try to win a competitive advantage at the 'quality' end of the market. Here it is assumed that healthy profits and incomes can still be made by companies and workers who are able to exploit the full potential of new technologies in the creation of niche markets for goods and services. The growing power of transnational corporations to determine where in the world significant investments are to be made has therefore created a *global auction* in investment, jobs, and new technology.

In such circumstances transnationals will invest in those nations where tax regimes and labour costs are low, while providing an infrastructure of a highly killed workforce, sophisticated transport, and financial communications. In effect, the state has to provide or create the conditions where a sophisticated infrastructure is delivered, while controlling tax demands and the costs of social protection. Consequently, there is a standard view in the literature that the changes in the nature of the global economy since the early 1970s has led to a weakening of the powers of the nation state. The removal of border controls in relation to capital, the rise in power of transnational corporations, and the enhanced communications afforded by the electronic revolution have set new challenges as to how the economy can best be managed.

Under these new conditions the policy instruments relating to Keynesian demand-management no longer work. In effect the nation state has one arm tied behind its back while having to confront the 'problems' created by the new economic conditions. However, there remains considerable debate about how far the influence of transnational business extends over national life and economic policy.

Nevertheless, in the Anglophone nations which have embraced the ideology of competitive individualism and market competition since the late 1970s, the breakdown of national barriers to trade have been positively encouraged. Indeed, the development of the welfare state, the social wage, and the powers of the trade unions are all seen to undermine the culture of enterprise which the New Right believe to be central to the ability of western nations to compete in the global economy.

This has led the New Right to reassert the principles of market competition in every nook and cranny of contemporary life, resulting in cuts in the welfare benefits on which the idea of a social wage depended. They have also introduced anti-union legislation to curtail the power of the trade unions who were seen to bid-up the price of labour 'artificially'. Whether these policies are a symptom of changes in the global labour market as Reich's position implies or an ideological response to the global auction, as Brown and Lauder suggest is a matter of debate.

However, as a consequence of such policies the link between economic growth and prosperity for all has been broken. There has been a polarization of wealth and income in Anglophone societies, with a significant decline in income for non-college graduates and a sharp increase in the level of unemployment. Coupled with the decline in welfare benefits, this has resulted in a sharp rise in the incidence of poverty, which has had a profound effect on children.

Global competition, technological innovation, and the shift away from the mass production of standardized goods and services has also led to a sustained attack on the bureaucratic paradigm of organizational efficiency. The bureaucratic paradigm has been identified as a competitive liability in rapidly changing markets for 'value added' products and services.

Management gurus such as Rosabeth Moss Kanter have spoken of the need for managers to apply entrepreneurial principles to the traditional corporation, creating a marriage between entrepreneurial creativity and corporate discipline, co-operation, and teamwork. The convergence of information technologies and their integration in the workplace, the need to free up and speed up the flow of information and decision-making, the increasing emphasis on teamwork and project work, and the need for flexible work practices, along with a new vocabulary of networks, empowerment, leadership, teamwork, downsizing, rightsizing, re-engineering, and contracting out, have all become part of the rhetoric of the flexible or adaptive paradigm. This, it is argued, has not only led enlightened organizations to invest heavily in new technology, but has also made them rethink and restructure their systems of recruitment, communications, rewards, and promotion as well as their structure of ranks and grades.

Kanter, for instance, argues that this is leading to a shift from position to performance and from status to contribution, where people are paid for what they do rather than for their ability to climb the corporate hierarchy, and for their value added contribution rather than their location in the organizational command structure.

This change in organizational paradigm has resulted in a massive process of corporate restructuring in both private- and public sector organizations. Enormous variations exist in the way organizations have responded to greater competitive pressures, volatile markets, technological change, and cutting costs. In most cases the progressive features of the flexible paradigm in terms of greater workplace democracy, job satisfaction, and social justice remain a promise rather than a reality. One of the most striking features of corporate restructuring in both the private and public sectors is an increase in occupational insecurity, redundancy, and the demise of the bureaucratic career, as American and British companies have energetically pursued 'downsizing' policies. These include cutting labour costs through layoffs, 'voluntary' redundancy, hiring freezes, and contracting out various activities to other companies, consultants, contractors, or self-employed workers.

In the United States, even during a period of rapid employment growth between 1985 and 1989,4.3 million employees who had been with their employers for at least 3 years were made redundant due to plant closure, business failure, or because they had been designated as 'surplus employees'. In 1992 American company layoffs amounted to around 1,224,000, whereas a year later they had increased to 1,314,000 employees.

In Britain the largest 1,000 companies shed about 1.5 million workers in the year to March 1993 as they tried to reduce their costs further. The demise of the mass employment organization offering long-term job prospects has forced all categories of workers to 'stay fit' in the market for jobs, as more people find themselves on short-term contracts, self-employed, under-employed, at risk of redundancy, or unemployed. Even the toddle classes, who depended on bureaucratic careers in medium- and large-sized organizations, have had to come to terms with uncertain occupational futures. The educational system itself, despite the golden postwar years of expansion, is far from being the safe haven of an 'ivory tower'. On the contrary, short-term employment on 'soft money' in colleges and 'supply teaching' in schools are determining features of academic employment.

Moreover, this sense of insecurity has been compounded by changes in household composition and structure. Single mothers and divorced women tend to drift towards the bottom of the income array, taking their children with them to new homes and new schools. Schools lose their community characteristics. The breakdown of economic nationalism has equally undermined postwar ideals about educational opportunity and social mobility.

But paradoxically, whereas there has been increased political conflict concerning the funding, control, and organizations of education, there is a new international consensus which recognizes education to be of even greater importance than in the past to the future of individual and national economic prosperity. Although the education system was being blamed for social and economic problems in the 1970s and 1980s, the power of education to deliver the will of its political elites has never been questioned in official circles. Indeed, there is now a new 'consensus' on both the left and right of the political spectrum which has defined education as the key to future economic prosperity.

The new consensus is based on the idea that as the walled economies at mid-century have given way to an increasingly global economy, the power of national government to control the outcome of economic competition has been weakened. Hence, at a time when severe limitations are being imposed on national governments in the sphere of economic policy, education has assumed even greater political significance.

Indeed, the competitive advantage of nations is frequently redefined in terms of the quality of national education and training systems judged according to international standards. If nations are unable to win a competitive advantage through investment in new technology, upgrading the quality of human resources, or reforming industrial relations policies as a way of attracting foreign inward investment to create new employment opportunities, there is little national governments can do to prevent a precipitous drop in living standards, stagnant economic growth, and increasing unemployment.

As in the era of economic nationalism, the new education consensus has led to what in many parts of the world amount to dramatic increases in post-compulsory education. In higher education there has been an increase from approximately 8 per cent to 30 per cent in the age cohort attending universities in numerous countries. Whatever reasons are given to explain political support for the new education consensus and the expansion of tertiary education, there are a number of issues over the centrality accorded to education in post-industrial societies that require further investigation and analysis. These include the changing relationship between education and the labour market. In particular, we need to ask whether education can lead to improvements in productivity, and to greater scope for individual creativity and fulfilling employment.

On the question of education and economic productivity there is little doubt that the new consensus maintains a long-standing trend towards a tightening bond between education and the economy in the twentieth century. However, whilst there is now widespread agreement that a high-quality general education is more appropriate to conditions of rapid technological change than a narrowly specialized vocational education, the exact relationship between 'vocational' and 'general' education remains unresolved.

This debate is likely to continue, given the recent argument outlined by Ashton and Sung that in the new economic competition there needs to be a much tighter relationship between education and work than anything that we have yet witnessed in the West.

In the United Kingdom, Gallie and White show that the introduction of information technologies has increased skill demands in jobs that remain in all but the unskilled manual sectors of the economy. Lidley and Wilson also estimate that the proportion of managerial, administrative, and professional jobs has risen from 20 percent in 1981 to 26.4 per cent in 1994 and is projected to reach 28.7 per cent in the year 2001.

In the United States, Block has suggested that oil tile basts of a variety of evidence about occupational trends since the late 1960s, the majority of American employees were in jobs where the skill demands of their jobs are quite substantial', and that technological innovation 'in blue-collar and white-collar settings is generally associated with rising levels of skill'. Moreover, figures published by the Department of Labor predict that between 1990 and 2005 there will be a 76.6 per cent increase in the number of 'managerial' jobs. Moreover, the increased demand for educated labour is often associated with the shift in employment from manufacturing to service industries.

In 1950 in the United States, 33 per cent of jobs were in manufacturing and 53 per cent in service industries. In the UK the figures were 46.5 per cent and 48 per cent. By 1987 the figures for the United States were 27 and 70 per cent respectively, and for the UK 30 and 68 per cent. Hence, while manufacturing is no less important to either economy the number of workers in factory jobs shrunk dramatically. However, the service sector is heterogeneous, and there are clearly many 'junk' jobs within it.

For example, Levy suggests that blue-collar workers who have entered the service sector receive 60 per cent of their former Wage on average in the United States. These figures relate to those who have secured a job; however, as we have indicated, white-collar jobs are increasingly insecure as, for instance ' clerical assembly lines are replaced by new technologies through the process known as 're-engineering'. Aronowitz and De Fazio take the view that the consequence of the current changes will lead to deskilling and even higher levels of unemployment than witnessed in the past decade.

Therefore, this somewhat confused picture of upskilling, reskilling, and deskilling is in urgent need of further research. Such research is important because changes in the structure of work will have major implications for the changing nature of the class structure in post-industrial societies. This, in turn, will inevitably have an impact on the distribution of educational success and failure of today's children.

The problem of understanding current trends is compounded by the fact that the intellectual history of attempts to chart the link between education and economic productivity have been strewn with good intentions and theoretical and empirical failures. The main problem is that it is very difficult, if not impossible, to demonstrate a causal relationship between education and economic productivity. There are two related reasons for this. Firstly, the link between education and productivity is mediated by issues of power most clearly seen in the phenomenon of credential inflation. And secondly, changes in the demand for skill are as much a social as a technical issue, subject to vested interests and social conflict.

Credentials are a positional good. A defining characteristic of a positional good is that it is scarce in a socially imposed sense, and that accordingly allocation proceeds through 'the auction of a restricted set of objects to the highest bidder'. Credential inflation simply increases the hierarchy of scarcity and demands that individuals invest more time in ascending the hierarchy to the scarcest and most valued credential. Screening operates by increasing the resources needed to attain the highest credentials in order to gain selection for a job. However, the resources needed to gain work may be more than intellectual.

Several theorists have hypothesized that the purpose of credentials is to screen personalities as much as cognitive achievement. This is an important issue, of great relevance to the current situation, and to which we shall return. Hirsch's analysis of credential inflation clearly undermines the human-capital assumption, reflected in the quote by President Clinton, that the higher an employee's credentials the higher her or his rate of productivity; and it points to the theory that credential inflation reflects the outcome of a competition within which higher socio-economic groups preserve and reproduce their privilege by raising the educational levels demanded for elite occupations. If this is the case then part of the explanation of the expansion of tertiary education should be located in the competition for credentials rather than in any straightforward link between education and economic productivity. Understood in these broad terms, the demand for credentials may well be a function of the pressure of an increasing middle class keen to secure their children's future.

If this hypothesis is correct it would explain why even right-wing governments, which in terms of their ideology would reject the expansion of tertiary education on the grounds that there is only an academic elite who can benefit from such an education, have promoted expansionist policies. The alternative would be to lose the middle-class vote. However, a consequence of educational expansion may be an increasing mismatch between the supply of higher-educated workers and the demand for employees with advanced technical and academic qualifications. We can therefore anticipate increasing political fallout from this situation in the future as the 'wastage of talent' is increasingly seen to be one of how to placate a growing army of ambitious and highly educated workers unable to realize their occupational ambitions.

There has also been a significant change in the definition of 'skill'. This is less a reflection of the secular trend towards a more technically skilled workforce than a change in employer definitions of individual competence, with the shift from bureaucratic to flexible paradigms of organizational efficiencies. This has led employers to emphasize the need for employees who have good personal and social skills, together with any technical 'know-how' which may be required.

At least among 'core' workers there is an expectation that they will be able to work in a rapidly changing environment, to engage in,rule-making' rather than 'rule-following' behaviour, to work in project teams, and to share the same 'personal chemistry' as others in the organization. Hence, the more organizational efficiency is seen to depend on the interpersonal skills, communication, negotiation, and teamwork, the more the bureaucratic legacy in schools, colleges, and universities is seen by employers as a form of 'trained incapacity'. Moreover, academic qualifications now tell employers less about what they need to know about potential recruits, given that they convey information about the individual's ability and motivation to jump through the appropriate test and examination hoops, rather than students' potential to work in teams or about their social and personal skills.

Consequently, calls from employers to have a greater say in the affairs of the school are increasingly less concerned about getting the educational system involved with programmes of specific vocational training, and more concerned with enhancing student business awareness, communication skills, and self-management. The use of 'profiling', which incorporates a broader range of student abilities, qualities, and attainment than that which is typically assessed in academic examinations is clearly an attempt to respond to an employer rhetoric of personal and social skills. However, the use of student profiles has as yet had little impact on traditional patterns of education.

Nevertheless, increasing external involvement in education does not rule out the possibility of a growing contradiction between the classification and framing of knowledge, interaction, and organizational practices operating in the educational system and in employing organizations. Some of the reasons for this are not difficult to understand, and again they highlight contradictions, unintended consequences, and 'forced' integration between education and the labour market rather than 'correspondence'. Part of the problem is that group work has tended to be frowned upon because the democratization of education opportunities has depended on the individuation of success and failure. Ability and performance, like the concept of meritocracy, is assumed to be judged on an individual basis.

Group assessment which could be introduced as a way of encouraging teamwork in a formal educational context is also rejected, because it is difficult to Mil Mite when individual grades need to be assigned. A greater emphasis on the development of personal and social skills in education is also unlikely to gain widespread support, especially from the elite schools, colleges, and universities. This is because the credibility attached to academic credentials remains based on the 'objective' assessment of 'knowledge' epitomized by the 'unseen' examination paper. In such circumstances, the formal teaching of personal and social skills represents the latest version of 'compensatory' education for those who lack the personal qualities which come 'naturally' as part of the informal social education of the middle-class child. The shift towards service-sector employment has also been associated with a rise in the proportion of women entering the labour market. This represents a considerable challenge to established assumptions about gender divisions in the pattern of socialization and social control.

Even in the so-called 'permissive' 1960s it was not difficult to find official statements maintaining the view that boys should be socialized for their future role as 'breadwinners' and girls for that of 'homemakers'. In England, the Newsam Report on the education of average- and below-average-ability students noted that gender divisions in future adult roles would inevitably lead males to show a far greater interest in science. 'A boy is usually excited by the prospect of a science course... He experiences a sense of wonder and a sense of power. The growth of wheat, the birth of a lamb, the movement of clouds put him in awe of nature; the locomotive he sees as a man's response-, the switch and the throttle are his magic wands. The girl may come to the science lesson with a less eager curiosity than the boy but she too will need to feel at home with the machinery.'

However, by the 1980s official statements on science education had changed. In the Department of Education and Science's consultative document on Science Education in Schools it was noted that: 'Throughout the period of compulsory secondary education every school... should adopt the policy of giving all pupils a broad science programme which... gives genuinely equal curricular opportunities in science to boys and girls. A similar shift in official thinking about what makes an appropriate education for girls and boys can be found in all the advanced Western economies, despite differences in the time in which this shift has taken place. But whereas the socialization of young women has been a focus of educational researchers over the last two decades, it is the socialization of men which has attracted more recent attention. When, for instance, Paul Willis described working-class resistance of 'the Lads' to school in the mid-1970s, it was based on an assumption that there would be physically tough jobs available at the local steelworks or in other heavy industries for them to fulfil their masculine potential.

Without formal qualifications his most likely prospect is a life of irregular employment in jobs such as that of security guard, shelf-filler, or cook in a fast-food outlet, if not one among the ranks of the long term unemployed. The 'problem' of male socialization is not, however, restricted to the working class. There is also evidence to show that middle-class males may in future lose out in the competition for credentials, although feminist researchers continue to demonstrate that there is some distance to travel before men and women leave education with the same academic profiles. Nevertheless, changes in the occupational structure and the improved performance of young women in the educational system will inevitably sharpen the focus on masculine identities, socialization, and social control.

At the same time, there is very little to suggest that the current 'backlash' against women will reverse current trends. It may be argued that women have benefited from changes in the structure of employment and from the redefinition of skill to include social skills, since women are often considered better 'team Players'. The changing definition of skill can be considered as a twoedged sword for women. Their social skills are now encouraged purely for their instrumental value and have been thereby co-opted for corporate profit-making rather than as a means of furthering the qualities associated with caring and human development.

In the past 20 years the family has become less stable and work more insecure, and hence it can be argued that the hold of these institutions on the processes of socialization and control has weakened.

By, the same token, the role of education has become more extensive and intensive. Paradoxically, as these institutions have weakened, the demand for greater involvement in schools, colleges, and universities, from employers, entrepreneurs, parents, and community groups points to the increasing diversity and diffusion of education into all comers of people's lives. Equally, the shift from education preparing people for employment to that of enhancing individual employability as a 'life-project' is not restricted to a question of enhancing technical competence.

The socioemotional world of the school child or the adult learner must now be fully and regularly interrogated. The demands made upon people to enhance their employability as well as social and personal skills places paramount importance on inculcating self-discipline, the virtues of self-improvement, and the art of self-management.

The educational system is increasingly expected to encompass much of the 'hidden curriculum' into its remit of explicit activities. This extension of the scope of education and training at the end of the twentieth century can, of course, be interpreted in significantly different ways. A technicist account of the expansion of education would see it as part of the inexorable move to a 'learning' society. For instance, the spread of certification to increasing spheres of our lives is seen as evidence of increasing social justice.

A woman who has taken time out from waged work to bring up young children, which involves the development of a range of skills, including patience, negotiation, time management, compromise, and so on, which arc,transferable' to the labour market, deserves formal recognition from employers and academic institutions for her 'prior learning'. Likewise the high-school student who performs badly at his or her academic studies, but who has shown considerable organizational abilities in organizing a big charity concert, should also have such 'skills' formally recognized by employers.

The ultimate success of the schooling instrument is the extension of its monopoly, first to all youth, then to every age, and finally to all areas'. Underlying the issues we have raised regarding the enhanced significance of education, two major problems remain. The first is this: how is it possible to promote higher standards in education, when an increasing number of children live in poverty.

One of the clear findings in the sociology of education over the past 20 years has been to establish a link between income and educational performance. The lower the family income, the more educationally disadvantaged students are. The second issue concerns the instability generated by the transformation of Western economies. If knowledge is at the heart of economic survival then the source of future knowledge lies in the education of the present generation of children. But children's education relies heavily on security and stability in the family and at work.

However, if working life is highly unstable for many then a crucial question that now needs to be asked, especially in relation to unemployment, is what effect is the instability in the labour market having on the raising and educating of the next generation?

Overall, the question raised by Levin and Kelly, 'Can education do it alone?' is highly pertinent. The key issue is whether a restructured, more effective education system geared to the economy can deliver on the expectations placed upon it, or whether, education is a 'waste-paper basket' in which difficult problems are simply dumped. The danger in focusing exclusively on policy formation 'from above' is that it negates the importance of competing interests, values, and power relations. Indeed, on many of the key issues confronting the education system today, including funding, testing, curriculum, school management, educational selection, and teacher training, there is significant conflict rather than consensus.

The reason why the educational system is likely to remain a site of struggle stems from what Durkheim observed and Parsons defined as the dual problem of 'socialization' and 'selection'. The question of access and selection in education has been inextricably connected to that of social justice and positional competition. At the same time educational selection takes the form of a positional competition between Students for access to credentials which can be traded in the labour market to 'Purchase' income, status, and employment. It is such sources of conflict which led Michael Young to note that the education system confronts a centuries-old conflict between the principles of selection by family and the principles of selection by merit.

Moreover, since the Enlightenment, education has been seen as necessary to human progress, not only technically and economically but also in terms of emancipation. It is for this reason that education has been intimately linked in Western thought to democracy. In this respect education has always been a focus of struggle between those with the power to define what constitutes legitimate knowledge and those excluded from educational decision-making. From the inception of public education systems in the latter half of the nineteenth century until the early 1970s the struggle over school knowledge was predominantly characterized in terms of class conflict.

More recently, with the re-emergence of feminism and the break-up of colonial rule, that struggle has also related to the emancipation of women and people of colour. Equally, whereas the sociology of education was previously dominated by issues of access, selection, and equality of opportunity, issues of knowledge, pedagogy, and the politics of difference have assumed far greater significance in the study of education as a site of struggle. This reflects broader debates within the social sciences about post-modernism and the cultural politics of difference. Cultural politics has brought the struggles of women and people of colour to the fore, in that it seeks to explain their oppression not only in terms of unequal opportunities, but in relation to the culture of their everyday lives, including education. Much of the inspiration for this new cultural politics has come from some of the many strands of post-modernist thought.

Postmodernism as a loosely textured set of theories has-its basis in changes in society which are identified as constituting a fundamental break with the modernist society of postwar economic nationalism. The inspiration for this intellectual movement came from France and placed great emphasis on the significance of images, signs, and language in the constitution of the self and society. From this emerged a cultural politics which sought to criticize the dominant white, male, metropolitan grand theories and images of the social and economic world which had placed women and people of colour in positions of oppression. The basis for this critique is the assumption that there is little or no justification for claiming that one specific theory or view of knowledge is a better representation of reality than another. Hence scientific claims to 'objective truth' are rejected.

The work of Foucault is particularly important in this respect, both for his 'discourse' analysis of thought and practice in which, he suggested, social practices and the self are constructed in such a way as to render social life an interminable conflict between 'dominated' and 'dominating', and that truth and power are inseparable. These ideas enabled him to criticize the grand narratives of the Enlightenment and particularly Marxism, which he understood not as a praxis for liberation but simply as another rationalization for a practice of domination.

The idea that knowledge is not about truth but is simply a weapon in the struggle between groups, and that individuals are socially constructed and represented in the image of oppressors, has clearly been attractive to some feminists and post-colonial peoples. For them, white, male, metropolitan knowledge could be seen merely as an instrument of domination, and the knowledge of women and post-colonial peoples that has been marginalized could be validated. In so doing it countered the persistent tendency in liberal societies to see the 'disadvantaged' as a problem to be solved and as victims of their own incompetence.

Despite the attractions of this position, it has also brought a series of intractable problems. For the educationalists amongst indigenous peoples, the relativism of linking truth and power so tightly conflicted with the claims that there was a past in terms of their own culture, which was authentic and material to the well-being of their people.

Similarly, relativism placed the theories of oppression they used to explain their position in jeopardy. After all, if knowledge is just the fiction of the powerful, what status do theories of colonial oppression have? For others there were broader problems in linking a politics of difference to relativism. One of the legacies of the Enlightenment has been that education has been seen as a vehicle for social and personal progress as well as for liberation.

A central problem for critical educational lists has therefore been to reconcile the relativism and nihilism of a set of theories denying the possibility of social progress with a politics of difference advancing the liberation of women and people of colour. There is no doubt that postmodern precepts have provided some important insights into the political processes of educational research. But in the case of Lather this has been at the cost of denying the relevance of quantitative analyses to complement qualitative analysis.

This is a point to which we shall return in the section on a new political arithmetic. However, more recently there has been something of a shift away from many of the tenets of post-modernism in educational theory. Bel Hooks has argued against the language which many post-modern critical educationalists have adopted. 'Postmodernist discourses are often exclusionary even as they call attention to... the experience of difference and Otherness...

As a discursive practice it is dominated primarily by the voices of white male intellectuals and/or academic elites who speak to and about one another with coded familiarity'. Kenway makes a similar point while noting the irony that at the very moment when post-modernism has denied the significance of grand theories it is one of the oldest of these, that of the 'free market', which has led to the axing of 8,200 teaching positions in her own state of Victoria in Australia.

For Kenway, the search is now on for a more adequate basis for a feminist politics of education. Whatever the difficulties with some of the post-modern and post-structuralist precepts of the new cultural politics, the major strength of this intellectual movement has been to draw attention to the need to make visible and understand the complex relationships between class, gender, and ethnicity in the restructuring of education.

If the new directions signalled by Kenway are indicative of a trend, then this particular post-modern turn can perhaps best be understood as one moment in the conflict between what Wallerstein has called the two modernities, of technology and of liberation, a conflict that has common roots in the Enlightenment.

In this context postmodernism can be seen as an aspect of the modern struggle for liberation. In the era of economic nationalism, Wallerstein argues, the two modernities seemed to come together and social progress and liberation were seen as embodied in the progress, security, and opportunity that the period offered. If the industrial working class was the driving force behind social change in the nineteenth and early decades of the twentieth century, it is the middle-class who are now seen to determine the destiny of post-industrial societies.

During the period of economic nationalism the burgeoning middle-class benefited most from the expansion of the welfare state, employment security, and the opportunities afforded by comprehensive education and the expansion of post-compulsory provision. Accordingly, within the sociology of education it was the question of working-class access and opportunity which dominated debates about class conflict and inequalities in the postwar period.

Now, it is not working-class resistance to education which represents the primary sources of class conflict as predicted by neo-Marxist analysts, but the exclusionary tactics of the middle classes at a time of profound personal and social uncertainty and insecurity. With the breakdown of economic nationalism, the demise of bureaucratic careers and the attendant risks of downward mobility have led the middle classes to reassert their vested interests in an attempt to maximize the reproduction of their class advantage.

Nationally this can be seen in terms of middle-class claims of over-taxation. Since the mid-1960s, tax revenues have risen steadily in all Western nations, initially to provide more adequate social protection while increasing expenditure on education and health, and latterly to fund welfare for the persistent high numbers of unemployed. The problem posed by the global auction of reducing public-expenditure costs while maintaining or increasing efficiencies has been exacerbated in the Anglophone countries by the perceived problem of 'overtaxing'. This had led to a concern by governments that the middle class would no longer pay the costs of welfare. Whether these concerns are well-founded is a matter of debate.

However, it is fair to say that the issue of overtaxing is more likely to have been canvassed by right-wing governments for whom high taxation is anathema, since they assume that it leads to a blunting of incentives to work and is more likely to advantage the middle-class state employees rather than the disadvantaged in whose name welfare taxes have been raised.

Galbraith has coined the phrase 'the culture of contentment' to describe the outlook of the middle classes in these terms. But this notion fails to acknowledge the underlying condition of the middle classes in the late twentieth century. Like their unskilled counterparts, the middle classes have been subject to relatively high unemployment and increasing insecurity as the social protection afforded by the state has been stripped away.

The cost of health, education, insurance, and pensions have all increased at the same time that far more of these costs have been redefined as a personal rather than a state responsibility. This increasing emphasis on self-reliance has contributed to a climate in which high taxation may appear to be an additional burden to be shouldered by the hard pressed middle classes, often to support those who are viewed as 'less deserving'.

The increased insecurity confronting middle-class families also has profound implications for the education system, given the importance of gaining credentials in the 'competition for a livelihood'.

As Bourdieu has argued; cultural capital in the form of academic credentials is essential to the reproduction of middle-class privilege. This, it can be argued, has led to intense class conflict over the question of educational selection, when concerns about ensuring 'equality of opportunity' have been superseded by primarily (although not exclusively) middle-class claims for greater 'choice' over the education of their children.

Consequently it has been hypothesized that the middle class will either seek to change the class mechanisms of exclusion and selection in education, or they will secede from state education. However, these hypotheses may be more applicable to one national context than another. For example, the issue of middle-class secession is at the forefront of debate in England, yet in Scotland the consensus concerning the importance of comprehensive (or common school) state education appears to be holding. Moreover, it would be a mistake to define this conflict in traditional terms as one involving the working class against the middle class.

As the 'new' middle class has grown exponentially in the era of economic nationalism, so aspirations have been raised for its children. This is clearly reflected in the buoyant demand for access to higher education. Therefore at the same time that the new middle class have been demanding increasing access to higher education for their children, the 'old' professional middle class is concerned to preserve its monopoly of access to the elite universities.

Hence the changing nature of the 'positional' competition for education at the end of the twentieth century may become increasingly dominated by class conflict within what can be broadly defined as the middle classes. There is a further intriguing hypothesis concerning the middle class and educational conflict which is worth entertaining.

Reich has argued that what he calls the 'symbolic analysts'-the design engineers, research scientists, bio-technologists, engineers, public relations executives, investment brokers, international lawyers, management consultants-are likely to secede from national commitments to education, health, and social welfare, not because of 'defensive' manoeuvring as a response to middle-class insecurities, but because they operate in a global labour-market, selling their skills, insights, and knowledge to global businesses. Hence, their objections to paying national, state, or neighbourhood taxes are likely to become more vociferous, because they are more likely to use portable private healthcare, welfare schemes, and prestigious private schools, colleges, and universities with international reputations.

For the moment Reich's argument has the status of a hypothesis with little or no empirical work on it. In the preceding discussion there was little mention of knowledge and pedagogy in the education system. This is because the middle class have a close affinity with the formal system of education, which in many respects is seen to mirror their ways of seeing the world and what they consider really useful knowledge. What this argument ignores, however, is the fact that class conflicts are cross-cut by those of gender. For women, the question of whether the state has enabled them to become full citizens in a democratic society has been long-standing, characterized by the notion of a patriarchal state, dominated by and run in the interests of men.

Recently the structural impediments to women realizing this goal have been added to by women's increased participation in paid work and the feminization of poverty. The issues for women include the question of curriculum and pedagogy: feminist educators have argued that their interests have been marginalized in a male-dominated curriculum, where the images, messages, and representations conveyed in educational institutions reflect the dominant male culture. The question, then, is how women's interests and perspectives can be fairly represented through pedagogy, curriculum, and assessment.

It is clear from the research that comprehensive education has, by and large, done little to change the dominance of a male perspective in the curriculum and the exclusion of girls in their interactions with teachers in classrooms. One significant consequence has been the increased demand for single-sex schooling. Whether single-sex schooling enables girls to escape the images of a male dominated society is a matter of debate. However, the criticism of comprehensive education as reproducing the ideologies and practice of patriarchy are really only the tip of the iceberg.

Underlying these criticisms are two further challenges to the received liberal view of the links between education and democracy. The first concerns what is taught in schools as part of the Western heritage of a liberal education. That heritage has been understood as partly comprising the great works of literature and philosophy, written largely by men, though, it could be argued, not exclusively from a male perspective. In the theories of its defenders, a liberal education is intimately linked to the creation of the dispositions needed in a democracy.

Every educational system has a moral goal that it tries to attain and that informs its curriculum. It wants to produce a certain kind of human being. Democratic education, whether it admits it or not, wants and needs to produce men and women who have the tastes, knowledge and character supportive of a democratic regime. Feminist criticisms of liberal education challenge the assumption that the male-dominated liberal canon of 'great' philosophy and literature constitutes an appropriate curriculum for senior secondary and university students. Rather than initiate students into the forms of knowledge and modes of rationality of Western civilization, a liberal education is an exercise in patriarchal power.

Power, in effect, masquerades as truth. Closely allied to this criticism is that of the notion of a public sphere in which the issues of a democracy are debated. The public sphere was constituted, in theory, on the idea that by recognizing and accepting man's natural rights, men found a fundamental basis of unity and sameness.

Class, race, religion, national origin all disappear or become dim when bathed in the light of natural rights, which give men common interests and make them truly brothers'. In an important sense this assumption is similar to the universalistic ideals of meritocratic education: in both cases the particular characteristics of individuals in terms of gender, ethnicity, and class are discounted in the wider national interest of democracy and equality. Bloom's analysis of what is required in order to sustain democracy is clearly open to question.

Nancy Fraser has argued that the liberal conception of the public sphere as represented by Bloom, although her work has focused on Habermas, is likely to limit rather than extend democratic participation. In her view, multiple public spheres representing the variety of cultures in a pluralist society are not only desirable but possible. For her, the possibility of a truly multicultural democracy is an empirical question. But Fraser's position is also open to question, since it raises the issue of whether groups from incommen-surable communities can talk to each other when they differ in their perspectives and values. This is, however, a vital question, since the move to different schools for different ethnic and social groups is likely to increase in strength in many Western societies. Only if the kind of vision articulated by Fraser is possible can a new set of links between education and democracy be forged on the basis of radical cultural diversity. The debate on single-sex schooling points to further aspects of gender and educational performance: the apparent increasingly superior academic performance of girls over boys. This trend has given a further impetus to the debate by the recent positioning of white working-class boys as anti-education macho, and right-wing.

The underlying problem which has led to this 'positioning' has been the process of deindustrialisation; the decline in unskilled blue-collar work and the consequent rise in working-class youth male unemployment. The research on the relationship between this relatively recent representation of working-class boys and the desire for single-sex schooling is in its infancy. However, it may be that the motivation for single-sex schooling in terms of providing girls with a more accurate representation of their lives and interests has now been coupled with what is, in effect, a fear of working-class boys.

As Connell has noted, the nature of masculinity is changing in the new historical conditions, and it is a question of whether the sub-cultures of working-class boys can adapt to the new realities. The mirror image of this representation of working-class boys is that of increasingly educationally successful girls from all classes. In this context, there is much talk of the twenty-first century belonging to women because they are becoming educationally more successful than boys and because the nature of work in the new century is more likely to suit them. Just as the new representation of working-class boys needs research, so this new image of women needs a critical eye.

In their paper Weiner, Arnot and David challenge the notion that girls are indeed outperforming boys at school, while the idea that the world of work in the twenty-first century belongs to women appears to be difficult to sustain. Throughout Western societies the participation of women in the labour force has increased dramatically, yet much of their work is part-time and low-paid. In the Anglophone societies they have been used to forge a neo-Fordist strategy in response to the global economy in which employers use lowpaid, casualised employment as a strategy to cut costs and increase profits. But women have also been at the sharp end of another significant trend in Western societies, the feminization of poverty.

The combination of the polarization of income in Anglophone societies and the increasing number of woman-headed families has meant that the incidence of poverty has fallen unequally on women. This in turn raises general questions about the ability of women in poverty to participate fully as citizens in a democracy and specific questions about the ability of women with families to have the time and resources to find work or upskill themselves, when the conditions under which they can freely enter the labour force have not been met. Education has been implicated in these issues because the universal provision of highquality, early-childhood education is a key factor in enabling women to enter the labour market.

Nevertheless, universal provision remains controversial, and a focus of struggle for women. The reasons for this are not difficult to find. The question of early childhood education stands at the intersection of several debates concerning the role of women in society and the appropriate education of young children. These include the question of the 'proper' role of mothers in the raising of young children, and whether paid work conflicts with conceptions of the mother's role.

These debates often assume, however, that women in general and mothers in particular have a choice as to whether they enter paid employment. If the state has been seen by women as biased towards the interests of the powerful in society, the same is true of groups whose history is characterized by colonialism.

Post-colonialism is the theoretical term that has been broadly adopted in discussions relating people of colour and education. The notion of post-colonialism draws attention to the fact that issues of racism have an historical context and that, for the most part, these are related economically, culturally, and politically to the impact of Western colonization over the past 500 years. At a time of increased global interdependency it also highlights once more the relationships between economy and culture and the problems that the new global economy poses for the once colonized.

The re-emergence of a politics of identity, culture, and autonomy among those who have been marked by colonization has been one of the most significant elements in education in the past 20 years. Whether it be the first peoples of North America, Maori in New Zealand, Aborigines in Australia, or the post-colonial peoples who have been drawn to the metropolitan societies like Britain and the United States, the struggle to break out of a Western-dominated mono-cultural and assimilationist society has been highly significant for education.

As Jordan and Weedon note, the cultural struggle is over the power to name, to represent common sense, to create the 'official' version of history and events to speak on behalf of or for other. In each case the history of postcolonialism has been one of conflict between the perspectives embodied in these powers by the post-colonial state and people of colour, the once-colonized. In this context the drive towards different forms of education and educational institutions for different ethnic and religious groups has constituted a strategy for taking power over these crucial issues of history, and culture. Educationally, it has been assumed that there are a series of crucial links between the security of a cultural identity, self-esteem, and educational performance. The educational rationale underlying this theory is that students learning in their own cultural context and, where applicable, their own language are likely to be more successful than if they are educated in ethnically diverse schools.

In recent educational debate, this theory is pervasive and has become almost axiomatic. It is, however, a theory which is in some respects testable. McPherson and Willms, for example, show that the raising of educational achievement in Scotland may largely be attributable to the greater socio-economic mix of students created by the comprehensive system. If so, then one inference to be drawn is that students who attend ethnically homogeneous schools but who are predominantly working-class may not improve their academic performance to the same extent as in ethnically and socially 'mixed' comprehensive schools.

The issue, however, is more complex than this potential criticism suggests. It fails to take into account the relationship between issues of power, pedagogy, and knowledge. While the projects of culturally autonomous schooling will take years to realize, and hence to evaluate, they need to be judged against the broader aims of the preservation of living cultures and languages and as a way of 'getting out from under': education here is seen as providing a platform for access to power and full democratic participation in society.

The project of culturally autonomous schooling is long-term and in the meantime the majority of students who may benefit from them remain in state schools. The educational outcomes of these students reinforce the view that they are systematically disadvantaged. For example, in the United States, Black and Latino students are far less likely to graduate from college, while in the UK patterns of mobility over two generations show that, while there are differences between ethnic groups, people of colour in the United Kingdom suffer a penalty, in terms of life chances, as a result of their ethnicity.

The most immediate threat to life chances of some ethnic 'minority' groups concerns poverty. The poverty of the 1980s and 1990s has fallen disproportionately upon people of colour and particularly on the women from these groups, especially in the inner cities. The state's role in relation to the question of poverty is a matter of debate; however, it is clear that the withdrawal of welfare support has created additional hardship for those in poverty. Most disconcerting of all is that changed policies of taxation and welfare have meant that children have suffered most from the withdrawal of state support.

In educational terms, children in poverty have begun school disadvantaged and are likely to be further disadvantaged by under-resourced, inner-city, ghetto schools. However, Western states have retreated from initiating large-scale programmes to deal with the problem of poverty and education in the inner cities. Over the last decade there has been a fundamental restructuring of education in Western societies. However, to understand the complex causes that have shaped this restructuring involves attempt to distinguish what is generally applicable to all post-industrial societies from what are specific to particular countries. Throughout the Western world, for instance, there have been similar changes in education, which seems to denote an international 'convergence' irrespective of national ideologies, politics, or power relations. These changes include the development of mass tertiary education with significant increases in age cohorts going to university as part of a overall increase in post-compulsory education; emphasis on life-long education; the attempts to break down the distinction between academic and vocational education; the devolution of educational decision making; and problems of funding.

At the same time, it would be difficult to believe that the state-led restructuring of education, particularly in the Anglophone societies, was merely epiphenomenal: that is, merely a reaction to underlying economic and social changes. The defining element in the restructuring of education in Anglophone societies has been the imposition during the 1980s of economic and cultural renewal guided by what has become known as New Right or Neo-Conservative ideology. This ideology guided the administrations of Reagan and Thatcher in the United States and Britain, and is equally influential in New Zealand and parts of Australia and Canada. New Right or Neo-Conservative ideology, couples a neo-liberal view of the virtues of individual freedom and the free market with a traditional conservative view that a strong state is necessary to keep moral and political order. In part this political project attempted to turn deep-seated economic and social change to its own account by interpreting the crisis in Western society and its antecedents according to its own theoretical presuppositions.

In post-modernist terms this could be seen as a 'totalizing' modernist project, imposing the grand narrative of the market and competitive individualism as an instrument of cultural renewal. In this specific sense, the advent of the New Right in the 1980s was similar to the kind of political projects advanced by the extreme Left and Right in Europe and the Soviet Union in the 1920s and 1930s. Nevertheless, despite the attempt to reconstruct societies according to their own ideological precepts, New Right theories had to connect with the common experiences of everyday life in a changing society. If they had not, they would have been rejected decisively in democratic elections yet that was the experience of neither Reagan nor Thatcher. While New Right ideology had to address the way people experienced underlying changes in work, family, and education, it was also the case that it was integral to economic trends in the 1980s.

The New Right political project was, for instance, instrumental in the development of the new global competition. The questions concerning an understanding of educational restructuring turn, then, on the way fundamental changes in the economy and society relate to the ideological currents of the New Right which have guided the restructuring of education in Anglophone societies. Distinguishing between these forces of change is more than a purely academic puzzle.

There is a practical policy pay-off to such an analysis, for without it, it is difficult to identify the causes of the outcomes of current policy formulations or the foundations on which alternative policies in education can be built. Clearly one of the major tasks for sociology of education is to attempt to assess the relative consequence of secular changes in the nature of post-industrial or post-modern societies as opposed to the educational and societal changes initiated by the New Right. The difficulty of this task should not be underestimated. Indeed, a failure to grasp the political possibilities of societal changes helps to explain why viable left-of-centre alternatives are currently thin on the ground.

However, one way in which research can illuminate the relationship between the New Right project and underlying change in Western Europe is to take seriously Skidelsky's theoretical view that all Western societies will have to conform to the New Right recipe for economic restructuring if they are to survive in the global economic competition. If this view is borne out it would confirm that there is an underlying and unfolding logic to the political economy of nations conforming to the interpretation of 'reality' advanced by the New Right. In a sense it would validate Mrs. Thatcher's claim that 'there is no alternative'.

Before looking at the impact of the New Right on educational restructuring more closely we need to make two cautionary notes. Firstly, the underlying economic ana social changes we have described apply unevenly to Western societies, and may have little application to other societies such as those of the Pacific Rim, as Ashton and Sung and Green make clear.

The demise of the state socialist societies of Eastern Europe has made social scientists far more sensitive to the differences between capitalism in contrasting cultures. This should alert us to the dangers of assuming that contemporary societies all conform to those of the West, and to the dangers of policy importation without due regard to the social, economic, and cultural context in which they have been,seen to work' and in which they are to be implanted. Secondly, as regards the New Right, a similar cautionary note needs to be made with respect to educational restructuring. As a term to describe the ideology behind market reforms in education, we should note that its precise meaning differs between societies.

Common to all New Right ideologies are a series of theoretical assumptions derived from neo-classical economics about human nature, society, and social progress which comprise the neo-liberal wing of New Right ideology. In the United States and Britain in particular, these assumptions have been coupled with varieties of conservatism, although, as Whitty has noted, there is a question as to whether these two elements of New Right ideology are in tension. Over and above differences in New Right ideology the way its theoretical assumptions are interpreted and implemented also varies in different contexts. For example, in Britain and the United States New Right ideology struck a chord of popular appeal, whereas in New Zealand its policy agenda was largely imposed.

However, despite such differences, there is a core of New Right thought that has set the terms for debate in Anglophone societies. We describe this core in what follows, and where appropriate we show its impact in the various societies where it has had a major influence on educational policy. In the early 1980s, the New Right argued that one of the fundamental causes of the decline of countries like the United States and Britain was cultural and in particular that state involvement in individuals' lives reduced their competitive and enterprising zeal.

Economically, it was asserted that there are two pathological effects of state intervention. The first is that every dollar spent by the state was a dollar that would not go into investment in private enterprise. In the jargon of the day, the state 'crowds out' the private sector. Moreover, in so doing it stifles both the entrepreneurial initiative and imagination of rich and poor. It reduces the capacities of the rich because it overtaxes them.

Therefore, with less disposable income the rich are not only less likely to invest in productive enterprises, but also the state itself loses out when the incidence of taxation is too high, as the rich will find ways of tax avoidance. For the poor, initiative is impaired because they come to depend upon state welfare 'handouts'. Hence the emergence of the notion of state dependency. In terms of the wealth and income polarization which has been a feature of Anglophone societies since the 1970s, the New Right take the view that individuals are the authors of their own poverty, and that state action to ameliorate their situation would be counterproductive.

At its most extreme, this position is captured by Gilder's statement, 'In order to succeed, the poor most of all need the spur of their own poverty.' While Gilder's writing represented the extremes of polemic, a similar point is made in a more systematic way by Murray and Herrnstein and Murray. The idea that the state cannot compensate for individual failure is part and parcel of the New Right view that the state is best out of people's lives.

In taking this view the New Right was attempting to reverse the assumption made during the period of economic nationalism that the state had a responsibility to alleviate poverty through policies of full employment, and to create security and opportunity. However, it can be argued that the conservative element of the New Right with its emphasis on a strong state simply changes the configurations of state power in people's lives rather than reducing it, as we shall see when we look at education.

The New Right nevertheless assert that economic and social renewal does not depend on state-led initiatives or changes to the underlying structures of society in terms of class, patriarchy, or racism, but on changing the incentives for individuals. It is through the creation of a culture of individual enterprise that economic success can be ensured in the new global economy. Consistent with this view is the assumption that economic reform could not be led by macropolicies, especially of the kind advocated by Keynes and which had guided the full employment policies of the period of economic nationalism.

Rather it is microeconomic reform that will lead to world competitiveness, through economic deregulation aimed at releasing market forces. This is seen as essential in order to reform the economy to approximate the neo-classical utopian vision of perfect competition. Given their general catechism—markets good, governments bad—it is not surprising that attempts would also be made to increase market competition within the education system. The themes of individual motivation, micro-economic change, the virtues of competition, and fiscal restraint all have their parallels in education restructuring.

The cornerstone of New Right education policy has been the introduction of market competition into all the education sectors. There are three aspects to this.

Firstly, the introduction of market competition involves a devolution of financial, staffing, and policy issues to individual educational institutions. In effect schools, colleges, and universities in the public sector become self-managing on the lines of small- to medium-size businesses. Here there is a parallel between the commitment to microeconomic reform for the private sector and micro-reform in education. For the assumption is that once the market context has been established with the appropriate incentives and market disciplines, competition between educational institutions will serve to raise standards or they will simply go out of business because they cannot attract 'customers'. Educational research primarily, then, focuses on what makes, for example, an effective school.

Secondly, it is assumed that schools could compete successfully irrespective of the nature of the school intake. This argument made in the work of Chubb and Moe is particularly attractive to the New Right because it assumes that raising educational standards for all is simply a question of school management and quality teaching. In other words, school success or failure is determined by the management of the school and the quality of the teachers. In effect, schools could compensate for society, so long, of course, as the appropriate leadership was in place to head the management team. This then enabled questions about family and child poverty and their impact on educational performance to be regarded as irrelevant. Indeed, the New Right have been quick to criticize any one who raised the link between pupil intake and school performance as evading responsibility. Well-managed schools coupled with pupil self-motivation, it is assumed, will make inroads into the eradication of poverty as individuals bettered themselves through education.

Thirdly, the notion of parental choice is treated as unproblematic. As James Coleman has succinctly noted:

> The movement toward choice is the first step in the movement toward getting the incentives right in education-incentives for both the suppliers of educational services, that is, schools and their teachers, and for the consumers of education, that is parents and children. The incentives for schools... would include an interest in attracting and keeping the best students they could. The incentives for parents and students would include the ability to get into schools they find attractive and to remain in those schools.

However, subsequent research, included in Part 4, has found this view wholly problematic with respect to overall academic achievement, equality of opportunity, democracy, and the impact of restructuring on the teaching profession. Ball *et al.*'s research has found that parents do not come to make choices with equal cultural and material resources. Moreover, the interests of parents and schools are not identical, as Waslander and Thrupp show, and for the privileged schools who could choose their intakes there has been little evidence of competition.

One of the major flaws in the marketization of education is the assumption that schools can achieve equally, and hence compete successfully, independent of the nature of their intake. As school-effectiveness studies become increasingly sophisticated so Coleman's original hypothesis that student mix within a school is a key factor in the overall achievement of the school is now a well-confirmed hypothesis. This being the case, there is an issue of whether overall standards of education will be raised by competition or whether, as unpopular schools go into a spiral of decline, the educational standards of the students in those schools will also decline: in other words, whether the introduction of competition into schools will lead to a polarization of intakes and educational achievement, thereby eroding the ethos underlying the comprehensive or common school and bringing back covert selection to successful schools.

A further issue then emerges with respect to equality of opportunity. If individual schools cannot compensate for society because their student intake's prior achievement is relatively low due to poverty, and if research can show that a socio-economically well balanced school can best raise their educational achievement, then some organizing principle for the system as a whole needs to be instituted in order to promote equality of opportunity.

However, equality of opportunity has been redefined by the New Right as 'equity', and this seems to mean something more akin to the right of each individual to a sound compulsory education with ever-rising standards, so that individuals can compete in the global labour market. In effect, it turns its back on state intervention to regulate the competition for credentials in order to reduce social disadvantage. This therefore signals a retreat from 'equity' as understood in the strong sense defined by Coleman. The significance of equality of results was that it applied to identifiable social groups rather than individuals, and implied active intervention by states to create equality of outcomes for different groups.

If the New Right version of equity constitutes a retreat from active state intervention, it is worth noting that equity can also be used in a more radical sense. For groups who have struggled for culturally autonomous schools it can be used to articulate a politics of difference whereby culturally different systems of schooling develop different qualifications. Equity would then be seen as similar to parity of esteem, that is, qualifications from different systems would be seen as commensurate.

Such a position is different from Coleman's concept of equality of results, because been envisaged the same outcomes in terms of qualifications. In this case, the shift in terminology from equality of results to equity reflects an underlying change from an education system with one relatively linear qualifications structure to a system of parallel structures, reflecting a radical pluralist rather than a bureaucratic and assimilationist society. This new terrain of contestation is an example of where fundamental social change has met the New Right head-on.

In relation to democracy, there are two broad criticisms that can be made about the marketization of education. Firstly, the question of the link between democracy and education is rejected. The realm of freedom for the New Right is that of private consumption, so that schools are not seen to play any part in the politics of liberation. Here there is something of a self-fulfilling prediction, for if students are socialized into a competitive market for education then a salient aspect of the hidden curriculum may well be to create the possessive individuals necessary to market behaviour.

Thus the marketization of education can be seen as a historically decisive moment, in that knowledge is not only structured to be economically productive but itself becomes wholly a commodity under market conditions. The introduction of market reforms in education can also be viewed as a mechanism for the control of teachers' practice in which rewards are based on individual performance, merit pay, and the threat of unemployment if schools do not perform. However, such rewards and sanctions are both highly problematic in an educational context.

Student achievement is the result of a collective effort over many years and cannot be seen as the product of a single teacher, while the reasons for falling school rolls may have little to do with the value they add to a student's learning. There is, therefore, an open question as to whether a market system, in failing to take account of teacher's sense of collective professional autonomy, can produce the higher standards claimed for it.

Moreover, it has also alienated teachers, since it is assumed that teachers will resist the changes because it is not in their interests to submit themselves to market regimes in education. This is a central New Right assertion based on what is called 'public choice' theory. According to this theory, teachers who work in the public sector are part of a state monopoly, within which teachers are 'featherbedded'.

Through zoning, they were guaranteed students, and hence a job, irrespective of their performance. This is known by public-choice theorists as 'provider capture' because of their belief that state education is run in the interests of middle-class providers rather than consumers (students, parents, employers, and taxpayers). This has led New Right governments to implement change rapidly and to attack the sources of teachers' collective strength, their unions and professional organizations.

Hargreaves calls this 'structural' change because it is imposed 'from above' without the consent of most teachers. What has been offered to teachers in compensation is a variant of what Hargreaves describes as post-modern and Whitty post-Fordist organization, which holds out the promise of far greater opportunities in the decision-making of the self-managed school, although comparative research does not tend to support this sense of promise. These arguments are supported by Darling-Hammond, who claims that existing educational policies in the United States with respect to funding and teacher education are wholly inadequate for a post-bureaucratic education system. These claims raise serious questions about the nature and strategy of educational restructuring and its impact on teachers and students.

There is a fundamental choice between restructuring as bureaucratic control, where teachers are controlled and regulated to implement the mandate of others, and restructuring as professional empowerment, where teachers are supported, encouraged, and provided with newly structured opportunities to make improvements of their own'. Hence what Hargreaves calls 'mandates' from the state will not themselves produce more desirable outcomes in education. What may be intended by state policy may be changed or subverted or adapted to teachers' assumptions about their professional role in the classroom.

Markets are always embedded within an institutional context over which the state continues to have a significant influence. The introduction of market policies in education has been accompanied by increasingly strong powers arrogated by the New Right state. What we have witnessed in countries where a New Right agenda has been close to full implementation is the devolution of certain powers of decision-making in relation to the self-managed school, and greatly increased powers of state regulation. This, then, is another example of the paradox of the strong state and the free market.

The increased powers of regulation of education have, in the New Right dominated societies, tended to take three forms. Firstly, in the light of the pressure exerted by the global auction and burgeoning public expenditure, the state has sought to weaken the institutional pressures on increasing state expenditure on education. Here the decentralization of educational resourcing involves the attempt to encourage market behaviour, and in doing so seeks to weaken the power of teacher unions, as national or state-wide employment conditions are replaced by schools determining their own employment policies.

The consequence of these policies of decentralization was a retreat from federal funding in the United States in the 1980s and the capping or reduction of expenditure on education in other New Right dominated countries. The catchphrase of New Right decentralization policies has been that of greater parental and community choice and control. Choice in relation to educational markets is problematic, but so is the notion of parental or community control. Control in this context can mean the management of schools by parents and communities, rather than bureaucracies.

It is a way of recruiting low-cost educational administrators and removing bureaucracies with expertise to challenge central policies. In effect, parents and communities merely become technical instruments of the state's will under these conditions. However, as Fine shows through her case studies of community participation in education, the control and management of education can never be simply a technical question; it always has a political dimension. In Fine's view, unless communities are prepared to mobilize politically, community initiatives in inner-city schools will fail. A further reason why the promise of devolved control cannot be taken at face value is because at the same time that schools have been given greater 'autonomy' over the allocation of resources and selection policies, the school curriculum has become increasingly centralized (whether it be at state or national levels in the United States, or embodied in national curricula as in Britain or New Zealand). This constitutes the second form of control.

The motivations for introducing these centralized curricula are not necessarily linked to economic productivity. Goodson has suggested that it is an attempt to reassert a national identity in the face of an increasingly globalized economy and weakened nation states, since subjects like history are particularly prominent while information technology is relegated to a minor role. Ball sees the introduction of the national curriculum in Britain as a struggle between restorationist and modernizing conservatives. The latter are more concerned to tailor the curriculum to post-Fordist economic possibilities while the former are, as Goodson suggests, more concerned with the shaping of a national identity.

Ball suggests that the restorationists have won the day in Britain. It can be argued, however, that these attempts to assert a national identity reflect the interests of the white male Elites. They are therefore a particular, contemporary variant of Green's view that education has been, historically, integral to the formation of the nation state. In this case, it is not so much the formation of the nation state which is at stake but its reformation in the light of the restructuring of the state-education relationship. Such curricula do, therefore, raise the question of whose knowledge is to be taught and what kind of national identity such curricula are designed to foster. There is, however, another side to the introduction of such curricula; it can also be argued that they serve to promote equality of opportunity because all students, irrespective of class, gender, or ethnicity, have to study them.

In this sense it removes, in principle, the link between a status hierarchy of subjects and the opportunities such status affords to those fortunate enough to be selected to take them. In the past, research has shown that the higher the status of a subject, the more likely it has been taken by students of a higher social class background. However as Apple argues, this is not the case at university, where technical and commercial knowledge is at a premium and is linked to a university's status and the social class and ethnic background of its students. At the school level, the consequence of the introduction of centralized curricula is that the power of parents and communities over a key aspect of education is removed, leaving them with the technical aspects of management. However, the removal of power is taken a step further by the third form of increased central control.

The New Right have also introduced new forms of accountability and performance indicators. These 'reforms' have involved an attempt to link the accountability of educational institutions, and where possible individual teachers, to the assessment of students. There are several reasons for this. The first is related to the programme of educational restructuring: as Torrance shows, assessment has been used to attempt to change teaching practice. The second is that it has been used to regulate competition between institutions. In Britain this has been most highly developed through various league tables of performance and the flow of resources. In educational systems based on choice and competition, resources follow students on the assumption that students will be attracted to the most successful institutions. Less successful institutions as indicated by league tables will suffer a decline in student numbers while the more successful will attract an increase, and funding will be regulated accordingly. Thirdly, there is clearly a political motivation for introducing modes of accountability which seem to link teaching performance to student success and failure, for it seems as if the state as representative of the people has finally opened the closed shop of professionalism to a set of transparent performance indicators that can be easily understood.

However, as Pollitt has argued, performance indicators in the public sector as a whole are at best proxies for efficiency. Most do not relate to effectiveness or quality: a point forcefully made by Torrance. This then raises the question of whether performance indicators are merely a matter of political expediency. If they are, their effects are none the less real, for educational institutions are being reshaped by them.

Indeed, it has been argued by Peters that the traditional purpose of the university education is undergoing fundamental change from an induction into a Western liberal education to one designed to enhance economically effective knowledge, and that performance indicators are instrumental in initiating this change. The preceding discussion should serve to remove any lingering remnants of the view popularized by Parsons and Kerr et al. that industrial evolution entails education moving inexorably from ascription to merit, dogma to democracy, and inequality to social justice.

Indeed, the study of education at the end of the twentieth century compels us to reconsider questions first addressed during the Enlightenment. In these terms it is useful to think of education in the modern, if not post-modern world, as a means of achieving a balance between equality, liberty, and community. We want here to reconsider all three. Though sociologists have contributed heavily to the debate about equality, the problem is much more than a sociological one. In 1651 Hobbes wrote:

> Nature hath made man so equal, in the faculties of body, and mind; as that though bee found one man sometimes manifestly stronger in body, or of quicker mind than another; yet when all is reckoned together, the difference between man, and man, is not so considerable, as that one man can thereupon claim to himself any benefit, to which another may not pretend, as well as he. Egalitarian claims and anti-egalitarian rebuttals are probably more strident now, and certainly more often couched in sociological terms, than they were in the seventeenth century. Yet Hobbes's formulation (substituting 'person' for 'man' and a pronoun for both sexes if the English language possessed one) defines the contemporary debate as well as anything written in the intervening 300 years.

The debate contains empirical propositions from both genetics and sociology, the one referring to natural differences and the other referring to the social psychology of people's perceptions of social rights. But the central assertion is an evaluative one, as it must be. For the debate is fundamentally about the values which ought to be reflected in the actual relations of women and men in society. Controversy goes on at three relatable but not necessarily related levels. First, there is a clash of priorities between different values presumed to be realizable in society; second, there is the philosophically and logically difficult intellectual task of clarifying the language of the debate; and third, there is the tedious labour of relating theoretical constructions to the changing empirical realities of the social world.

The distinctive contribution of sociology must clearly be at the third level. It is well known, of course, that the political persuasion of many western sociologists has leant towards egalitarian politics, by contrast with the typical orientation of biologists and psychologists since Herbert Spencer and Social Darwinism. Perhaps there is a sociology of intellectual culture which might partly explain these persistent political differences in terms of the social consciousness induced by work in the different disciplines and the selective effect of their popular representations on the recruitment of personalities to them. At all events, whatever the provenance of ethical discussion, the premises of argument are set by a moral affirmation about the value of equality in relation to other values such as liberty, efficiency, prosperity, or community sought by people in their dealings with others.

In this sense the debate, we suspect, is unresolvable, and for that reason all the better phrased in the blunt banality used by R.H. Tawney to dismiss the inegalitarian—'if a man likes that sort of dog then that is the sort of dog a man likes'. Yet to begin with this fundamental simplicity is in no way to detract from the work of those who have contributed to the second level of discussion by seeking greater conceptual clarity as to the meaning of the terms used in the debate. John Rawls's *A Theory, of Justice* is now a classic case in point. He adopts the device of the 'original position'—an 'as if' story of the rational choices that might be expected from an individual contemplating different societies with known different systems of social relationship and distribution but an unknown position within them for the contemplator-to illuminate the problem of value choice.

Brian Barry's *Political Argument* is another example of a book which educates us to avoid terminological confusion and to use words to the fullest extent of their potential for precise distinction. Yet if we only consider Brian Barry's short book on The Liberal Theory of justice or Rawls's long one, it becomes clear that no amount of conceptual clarification, however sophisticated and erudite, solves the problem of what we have referred to as the first level.

Thus Barry, through an argument of delicate philosophical dissection, clearly demonstrates how a minimal adjustment to Rawls's social and psychological assumptions opens up the possibility of a crucial shift from liberal to egalitarian forms of society. Nevertheless, the problem at the first level remains, and Barry ends with a personal statement of preferences which he does not offer as compelling, only as consonant with his preceding argument.

A strong attachment to liberalism in relation to ideas while believing that in matters of political, social and economic organization altruistic collaboration is worth giving up a good deal of efficiency for, and fearing that hierarchy is more soundly based in human psychology than 'would altogether like'. At the same time, this passage indicates the existence of a third level of argument which sustains the first and second levels by challenges to test concept against relevant fact, typically under conditions where either the pace of social change or the ingenuity of theorists outpaces the capacity of empirical enquiry.

Of course, politicians can be more or less serious even at the first level. Thus, when a Labour or Democratic politician tells us that she does not like the private sector of education but that the cost of abolition is too great a financial burden to face for the time being, she is offering an honest if debatable ordering of priorities. When we hear Conservative and Republican politicians suggest that all children should have an equal opportunity of acquiring intelligence, and of developing their talents and abilities to the full, and then go on to tell us that they favour a market system of education, the reader or listener is under standably baffled as to what priorities are being offered.

It is only, by hearing the firs affirmation as amiable rhetoric or the second as assuming the (false) empirical proposition that opportunity to develop intelligence is equal as between children in a market or comprehensive system that the two assertions can be reconciled. In the latter case given conceptual clarity, empirical enquiry can settle such debate. This we take to be the distinctive business of the social scientist; and we will return to the question in considering a new political arithmetic shortly. There has been widespread disillusionment and now, again, some renewed optimism concerning the possibilities of reaching a more egalitarian society through educational reform.

Much sociological effort is needed to determine what education might contribute to wider participation in the material and cultural abundance potentially available to the members of a rich society. We are, of course, invited on every hand to espouse various utopias, among which Ivan Illich's outline of a convivial society was a previously fashionable one. Nevertheless, whether we lean towards Illichian or other nostrums, there is inescapable controversy as to the relation between theory and policy, or what means might appropriately and effectively turn our dreams into realities. Our own view is basically that the society of equals has to be created by economic and political reform, and that the role of education must largely be to maintain such a society once it has been attained.

A good deal may be learned by looking back over the debate on the relation between equality and education, and in this connection Silver's review of British and American official polity towards poverty from 1960 to 1980 gives a fair picture of this element of intellectual and political history.

But, as we shall argue, the origins of the mainstream of theory on which policy has been floated are to be found further back in the nineteenth century. Looking back over the history of official policy in Europe and America, one can see throughout it an unmistakable thread of egalitarianism. No less striking, however, is the fact of failure to realize egalitarian ends by educational means—a failure to which the virulence of current debate is itself a major witness.

The basic reason is that the theory which has formed the foundation of Western policy is a false one, consisting of liberal concepts which have not stood the test of historical experience. This liberal theory came out of the tradition of political economy in which, in Britain atleast, the boundaries between economics and sociology were not drawn as sharply as they are now. The classic statement of the theory is to be found in a paper written by Alfred Marshall more than 120 years ago and delivered at the Reform Club in Cambridge, England, on 'The Future of the Working Class'. This famous essay is the *locus classicus* of liberal theories about the relation of education to social class. It is worth reconsidering because he was commenting on social change of a similar magnitude to the social transformation we have described in this chapter.

Looking at views of social change can help to throw our own situation into sharper relief. Marshall was, of course, writing at a time and speaking in a place when women's contribution to intellectual life was virtually unrecognized, and when the division of labour between the sexes was such as to place women in the class system derivatively from the occupation of their fathers or husbands. He was in fact a devoted liberal who, in writing his Principles of Economics, was highly appreciative of Mrs. Mill's contribution to John Stuart Mill's book on the same subject. The question, as Marshall put it, was 'whether it be true that the resources of the world will not suffice for giving to more than a small proportion of its inhabitants an education in youth and an occupation in afterlife, similar to those which we are now wont to consider proper to gentlemen... The question is not whether all men will ultimately be equal-that they will certainly not-but whether progress may not go on steadily if slowly till the official distinction between working men and gentlemen has passed away; till, by occupation at least, every man is a gentleman.'

Marshall's high-minded Victorian conception of the stratification system was focused on culture and character. These were the defined class attributes to which policy had to be directed. The theory was that culture and character were functions of education (which determine occupation) and occupational experience. The mediating variable was experience in work. The occupations of 'gentlemen' he saw as directly promoting high culture and refinement of character—qualities which require a careful and long-continued education. He further saw the occupational structure of his day as descending (in terms of its propensity to generate admirable personal qualities) through fine gradations from the high professions through the 'intermediate classes' down to 'that darker scene which the lot of unskilled labour presents... Vast masses of men who, after long hours of hard and unintellectual toil, are wont to return to their narrow homes with bodies exhausted and minds dull and sluggish.'

Marshall's proposals for liberation from mid-nineteenth-century conditions were contained in a sketch of a 'fancied country" from which the brutalizing effects of long hours of toil had been excluded, and in which no one would have an occupation which tended to make him anything else than a gentleman. This would be assured by technical progress, extensive education, and short hours of work. He argued that such an education, economy, and society would be practical:

> We know, then, pretty clearly what are the conditions under which our fancied country is to start; and we may formulate them as follows. It is to have a fair share of wealth, and not an abnormally large population. Everyone is to have in youth an education which is thorough while it lasts and which lasts long. No one is to do in the day so much manual work as will leave him little time or little aptitude for intellectual and artistic enjoyment in the evening. Since there will be nothing tending to render the individual coarse and unrefined, there will be nothing tending to render society coarse and unrefined.

Marshall went on to rebut the objections which were seriously advanced in Victorian England.

First, he argued against the fear that a great diminution of the hours of manual labour would lead to economic ruin. This argument was the stock-in-trade of British employers from the middle of the nineteenth century and survived not only to the slump years of the 1930s, but as far as the Eurosceptist opposition to the Maastricht Treaty in the 1990s. Thus, when the Bill presenting the Fisher Act of 1918 was before Parliament, we find R. H. Tawney repeating the Marshall argument against a memorandum of the Education Committee of the Federation of British Industries.

The proposal was to abolish all exemption from school attendance for children under 14. The Federation of British Industries argued that: 'A period of eight hours a week taken out of working hours would impose a burden upon many industries which they would be quite unable to bear except on a basis of very gradual development.' Gradual indeed: for resistance to the Maastricht social protections remain lively. Tawney couched the rebuttal in terms of outraged irony:

> To suggest that British industry is suspended over an abyss by a slender thread of juvenile labour, which eight hours of continued education will snap, that after a century of scientific discovery and economic progress it is still upon the bent backs of children of fourteen that our industrial organization, and national prosperity, and that rare birth of time, the Federation of" British Industries itself, repose-is not all this, after all, a little pitiful?

Marshall's version of the argument is more sober, but otherwise identical. It is based on technological progress and the high return to skilled labour exploiting technologically advanced forms of capital. That knowledge is power was already a well-worn cliché, but that people could possess it with reduced toil was revolutionary thought, contrary to the common sense of all previous experience. None the less, Marshall went so far as to assert that the total work done per head of the population would be greater than it then was. All labour would be skilled and there would be no premium on setting people to tasks that required no skill.

Inventions would increase and would be readily applied. His argument at this point reads like the familiar contemporary thesis of official policy throughout the industrialized and industrializing world-that investment in human resources is the cure for all things but, as was consonant with his elevated view of human nature and society, he stressed the vigorous exercise of increased faculties and saw the direct outcome as an improvement in the level of civility and sensibility and only indirectly as an increase in material wealth.

When Tawney developed this theme in the twentieth century the paramountcy of social over economic values became even more sharply emphasized. In arguing the possibility of maintaining the new society once it had been attained, Marshall also dealt with the objection that a high standard of education could not be kept up because some parents would neglect their duty to their children:

> A class of unskilled labourers might again grow up, competing for hard toil, ready to sacrifice the means of their own culture to increased wages and physical indulgences. This class would marry improvidently: an increased population would press on the means of subsistence, the difficulty of imparting a high education would increase, and society would retrograde until it arrived at a position similar to that which it now occupies-a position in which people, to a great extent, ignore their duty of anticipating, before marriage, the requirements of the bodily and mental nurture of their children; and thereby compels Nature, with her sorrowful but stern hand, to thin out the young lives before they grow up to misery.

We see here the Malthusian spectre which continued to haunt the Victorians into the 1870s. Marshall pinned his faith on the two forces of self-respect and external restraint. At the present time, debate over adaptation to the competitive global economy has divided conservatives from socialists along lines of labour protection and social security. The Maastricht Treaty in Europe is the focus, in which Britain and the United States are pitted against the priorities so far followed by Germany, France, and Scandinavia. The ghost of Marshall is ignored in the Anglo-Saxon world, while the French President Chirac insists that job creation must not take precedence over the established worker protections of health, security, and minimum wages.

Yet to look at Britain or America now, a century later, is to see that the preconditions postulated in Marshall's 'fancied country' have, if anything, surpassed his youthful expectations in the era of economic nationalism. If unskilled labour is the measure of degradation and brutality, its proportion in the total occupied population of Great Britain had fallen from 14.8 per cent in 1931 to less than 8 per cent in 1971. Indeed, the white-collar occupational groups grew by 176 per cent between 1911 and 1966 and now exceed 50 per cent of the total. Moreover, within their ranks the growing number of skilled scientific and technical workers has proliferated, reflecting a vast investment in human capital and an increasingly scientific and capital-intensive technology. Meanwhile, from the end of the war until the mid-1970s, hours of work were reduced from 54 to 40 a week, and there was a marked increase, especially since the Second World War, in paid holidays.

By 1972 three-quarters of the manual workers in the United Kingdom were enjoying 'weeks' paid holiday, compared with 1 per cent in 1951. There were rising standards of housing and health. Affluence accumulated: the national product had quadrupled since 1900. In some respects at least, the material conditions of the ordinary person were superior to those of the gentleman in Marshall's day. Moreover, the position of women in society changed fundamentally as women won greater personal, economic, and social independence with the transformation of patriarchal society. On the other hand, the redistribution of what in Victorian Britain was an almost exclusive concentration of private capital ownership in the hands of the richest 5 per cent of the nation—conditions approximating most closely to a simple Marxist definition of class-proceeded at no more than a snail's pace. In 1911 it was 86 per cent; by the 1950s, 67 per cent; and by 1970, 55 per cent.

Since the 1970s this trend has been reversed, with the rich increasing their share of national wealth in both Britain and the United States. Moreover, the small minority of the extremely wealthy is matched by another and larger minority of the poor. At the end of 1971 3 million people were receiving supplementary benefit in Britain and these, with their dependants, numbered 4½ million, including about a million children under sixteen. In the early 1990s Field suggests that half the population live in households drawing one of the principal means-tested benefits; though the middle mass of white-collar and affluent workers have enjoyed a considerable material prosperity, a steep hierarchy of income, power, and advantage remains.

However, in the United States many 'middle' Americans have seen a decline in their living standards over the last 20 years. Universal compulsory education to age 16 has arrived, together with dramatically expanded provision at the secondary and further stages. But educational inequality has also remained. Its documentation is a recurrent theme of the sociology of education. The major burden of recent work is to show that the disparities persist despite educational expansion.

Thus, educationally at least, there has been no assimilation of the working class into the middle class, though studies at various points in the century show a rising trend of aspirations for the education of their children among working-class families. Marshall stood at the Victorian horizon of a century of liberal theories concerning the relations between education, occupation, and class. Halsey has traced the subsequent history of this tradition and theory elsewhere and has argued that it has failed even in its own terms. Its aim—equality of opportunity in education-has eluded the policymakers. It may be, as James Coleman argues, that, as a pure object of policy, whether defined in input or output terms, the concept is useless in a pure form. Of course, if there were universal provision of all stages of education, the aim would be achieved definitionally: but in fact, selection and differential attainment between gender, class, and ethnic groups have remained an integral feature of passage to further stages of education and of entry to the hierarchy of occupational advantage.

Marshall himself, it may be noted, avoided the meritocracy problem which has faced later versions of the liberal theory, by building in the supply, demand, and price argument with respect to different kinds of labour on the assumption of technological advance. This advance has been realized and, in the post-war period, has resulted in more diverse origins among those in the most elevated occupational destinations. But this pattern of recruitment to 'the top' co-exists with a very large measure of self-recruitment among manual workers.

Education in industrial societies has remained predominantly an avenue for the stable transmission of status from one generation to another, though this has not been incompatible with some inter-generational occupational mobility, not only through the relative expansion of skilled work (because of technical advance) and through the 'replacement' of 'deficient' numbers among the highborn (because of an inverse relation of social class to fertility) but also through successful educational and career competition by a minority of children born in the lower strata. The details of how much social mobility has been experienced in industrial countries in the twentieth century is summarized as 'constant flux' by Erikson and Goldthorpe.

The statistics show the steepness of the remaining inequality, with the upper-middle-class children having three times better-than average chances, and the lower working class having less than half an average chance. Nevertheless, the degree of inequality has lessened with reduction at the top and slight relative improvement at the bottom of the hierarchy of social birth. So much for the progress of educational equality. Marshall was, in essence, advancing a particular version of the embourgeoisement thesis, the theory that class is inexorably abated by the assimilations of the working class into the middle class as industrial society advances to ever higher levels of wealth and income.

For Marshall this assimilation was assured by technological progress leading to an amelioration of economic circumstances in work and social opportunities and attitudes in non-work for the working-classes. Normative assimilation was also crucial to his theory the spread, that is, of 'gentlemanly' character and culture, partly from occupational experience and reinforced by increased and prolonged education.

Characteristic differences in the work situations of manual and non-manual employees still widely persist. Hence these writers regard with some scepticism the broad evolutionary perspectives of Western industrialism in which 'the emergence of a "middle-class" society is seen as a central process resulting more or less automatically from continuing economic growth'. Rising affluence and advances in the technical organization of industry are not likely in themselves to bring about a radical restructuring of the stratification hierarchy. At best there is a classless inegalitarianism. And the interpretation which Goldthorpe puts on the developments that have occurred is rather one of 'normative convergence between certain manual and non-manual groups'.

Marshall's version of the embourgeoisement prediction has not, therefore, been confirmed by events. Not only has there not been a 'one-way' assimilation of the character and culture of working-class into middle-class life, but it has also not taken the direction of universalizing the life-style of an ideal late-Victorian Cambridge don. Marshall did not address himself to the complications of a sophisticated theory of social consciousness. He in effect assumed that the 'gentlemanly' culture of his day would be the common culture for both the women and the men of a rich society. He was only dimly aware of the high cost in cultural terms of the extreme forms of divisions of labour that have been necessitated by technologically-based economic growth.

At the turn of the last century, he could not anticipate the consequences of the breakup of colonialism. Hence he could not foresee the development of socially and ethnically pluralistic societies, within which assimilationalist policies and educational programmes would be rejected for failing to recognize the authentic diversity of cultures, lifestyles, and individual preferences, which would characterize post-modern visions of Marshall's 'fancied country'.

But what cannot be denied is that, quite apart from its intricate relation to liberty, equality also presupposes a solid basis in community. It is, of course, for this reason that American scholars, including Coleman, Bellah *et al.*, and Gans have examined the relationship between individualism, community, and society. In an educational context, John Dewey's Democracy and Education has profound contemporary relevance. Equally, the idea of socialism as fellowship is central to the British native brand of political thought which runs through Tawney to Titmuss.

The liberal conceptions underlying official policy have always lacked an adequate theory of learning. For example, the experience of the American Compensatory Education movements or the British Education Priority Areas (EPAs), has had the effect of locating the origins of inequality at earlier and earlier stages in the life-cycle. But in the end the criticism of the liberal approach becomes an attack on the conception of class held by Marshall and later liberal theorists. In its recent history, particularly in the hands of economic liberals, the concept of class is trivialized to the point where differences of parental attitude are conceived of as separate factors rather than as an integral part of the work and community situation of children.

There are, of course and always have been variations of ambitiousness and levels of aspirations at any given economic or income level. But it is essential to insist that the effect of class on educational experience is not to be thought of as one factor from which parental attitudes and motivations to succeed in education are independent. A theory which explains educational achievement as the outcome of a set of individual attributes has lost the meaning of those structural forces which we know as class. An adequate theory must also attend to those structural inequalities of resource allocation which are integral to a class society. Thus, any attempt to free education from its antecedents and consequences in the class system has to include structural forces as well as individual attributes.

Both within and outside the formal educational system, there are social forces which weigh systematically against working-class children in respect of those types of learning which make for educational success and subsequently for advantageous occupational placement. These include the quality of linguistic and other stimulation in family and neighbourhood, the expectations of teachers, the efficiency of co-operation between teachers and parents, and the occupational horizons which can be seen by children at different social vantage-points. Above all, it is a matter of resources. At every point, again both inside and outside the schools, working-class children have a great deal less spent on their opportunities for learning than have their more fortunate middle-class contemporaries.

The association of social class with educational achievement will not therefore be explained by a theory or eliminated by a policy which falls short of including changes in public support for learning in the family and the neighbourhood, the training of teachers, the production of relevant curricula, the fostering of parental participation, the raising of standards of housing and employment prospects and, above all, the allocation of educational resources.

The translation of such a theory into action would require political leadership with the will to go beyond the confines of traditional liberal assumptions. There are three persistent types of argument against the viability of egalitarian theory which deserve specific consideration. The first concerns the immutability of occupational hierarchy, postulating a *de facto* necessity for some jobs to be more distasteful, unrewarding, and injurious to health than others despite (and possibly because of) the technical advances on which Alfred Marshall pinned so much hope.

The global economy and strategies of competition designed by national governments to invest in the skills of the national workforce, are in effect, the globalizing of occupational hierarchy. Given that life-chances in wide measure are determined by the individual's occupation, a hierarchy of social advantage seems to be inescapable and equality as opposed to equality of opportunity therefore unobtainable. But even accepting this postulate, a more egalitarian society is not thereby rendered sociologically impossible. It is not difficult to imagine a wide range of counteracting social policies.

There are other such institutional reforms, both inside and outside education, which can be brought into play without making outrageous assumptions about 'human nature' or the price to be paid in terms of other widely held values in society. The development of the social wage into a citizen or participatory income, recognizing service to society other than by direct involvement in the labour market, is one such, and a radical step towards worldwide egalitarianism. Value choice is again the nub of the issue.

Hence, with a view to suggesting that equality and liberty need not conic immediately and directly into conflict when a more equal society is sought, we may refer to the set of ideas which are labelled recurrent, or life-long, education, and the views of the Swedish economist Gosta Rehn. The average full-time industrial worker spends something like 100,000 hours of his or her life at work. There is here, therefore, a large arena for the application of both egalitarian and libertarian ideas.

Responsible government on behalf of individual liberty has to go beyond the enforcement of contracts voluntarily entered and the natural tendencies of people to conspire against the rigours of the free market. Post-industrial society has to be committed to the efficient production of abundance, the maintenance of full employment, and the abolition of all unnecessary labour. On these assumptions it is possible to arrange deliberately for greater variation and diversity in the life-patterns of education, work, leisure, and retirement, in such a way as to transfer decision as far as possible from the bureaucracy to the individual. The underlying conception is of a modified social contract. The individual has a life-long bargain with society to work in exchange for material rewards and social security.

In such a society the individual, within a broad framework of agreed rules, would determine the phasing and placing of the exchange, week by week, year by year, and over the course of the individual's whole lifetime. The sharp divisions of the life-cycle and the established patterns of education, leisure, and work, bequeathed by the harsh necessities of preindustrial society and entrenched in the rigid formulae of statutory school-leaving ages, weekly hours, annual holidays, and compulsory retirement ages would go. Instead, there would be 'flexitime', study rights at personal discretion, vacation rights not tied to calendar years, sabbaticals, and temporary retirements not tied to old age.

In order to effect these new freedoms, which are in any case gradually and patchily appearing in the rich countries, it would be desirable, though not absolutely necessary, to systematize the present piecemeal arrangements for providing income to those who are not in paid employment because they are young and in school, or unemployed, or pregnant, or sick, or old and therefore retired. Collectively, it would require decisions on the generalized drawing rights to he allocated to each citizen. Obviously, there would have to be safeguards against improvidence and the absence of 'deferred gratification patterns'. But the general idea is one of institutional movement towards the reduction of bureaucracy and enlargement of personal choice. For example, there would be an age of compulsory schooling, but not as high as that currently set in the richer countries.

Then everyone would have a basic study credit, which could go to all age groups, not only to children and the unborn, to cover living and tuition costs for a given number of years. The individual could claim her educational rights according to her own career management, and would not be pressed to extend her childhood as she characteristically now is. People would thus be encouraged to have low-skill jobs in youth, and occupational status could become more a matter of age than class. And the right to further education could be transferred to leisure or to more affluent retirement if the individual so chose. The point here is that lifelong education may in principle serve to increase both equality and liberty. The possibility of bringing about greater equality between generations is obvious enough. The danger is, however, that it could so easily be trivialized into gestures towards a more generous provision of adult education classes, sabbaticals, day-release courses, and distance-learning programmes.

It would only be if lifelong education were taken seriously as a citizenship right, like social security or pensions, that the transformation of the established system in an egalitarian direction would be possible; and this would require ambitious institutional inventiveness, much more flexible relations between work and education, a move towards learning organizations, more optimistic definitions by teachers of educability and curriculum, a vast development of community schooling, and more bounteous educational budgets.

We have here a problem which is becoming central to educational policy and the correct forecasting of future demand for labour. The traditional theory was simple. Human wishes are limitless, therefore labour supply is essentially a matter of adjusting the flow of trained workers for the demands of an advancing industrial system. By and large, the twentieth century has seen more or less efficient adaptations along these lines.

Moreover, the idea of human investment has gained in popularity despite the concurrent rise in determination to reduce public spending. The other, more contentious theory is that technology is substituting for human labour in every field from manufacturing to surgery. The evidence according to R. Dore is that unemployment, especially among the unskilled or minimally educated, increases from slump to slump and never fully recovers in subsequent booms.

The second obstacle to be considered may be termed the Jencks pessimism. We are not here concerned with the relation of educational opportunity and educational attainment to social origin, which has always been close and continues to be so, but with the linkage of education to subsequent life-chances, and therefore the possibilities of' education as instrument for changing social distributions. This issue lies at the centre of the controversy which was so explosively refuelled by Christopher Jencks.

Jencks argues that the American occupational structure is open in the sense that a relatively loose relation between social origin and occupational destination is largely to be accounted for by factors which, as far as the individual is concerned, might be regarded as luck, even though some of them have a structural basis. Again it needs to be remembered that this argument is based on a study of male workers. Nevertheless, in his formulation, largely derived from the Blau and Duncan findings, Jencks writes:

> While occupational status is more closely related to educational attainment than to any other thing we could measure, there are still enormous status differences among people with the same amount of education. This remains true when we compare people who have not only the same amount of schooling, but the same family background and the same test scores. Anyone who thinks that a man's family background, test scores and educational credentials are the only things that determine the kind of work he can do in America is fooling himself. At most, these characteristics explain about half the variation in men's occupational statuses. This leaves at least half the variation to be explained by factors which have nothing to do with family background, test scores or educational attainment.

Jencks is concerned to stress a different set of causative factors: 'Much of the variation is probably due to chance (one steel worker gets laid off and takes a temporary job as a painter, while another keeps his job because his plant happens to be busier). Some is due to choice (a businessman decides to give up making underwear and become a clergyman).'

On income equality, Jencks adds: 'Income also depends on luck: chance acquaintances who steer you to one line of work rather than another, the range of jobs that happens to be available in a particular community when you are job-hunting, the amount of overtime work in your particular plant, whether bad weather destroys your strawberry crop... and a hundred other unpredictable accidents.' Jencks's argument was a response to the previously orthodox view that education reform was the best mechanism for breaking the inter-generational curse of poverty. In one sense, then, he produced an essay in the demolition of popular explanations of' economic inequality, given that we cannot blame economic inequality primarily on genetic differences in individual capacities for abstract reasoning:

> since there is nearly as much economic inequality among men with equal test scores as among men in general. We cannot blame economic equality primarily on the fact that parents pass along their disadvantages to their children, since there is nearly as much inequality among men whose parents have the same economic status as among men in general. We cannot blame economic inequality on differences between schools, since differences between schools seem to have very little effect on any measurable attribute on those who attend them.

Academic critics questioned Jencks's statistical analyses. No less an authority than James Coleman was not entirely satisfied with them. He criticizes Jencks essentially for failing to distinguish clearly between two meanings of inequality-inequality of opportunity and inequality of result. He argues, quite correctly, that Jencks's intention is to discuss inequality of result but that in fact he spends his time on inequality of opportunity.

What Jencks demonstrates, of course, is that equalizing opportunities through schooling will not change inequality of income between individuals. Schooling explains only about 12 per cent of the variance in income. Coleman complains that the explanation for the inequality of income accruing to jobs cannot explain the people who happen to occupy those jobs. The former problem is not directly tackled by Jencks. By demonstrating the absence of a relation between income distribution and distribution of schooling and family characteristics, on the one hand, however negatively, he points to the direct truth that the basic trouble with the poor is that they have no money.

But on the other hand, by the form of analysis adopted, the is left with a large unexplained variance in income which, in various formulations, he attributes to luck and a capriciously if not arbitrarily distributed competence. Then followed, however, a second analysis. The $400,000 (Jencks et al.'s estimate) spent on this new analysis purchased a restoration of the common picture of the universe we know and do not necessarily love. But sociologists will do well to resist this over-reaction, as they resisted when previously encouraged toward nihilistic despair about the possibility of educational paths to equality. The more sensible judgement is that the Jencks team is to be commended for taking criticisms of inequality seriously, for defining more rigorously the variables of family, personality, and schooling, for using these definitions in a Herculean effort of reanalysis, and for adding to the value of the answers by refining the questions. That way lies the progress in social science to which the profession aspires.

The restoration is, in any case, by no means complete. The old figure for the percentage of variance in occupational status explained by family background was 32; the new figure is 48. The old figure for schooling was 42 per cent; the new is 55 per cent. Combining the variables of family background, test scores, years of schooling, and personality traits, it now appears that the characteristics which people take into the market on first entry explain between 55 and 60 percent of variance in adult occupational status and between 33 and 41 per cent of variance in male annual earnings.

Thus the general thrust of the *Inequality* argument is not blocked by recalculation.

For example, whereas in inequality the expected difference between the occupationa. status of brothers was 82 per cent of the expected difference between pairs of unrelated men, the new percentage is 72. Clearly the revised figure does not afford dramatically enlarged scope to the social engineers. Yet readers are likely to notice a marked change in tone between the two publications. This is partly because *Who Gets Ahead*? has a lot less to say about public policy. More fundamentally, it is due to a shift in statistical presentation: the earlier book focused on within-group differences.

Inequality attacked the utopian hopes of the Great Society for widespread reform through educational engineering. The dramatic effect of that essay in demolition, however, rested largely on its demonstration of the limits of social action. People with similar family backgrounds, test scores, and schooling subsequently scattered themselves over the range of occupational statuses and incomes to about three-quarters the extent of the scatter of people in general.

In that sense, American society was an open lottery. But by the same token, the scope for social engineering on behalf of a principled allocation of life chances was woefully small. If schooling explained only 12 per cent of the variance in men's incomes, then complete equalization of schooling would at best reduce income inequality by only 12 per cent. The critics rightly complained that to assume it is possible to change the value of one variable without changing the totality of relations between variables in a system of plural causation is statistically convenient but sociologically invalid.

If America gave everyone the same schooling, it would, in the process, completely change the class structure, the labour market, and indeed its whole social self. In *Who Gets Ahead*? these objections are accepted. Moreover, Jencks et al. also accept criticism of the undue importance they previously attributed to luck, narrow their definition of the variables listed above, and discuss the implications for the labour market of a radically equalized distribution of human capital. Paradoxically, however, one of the features of social life in the 1990s is the increased sense (and reality) of economic insecurity experienced by all social groups.

Consequently, occupational biographies and careers may be increasingly determined by 'luck' in that corporate organizations are subject to restructuring, rationalization, down-sizing, re-engineering, takeovers, and so forth, irrespective of the individual's competence and commitment to his or her employer.

The third obstacle is the alleged structural feature on which Jensen, Hernstein, and Murray in America and Eysenck in Britain lay so much stress-the argument that differences in educational attainment are rooted in genetic differences between races and classes. A notorious formulation of this argument was published by Arthur Jensen in the *Harvard Educational Review* ('How Much can we Boost IQ and Scholastic Achievement?'), of which his Genetics and Education is an extended version and of which a popular version was published by Hans Eysenck under the title Race, Intelligence and Education.

Much of Jensen's extensive marshalling of the evidence is uncontroversial. Whether you take social classes or racial minority groups in America, there are incontrovertible differences in the average scores. On all this it may be said that the scientific mapping of measured performances is necessary to informed discussion; but the explanation for test differences, and even less the question of the relation between test scores and the distribution of whatever we might mean by intelligence remains. The distributions and correlations of test scores are not at issue. The importance of Jensen is that he advances a theory about causes together with advice about consequences. In both of these realms reasonable people can differ.

On the side of causes or explanations, the question he asks is whether the average difference between American blacks and American whites in IQ (a difference of ten to fifteen points) is either genetic, or a combination of genetic and environmental influences, or environmental. Eysenck polemically called the second type of theory hereditarian and the third type environmentalist, whereas obviously the first is hereditarian, the third environmentalist, and the second a combination of the two. Jensen is more careful acknowledging that one cannot formally generalize from within-group heritability to between-group heritability, but concludes that 'a largely genetic explanation of the evidence on racial and social group differences in educational performance is in a stronger position scientifically than those explanations which postulate the absence of any genetic differences in mental traits and ascribe all behavioural variation between groups to cultural differences, social discrimination, and inequalities of opportunity-a view that has long been orthodox in the social sciences and in education'.

Jensen thus places himself behind the second type of explanation, excluding the purely hereditarian view and regarding the purely environmentalist theory as dubious almost to the point of impossibility. Our view of the evidence is that the purely environmentalist theory is much less implausible. For one thing, we take seriously the calculations of heritability produced by Christopher Jencks in his Inequality. Curiously enough, Jensen ignores Jencks's calculations, which yield much lower estimates than his own of the variance in IQ attributable to genetic factors. Still more important is the issue of consequences, for these take us from science to politics. Jensen is last, if not first, an American individualist, and he pleads for diversity of opportunity and treatment in a way which reflects his appreciation, perhaps over-appreciation, of the huge variability in genetic make-up which is such an important fact about the human species. No reasonable person could quarrel with that as such.

But, like Eysenck, Jensen has the blinkers of a psychologist and vastly overestimates the importance of IQ He half-recognizes this when he notices that IQ differences are relevant to differences in levels of performance in traditional school structures. But he assumes, along with many of his environmentalist opponents, that IQ is overwhelmingly important in determining the placing of individuals in the economy. In respect of income distribution in America this is certainly not the case. In addition to Jencks's evidence, Bowles and Gintis have shown that IQ is of negligible importance by comparison with socioeconomic background and years of schooling in determining economic success as measured by a combination of occupational status and income. But if the Bowles-Gintis argument is taken seriously, the Jensen wrangle becomes largely irrelevant to the underlying questions of political and economic justice for American blacks and the American working class.

In this sense, the Jensenist controversy is but a storm in the academic teacup. However, the hereditarian controversy was fanned into fierce flame again in 1994 by Richard J. Herrnstein and Charles Murray in their *The Bell Curve: Intelligence and Class*

Structure in American Life. It is a cunning book. Apparently even-handed and reasonable, it is in fact an explosive intervention from the political right. With respect to the genetics and environment debate no new data are produced, and European contributions e.g. from Bernstein, Bourdieu, or Boudon are ignored. Class is not defined, and the international studies of class mobility are not mentioned.

Instead we are presented with a theory of class polarization which argues that the educational selectivity of the system works steadily along lines of IQ segregation to produce a 'cognitive élite' and an unqualified underclass. American blacks are doomed to belong to this underclass because they score a clear standard deviation below whites in IQ tests, and the hereditary component of capacity to show intelligence iii tests is, according to Herrnstein and Murray, 60 per cent. A critical review of their book edited by Steven Fraser, The Bell Curve Wars, goes a long way towards neutralizing Hernstein and Murray's polemic. Indeed, Stephen Jay Gould had already anticipated the main argument in his *Mismeasurement* of Man. He deals with the 'four shaky premises' of the Bell Curve authors-that Intelligence is: firstly, a single number; secondly, capable of ranking people in linear order; thirdly, genetically based; and fourthly, effectively immutable.

Students of the sociology of education, perhaps especially Americans whose culture specifically enjoins the pursuit of equality, must absorb the evidence on genetic and environmental interactions in education and society. The idea of a new political arithmetic as a form of 'social accountability' is in our view a powerful one. When we think about all the claims to empirical 'truth' made by politicians and journalists over the last two decades, the need for independent research which subjects such assertions to account is crucial to the future of democracy. Political arithmetic has also represented an important 'methodology' for studying the nature of society and social institutions.

This methodology can be traced back to Booth and the Webbs, if not to William Petty in the seventeenth century. In more recent times it has been used in many studies of social policy and social stratification, including that conducted by David Glass in the 1950s and by Halsey *et al.* in the 1970s in order to survey the relationship between family, class, and education in postwar Britain. In their introduction to political arithmetic, Halsey *et al.* note that early proponents were:

> concerned to describe accurately and in detail the social conditions of their society, particularly of the more disadvantaged sections, but their interest in these matters was never a disinterested academic one. Description of social conditions was a preliminary to political reform. They exposed the inequalities of society in order to change them. The tradition thus has a double intent- on the one hand it engages in the primary sociological task of describing and documenting the state of society'; on the other hand it addresses itself to central social and political issues. It has never, therefore, been a 'value free' academic discipline, if such were in any event possible. Instead, it has been an attempt to marry a value-laden choice of issues with objective methods of data collection.

At a time of increasing social inequalities and injustice, when the 'self-regulating' market threatens to undermine the foundations of social solidarity; when the advances of postwar welfare reforms have been reversed; and when the dominant ideology of meritocracy in liberal democratic societies has been seriously weakened at the same time that right wing politicians proclaim the 'classless society', a new political arithmetic must be asserted as a vital tool of democracy as well as of sociology. For this to happen, citizens must first have,access to collective self-knowledge independent of government'. Second, there needs to be a sufficient number of trained and motivated researchers to take up the challenge of 'mapping' the changing contours, contradictions, and complexities of advanced post-industrial societies. On both counts there are considerable grounds for concern. It is also clear that the widening inequalities in some of the advanced economies has been mirrored by a drift into post-modernism with its rejection of everything political arithmetic stands for.

By rejecting quantitative methods, post-modernist researchers such as Lather turn their back on the vital task of holding the state to account for its policies. The currency of official justification is statistics, and there needs to be some critical check on the figures used to support policy initiatives and their outcomes. The social context and understanding of research methodology in which we now work is quite different to that in which political arithmetic was initially developed; but the aim of a form of social accountability remains crucial. The work of post-modernists contains important insights into the self-reflexive nature of individuals which corresponds to the wider changes in society referred to by Beck and Giddens as reflexive modernization.

Social reflexivity is both condition and outcome of a post-traditional society. Decisions have to be taken on the basis of a more or less continuous reflection on the condition's of one's action. 'Reflexivity' here refers to the use of information about the conditions of activity as a means of regularly reordering and redefining what that activity is. It concerns a universe of action where social observers are themselves socially observed and it is today truly global in scope. A new political arithmetic would acknowledge the insights relating to these wider changes but deny that they entailed the eschewal of quantitative methods. Quantitative methods are not logically linked to empiricist methodology with its functionalist assumptions about the theory free nature of observation. There is a distinction to be made between methods such as those used by quantitative researchers and the methodological assumptions in which they are embedded. Proponents of the new political arithmetic would not only take on the role of social accountant, but may view it as part of a committed policy scholarship, and would certainly seek to be aware of the presuppositions that inform their research. In addition, a new political arithmetic would not only involve counting inputs and outputs, but is also dedicated to an analysis of 'what counts' and why.

This is necessary in order to avoid the problem of the 'black box' which was a common criticism of political arithmetic in the 1970s. Studying what counts involves studying 'process' as well as outcomes. In a context of rapid social, economic, and institutional change it has become more important to find ways of linking quantitative and qualitative methods of social research. Actors must be recognized as knowledgeable. Their ideas clearly count in shaping outcomes. Hence, social and educational researchers need to use the knowledge they generate to engage in a dialogue with people about post-industrial possibilities in relation to the society they live in; and a new political arithmetic must be involved in a process of theory-building as part of a political project dedicated to 'institution building'. In this sense, it offers the prospect of addressing enduring questions of political economy as defined above, in a context of changing educational, social, economic, and political conditions at the end of the twentieth century.

6

Reformation of Teaching Technologies

Within the context of the effective integration of technology into the teaching and learning process, we have found that these three keys are fairly simple, but are often overlooked by an institution of higher education. The first key is to actively encourage and train faculty in the use of educational technology in teaching and learning. The second key is to use technology to assist overall student productivity, and in particular, to help support a student's own individual learning activities. Finally, the third and perhaps most important key is to specifically plan curriculum activities to accomplish with the technology.

We have found that each of these three 'keys' can be essential to unlocking the potential of technology in the teaching and learning process at an institution. To help faculty embrace technology and recognize its importance in teaching and learning, we have found that several elements need to be present at an institution. First, at least some equipment must be available for both faculty and student use. A computer on each faculty member's desk is a useful first step in encouraging faculty use of the computer in teaching. In addition, providing appropriate software, an adequate network, and a good connection to the Internet are effective follow-up steps. When the computer becomes a necessary tool for the professor, then use in the classroom is often the next logical step. However, much more than just access is needed to empower faculty, and encourage their use of technology. Another element that needs to be present is an ongoing faculty training and coaching process.

Usually, faculty training is most successful if it also includes efforts to build a general awareness of the practical uses of technology, followed by hands-on sessions, where faculty members can actually develop personal applications of the technology. Such faculty support is similar to the coaching and mentoring techniques that have been used successfully in precollege secondary schools, where teachers also specialize by discipline, but often overlooked at the university level. While many higher education institutions hire outside consultants to train their faculty members, some colleges and universities encourage their own staff and faculty members to facilitate the training and coaching process. The advantages of in-house training are many, including an important comfort level in knowing that the 'expert' is always available if a problem or question arises later, as well as a more personalized understanding of the teaching responsibilities of individual faculty members. Training topics should be wide in variety, and include such high interest topics as office packages, multimedia and use of the Internet.

The institutional expectation that all faculty will actively include technology in academic activities is also a critical element for encouraging faculty to use and become empowered with technology. Faculty members need to feel that effective use of technology is expected for all appropriate courses and situations. They need to feel they are being supported by the institution, as well as encouraged to use and model teaching techniques that take advantage of technology. Faculty members must also believe that their institutional environment is supportive of the 'risk taking' necessary for trying such new teaching/ learning techniques. In order for technology to be integrated effectively into the teaching and learning process at an institution, it takes more than faculty empowerment. The individual student, and their ongoing needs within the learning process, must also be carefully considered. Kearsley et al., researchers in the midst of implementing technology integration in classrooms, see the facilitation of 'student productivity' as the major goal in this area.

In reality, most institutions have not yet implemented technology so as to maximize student productivity. Many faculty may not have enough knowledge about the new technologies to realize the distinctions between productive and meaningless computer activities. When appropriately used with students, technology can provide a variety of ways to help students be more productive, become more engaged in the instructional activities, and learn more efficiently. Effective student projects often include connections to the real world which can be facilitated by technology. For example, a student can often be less than motivated to pursue learning unless he or she has a clear mental picture of how the skill or topic to be learned will be useful. Using multimedia technology, or such information related tools as the World Wide Web, students can be provided with very current examples of how a particular instructional activity relates to business, or other contexts.

Uses of technology to facilitate research within a student project, such as having a student develop a hypermedia program to teach a particular topic, can also help make the maximum use of student instructional time. Such a blend of student research and technology can enable students to work on self-paced and meaningful projects while avoiding the typically unproductive time of waiting for help or waiting to be told what to do next. The Internet is a wonderful research tool within the context of such student projects, and can greatly help students practise making sense of information. Perhaps the most important key to the successful integration of technology into the teaching and learning process, and essential for supporting both faculty and student use, is to carefully modify the curriculum to include specific technology appropriate activities. In particular, such new tasks must target core components of the curriculum, rather than represent superficial add-on tasks.

The incorporation of specific tasks within the core curriculum has been shown to be a critical link to whether an institution will successfully use technology. At some institutions, it works well to have a standing committee, representative of the faculty, to help plan for such ongoing integration. But how is a curriculum targeted for modification? One of the most effective ways of examining the curriculum related to technology is first to consider the potential roles of technology in the teaching an learning process. An excellent and well establish model is that developed by Taylor which suggests three distinct categories for the use computer based technologies in the teaching and learning process. These categories consist of the use of computer technology in three ways, as a tutor, to and tutee. Within the tutor role, the computer-based technology is used to present material and content to the student much as a traditional teacher would do.

Commercial packages can be purchased for teaching particular topics, and can the be used as either a classroom demonstration, or within the context of an individualized student learning activity. When the technology is used as a 'tutor' this way, it is being used to directly teach the concept or topic. In contrast to the tutor role, the use of technology a 'tool' provides more of a general partnership between human and machine. In the tool category many of the more traditional tool applications a recognized by both faculty and students, such word-processing, spreadsheets and databases. However, many newer tool applications also exist, such as computer-assisted presentation packages, and can represent powerful and motivating aids to the teaching and learning process.

Often, planning for each institutional course to take advantage is a use beginning for integrating such tool applications in the curriculum. In contrast to both the 'tutor' and 'tool' roles, the use of technology within a 'tutee' role involves the student in much more direct control of the computer. The human student learns by 'teaching' the computer a particular concept or task, or guiding the comput in the creation of a some instructional product. In the approach, the human student is much like a professional curriculum developer, who targets important components of the topic, and then builds instruction to teach the material. An example of this process might be when a student uses a hypermedia package to develop an instructional overview of lunar eclipses. The student learns a great deal about lunar eclipses while in the process of developing such an instructional lesson and retrieving relevant information. In essence, the human student is 'teaching' the computer, which is acting like a patient 'tutee'. Such a constructivist approach to the use of technology for building student understanding has long been identified as a very powerful application of technology within the teaching and learning process.

Each of the three categories of curricular application, tutor, tool and tutee, offers potential advantages to a faculty for refining a curriculum to take full advantage of technology in the teaching and learning process. In basic terms, one might view the three roles of tutor, tool and tutee, as simply different levels of student control for technology related tasks, where some tasks require little student control (tutor), some require more of an equal partnership (tool), and some require considerable student control (tutee). We have found that this three category model is a very useful and simple one for faculty to consider when developing instructional activities that support a comprehensive integration of technology. When students and faculty work together effectively on technology-based tasks that are integral to the instructional plan at an institution, effective technology use can indeed be a powerful catalyst to improved teaching and learning. However, such institutional efforts do not happen easily, or without careful planning.

We have found that such efforts require substantial and formalized commitment by all involved, especially the institution. Technology planning must become an integral part of the institutional culture, rather than just a periodic interest at available budget opportunities. We believe that truly to become a part of the institutional culture, the three keys discussed within this article provide a useful model for the successful this integration of technology into the teaching and learning process. Thus, an ongoing faculty training and support process must be initiated, student productivity must be ensured, and most importantly, the curriculum must be adjusted to include technology appropriate tasks.

When all three keys are present, and carefully considered within the technology planning process, we believe that an institution is on the right track for effectively integrating technology into the teaching and learning process. Obviously, the institutional process represented by such technology planning is never fully completed, and must continue from year to year, but it is a process with considerable potential impact for the institution. Although technology integration can indeed seem like the 'immovable object' of higher education, once rolling, the momentum of technology integration can indeed be a satisfying one, especially when everyone is helping push on the stone context. A third form of communication ability is the visual. Collaboration and teamwork are characteristics of the modem work environment. Written, oral and presentation skills all contribute to the functioning of a team as well as to interaction at a social level. Despite the increase in telecommunication capabilities, people still travel to a work-place to interact in person with other people.

Students should have the opportunity to practise collaboration and teamwork within a learning environment and thus develop and refine their communication skills. An ability to think critically should be an essential outcome of effective learning. Critical thinking includes: identifying and challenging assumptions; challenging the importance of context; imagining and exploring alternatives and having reflective scepticism, Norris and Ennis identified four elements of critical thinking: reasonble thinking that is based on sound evidence; reflective thinking that examines the worth of one's own and others' thoughts; focused thinking that is purposeful and deliberate; and thinking that leads to decision or judgement.

Critical thinking is an essential component of active knowledge, for knowing quires an appreciation of how something is known d what it is worth. The ability to deal with real-life problems is a;desirable quality of graduates particularly those in professional fields. A test of whether knowledge is active or is merely surface-learned information is if an be applied effectively to problem situations. It be argued that practice and exercise in problem-solving is necessary to develop active knowledge. Problem-based courses promote the acquisition of knowledge in ways that the potential to improve problem-solving skills in general. Real-life problems are often considered to be illstructured and to lack the information necessary for a solution. In this case, action to solve the problem must be based on the conviction that progress is possible even if the direction is not immediately apparent. In these situations, heuristic procedures may increase the chances of finding a solution.

Heuristic activities require feedback in a reasonably short time-frame to be an effective way of learning; conventional learning environments may not be responsive enough for this. Lifelong learning attitudes are necessary for today's graduates in a world where employment is increasingly of a short-term nature and changeable. Conventional teacher/student relationships tend to place the student in a dependent position and to leave them ill-equipped for the real world. A personal sense of being in control of one's own learning is at the heart of lifelong learning attitudes. That control can be assigned from the outset of a course of study through a learning contract between student and teacher where the student assumes responsibility for their own learning. Approaches to the encouragement of lifelong learning include: self-directed and peer-assisted learning; experiential and real-world learning; problem-based learning; reflective practice and critical self-awareness. The range of technology used in a classroom may extend from the overhead projector which is cheap, easy to use and accessible to all to an exclusive fully immersive virtual reality where students interact with each other and objects in cyberspace.

Virtual reality may be considered irrelevant to today's common teaching practices although this may change in the future. For the purposes of this discussion, technology is defined as the use of computer software and telecommunications. In a high-tech classroom, a teacher may continue to provide a constant supply of information, in various media, to an essentially passive audience in the belief that variety will provide stimulation, interest and learning. But more than a didactic form of information delivery is required to promote effective learning. Whatever the range of software media utilized in the classroom, its purpose should be to promote active knowledge acquisition through communication, the consideration of different viewpoints and reflection.

We now examine how the use of technology can contribute to the learning outcomes identified above and how it can, therefore, contribute to effective teaching and learning. In incorporating technology into the teaching and learning process, perhaps just because it is available, we must have justifiable confidence that the new learning environments will have outcomes at least comparable to proven effective practices. It is difficult to conceive of a stand-alone computer program that could give a student a holistic appreciation of any particular subject or discipline and see the relationships with other disciplines. It is also difficult to conceive of anything more holistic than the Internet. The content of the Internet is continually growing as are the links between related topics. The Internet may be considered an effective learning tool because of the diversity of information related by hyperlinks that the student is free to follow. However, in following those links, students are doing just that - following, and not necessarily making the connections for themselves.

Nevertheless, the sheer multiplicity of links may in itself be educational and achieve some degree of holistic appreciation in students. Knowledge that the learner has personally constructed and compared to that of others is active in the sense that this knowledge is based in the learner's personal experience of the real world. In the real world, that process of comparison and construction may take considerable time. Technology can be used to construct simulations of the real world environment wherein the user can interact with the environment. Simulations can provide a realistic context for exploration and heuristic activities which enable the learner to construct mental models apposite to the environment and past experience. The interactivity provided in a simulated environment can enable learners to see the results of experimentation, and thereby gain experience, in relatively short time periods.

Koppi and Chaloupka have developed a first-person, interactive realistic simulation of soil analysis in the field and laboratory that permits exploration and heuristic experimentation in a few hours that would take many weeks to complete in the real world. Programs like this enable the components of Kolb's experiential learning model to be enacted in the classroom. For simulated environments to be effective for learning, they must be credible and permit sustained engagement of the imagination as well as giving the learner control which is a key factor in sustaining student stimulation and motivation. The challenge in developing this type of learning environment is to facilitate imaginative immersion that enables experiences, learner control and reflective reasoning. Since communication and dialogue are at the heart of teaching and learning, technologies that facilitate the process over a network, particularly for learners distant from each other and the teacher, are probably the most important. O'Malley has given an outline of computer-supported collaborative learning (CSCL) technologies of which there are several types. The essential functions of CSCL for teaching and learning include one-to-one and one-to-many communication and the ability to work collaboratively in groups. Another facet of this mode of communication is that it may be synchronous or asynchronous.

Teaching and learning over a network (on-line) has resulted in changes in the roles and behaviour of teacher and student. It seems that students may become more involved in the learning process and that the authority of the teacher can be lessened. Reasons given for this include greater freedom for the student to explore the hypertext links in web documents, thereby following their own learning pathways, and the possibility for individual teacher contact that may be missing from the conventional setting. In studies of computer-supported collaborative learning programmes, students gained worthwhile skills and quality learning. Important aspects of collaborative learning are the contributions of individuals to the group and the opportunities for dialogue between students and their teachers, and for discussion among peers.

An advantage of asynchronous communication between peers is that students who are left out of synchronous or live discussion because they are busy developing mental arguments while the topic moves in, have the opportunity to contribute by using the extra reflection time afforded by e-mail. Also, with asynchronous communication the argument is not lost and can be revisited whenever appropriate. Perhaps the most useful function of the Web from an educational view is that it can be used effectively as communication medium for student collaboration, an information resource, a search tool and as a medium for publication. At present the Web is mostly used for static presentations and the delivery of information. Problem-based learning can take place without using technology but, in the classroom setting, the opportunity for experiential activities may be lacking, eg in the training of aircraft pilots.

Problem-solving is -encouraged by programs that allow discovery learning response to problem situations that mimic real life, *Investigating Lake Illuka*. Given that real life problems are often illstructured and lacking the information for a solution, mimetic programmes like these probably best used as part of the problem-solving activities in which students can collaborate on the investigative strategies interpretation of results. The interpretation of results from heuristic activities.the prediction of consequences is probably and the scope of computer-based learning, at least until artificial intelligence becomes more sophisticated. The more that programmes allow students the freedom to construct personal knowledge, the more it becomes necessary to compare that knowledge with the experience of others. It is common for programmes to include expert 'answers' for students to use as a comparison. There are limits to the usefulness of this approach because it may not be clear to the learner whether their answer is right or wrong if it differs from that of an expert.

With the cooperation of the teacher, technology can provide learner control in several essential ways:

study or reference materials can be conveniently accessed on the Internet; the process of knowledge acquisition can be given over to the student; and communication can be direct with the teacher and peers. One way of allowing students to choose their own manner of investigation is to provide documents with hyperlinks to other information perceived as relevant by the teacher. However, despite the apparent freedom offered to the learner by hypertext and hypermedia, the student is only free to follow predefined paths. Laurillard notes that 'Hypertext, accessing a text database, is not interactive, because there is no intrinsic feedback on the user's actions: the information in the system does not change as a consequence of the user's actions on it: it only changes if they change the system itself, by changing the information of the links directly.

So it is no more interactive than writing in the margins of a book, or editing the book yourself, or annotating it with your own references to another point in the book... as an educational medium, enabling students to develop their academic understanding, it has little to offer'. In hypertext/hypermedia, navigation is an explicit action of the interface, ie pressing the forward button delivers another page of information thus leaving the student to do whatever a person does with the information. Therefore hypertext/hypermedia as a primary learning tool shows that limited thought has been given to the cognitive aspects of interactive, leaving the student to become passive agent to a narrative. The internet and the facilities of World Wide Web offer unique opportunity of near instant communication. One can access the information and individual throughout the world. This communication network has created a 'cyberspace', where one is free from the boundaries created on the basis of geography, language, religion or culture.

Microteaching

In any highly skilled profession, whether it is law, medicine or teaching, training for the persons involved is most essential. One of the factors that contributes to the quality of education is the competence of the teachers to teach. Since Independence, one of the sectors in education that has not received adequate attention is that of teacher education. In spite of sporadic efforts to enhance the competence of student teachers through innovation like interaction analysis, sensitivity training, team teaching microteaching, the standard of teacher education still remains uncertain, if not low.

The Education Commission observed, "Methods of teaching and evaluation in training institutions are extremely important and the attitude of the student teachers will be influenced more by the methods used with them than by what they are formally taught about the methods they should use in schools. Unfortunately, there is little realisation of this and the methods of teaching and evaluation used in the training institutions continue to be largely traditional". The advanced countries have revolutionised their teacher education programmes in the light of new technologies and contemporary requirements. However, in India training schools and colleges still follow the beaten track of traditional strategies.

The teacher training programmes should be planned and organised to develop the 'spirit of enquiry, initiative, scientific temper, manual dexterity, conceptual clarity and linguistic skills' of the trainees. So there is an urgent need for change in the curriculum and methodology in the teachers' training institutions. The curriculum should correspond to the present state of knowledge and communication techniques in each discipline.

Teaching is becoming the last choice in the job market and as a result, persons with questionable calibre and motivation enter the profession. So teacher training programmes are to be rigorously designed to update these new entrants by imparting them attitudes, skills and proficiencies essential for the profession. The workshop on teacher education by the UGC in 1976 and the National Conference on Teacher Education sponsored by the UGC and the National Council of Teacher Education in 1977 emphasised the need to separate teacher training programmes form the teacher education programmes and courses. This could be done by organising preservice and inservice training programmes and devising more effective methods to inculcate teaching skills and behaviors in teacher trainees.

The National Policy on Education promises that the methods of recruitment of teachers will be reorganised to ensure objectivity, merit and functional competence. It envisages the establishment of State level agencies to sponsor, plan and evaluate the inservice programmes for teachers and instructors at all levels. At present there are about 1200 institutions for training elementary school teachers and 360 colleges for training secondary school teachers.

The curricula, training practices and orientation of these teacher education institutions are to be overhauled in tune with the changing educational and national goals. The purpose of any teacher training programmes is to mould and sustain a good teacher capable of dealing with any teaching-learning situation. A good teacher is at first a good individual, but he is also a learned and trained individual. The main characteristic of a teacher as a professional is that he uses knowledge to organise and assist certain approved kinds of learning through a system of formal education, namely, schools, colleges or universities.

Today this role is extended to forms of informal education like extramural, correspondence and open university education also. Teaching is an activity aimed at the effective transmission of knowledge and skills to the pupils with a view to making them capable of proceeding further without external assistance. This demands that the teacher should be adequately trained in various teaching skills, disciplined in his learning and behavior and initiated into the several facets of pupil personality. Traditional teacher training programmes have been based on four fundamental concepts, namely, curriculum content, professional knowledge, educational theory and class room practice of skills.

Though all the components are important, recent studies in advanced countries tend to place a greater emphasis on training to acquire class room skills and behavior than on the other three. This stress on teacher activity inside the class room rather than on teacher learning proceeding it has revolutionised teacher training programmes in the West. As a result several innovations have taken place and have slowly spread to less advanced countries. One such innovation which has a universal application is microteaching. The first microteaching programme began in 1963 at Standford University, USA as a new technique for teacher training. Since then it has spread to several other countries and today this technique is being practised in teacher training at a few places in India also. A hypothesis central to microteaching is that teaching can be described in terms of component skills.

Microteaching is programmed teaching. Four essential features of mircoteaching are small unit classes, concentration on one teaching skill at a time, effective feedback through analysis and critique, and reteaching. Under this system the student teacher teaches for about five or ten minutes a group of five or ten pupils. During the microteaching session the emphasis would be on any particular skill. For instance, the student teacher may devote a particular microclass or a series of them to exercise and master the skills of evoking pupil response to questions or for judging degrees of correctness in pupils' answers.

While the microclass is in progress it is being observed critically by the supervisor and a small group of other student teachers whole would make a record of their observations relating to the particular skill in practice. After the microclass, the student teacher, the supervisor and the peers sit together and make a critique of the performance. This feedback process enables the student teacher to spot out his deficiencies and to improve upon his performance during the reteaching of the same microlesson with another group of pupils. The cycle of teaching, feedback and reteaching may go on until the student teacher attains perfect mastery over a particular skills or groups of skills.

The role of the supervisor is to help the trainee transfer the skills acquired in microteaching to the actual class room. Microteaching is skill-oriented rather than content-oriented. So each course is comprised of various microcourses based on various teaching skills. For instance, a course in 'effective questioning and eliciting responses' may comprise of skills like prompting, judging individual responses, encouraging pupil participation, praising pupil achievement and so son. Thus the introduction of microteaching should be proceed by the formulation of a set of microcourses in each branch or discipline.

These course packages may be subjected to experimental field test by supervisors prior to their actual introduction as components of the training programme. Simultaneously with the preparation of the microcourses, model microclass lessons based on particular skills may be got ready in the form of films, tapes and slides to be used as an introduction to the new student teachers. Two aspects of the microteaching process deserve special mention—modelling and feedback. Modelling is the mode of introducing a skill to the student teacher. This can be done either by showing a videotape or film to the trainees to initiate learning by imitation or through verbal/written instructions.

Modelling procedures should be supported by the supervisor's assistance in locating the essential skills. Feedback is the process by which the student teacher is enabled to assess the effectiveness of his own performance at microteaching sessions. This includes the skills acquisition of the student teacher and the effect of the supervisor on his performance. The most effective method of providing feedback is to use a closed circuit television equipment or video-recording. But in all developing countries this facility may to be freely available at present. In such a situation, video-recording may be replaced by audio-recording and the feedback analysis and critique may be done accordingly.

However, the real excellence of video-recording is that a series of such recordings may be sent to a supervisor and got back with his comments recorded on the second sound track. The complaint that the presence of the television camera inhibits the student teacher and the pupils is trivial because familiarisation takes place in due course. In microteaching there is instant feedback possibility through discussion, analysis, critique and reteaching. Feedback results are put into the reteaching lesson and the performance of the student teacher is improved through each lesson as every reteaching lesson is a step forward in eliminating the various drawbacks and blemishes.

The combined effect of the use of video-recording, models and microcourses, the instant feedback performance, analysis together the teaching behavior of the student teacher. Thus teaching becomes 'a complete information process activity, perhaps better described as an orchestration of skills'. A workable, rational and flexible evaluation scale will have to be devised before the introduction of microteaching practice. The scale of evaluation should help judge student teacher performance with respect to each constituent skills. A series of such evaluations would result in a 'microprofile' of the student teacher. This profile would be more reliable than the traditional assessment because each profile focuses on short teaching sessions with pupils and is related to each constituent skill.

The microteaching technique has certain clear advantage over the traditional class room teaching practice. It deals with real teaching situations and introduces tighter control over teaching practice and teacher behavior. It reduces the complexities of normal class room reaching because class size, scope of content and teaching time are reduced. A high degree of control is inbuilt in the system and a phased accomplishment of each skills is possible because the practice is concentrated into a small span of time.

Instant feedback helps knowing the results and facilities possibility of improvement. The student teacher is relived of his initial fear as he is phased into real teaching instead of being dropped into it all a sudden as in the traditional class room method. Above all, pupil participation and response is maximum in a microteaching class because the intense teaching activity in a microclass draws the pupils into its stream automatically. Researches have shown that microteaching-based training programmes help increase the competence of the teachers to integrate various teaching skills effectively.

Microteaching experience persists in the overall teacher behavior modifying and disciplining the teacher habits and teaching devices even after the termination of microteaching-based training. Microteaching is still in an experimental stage in most developing countries. The basic philosophy and method of microteaching are unexceptionable. The highly industrialised and technological nations could gear their resources towards experimentation in the field of education. However, in a developing country where resource mobilisation falls short of developmental needs, costly experimentation in education will have to be undertaken after sufficient introspection. Successful practice of microteaching technique largely depends on a sensitive academic milieu, availability of trained personnel, the demand for teachers trained in diversified skills and the identification of the skills themselves.

Teamteaching

All teaching aims at producing learning in pupils. Teaching as a function involves several activities. But all of them are not its essential elements. The pure activity of teaching is the part of the process that directly contributes to the acquirement of learning by the pupils. Though pupils may learn many things even without the assistance of teachers, the quantum of learning may be enhanced and disciplined if the teachers creatively assist.

Skinner is of the opinion that it is possible to teach almost anything to anybody in a worthwhile form provided we evolve the appropriate structuring and presentation of the learning materials. The purpose of all learning is to produce a relatively permanent effect on man's activities after the period of learning. The aim of teaching is to bring about learning and the aim of learning is the achievement of an 'end state'. The 'end state' may be a belief, a value, a skill, an attitude or any other complex achievement which may not be evaluated in tangible terms. Thus it is clear that teaching is related to the end achievement through various stages.

These various stages correspond to the systematic development of the mental and emotional faculties of the pupil through a long period of exposure to teaching. One of the factors that militates against the development of the pupil's faculties is the lack of flexibility in the institutional and structural patterns of the school. A teacher has to teach, has to stimulate the pupils' enthusiasm and to show them how from specific relations and instances, they must generalise into a precise code of values and behavior useful to them in later life.

Today there is an increasing recognition of the view that the purpose of education is to guide the pupils to the several sources of knowledge and to enable them to possess self-generating knowledge rather than simply to pick up scraps of information from books and teachers. To realise this purpose, several innovations have been introduced in the technique of teaching in recent times and experiments in the methodology and content of teaching have been carried out at different levels. The style of teaching has changed from oracular methods like lectures and dictation to participatory methods like tutorials, seminars, group work and so on.

One such method aimed at maximising the teaching impact on pupils is team teaching. It combines the graces of traditional teaching and unconventional teaching strategies. It is one of the most widely spread developments in teacher cooperation to attain definite goals of learning achievement and has been successfully practised in the West since 1957 when at Lexington, Massachusetts, the technique was first introduced. In its simplest sense, team teaching is the form of instruction in which several teachers competent in the same subject work together in planning and presenting the lessons to groups of students and evaluating their learning experience and achievement.

It is one of the most effective ways of managing and controlling the teaching environment so as to derive the maximum learning benefit with the lest dissipation of human and material resources. It facilitates a more intimate and wider area of contact between the pupils and the teachers and creates situations conducive to the absorption of self-generating knowledge without being acutely conscious of the drudgery involved in the conventional process of learning. The first task in the administration of team teaching is the formation of teams of teachers in each discipline or subject. The teachers working together in a team have to assume joint responsibility for all or a substantial part of the instruction of a group of students in any particular subject or topic.

Teams may be formed with two or more teachers. It can be hierarchical or otherwise with a leader who has greater experience in teaching or better ability to organise and supervise the work. The number of members of the team depends on the level at which the subject is taught, the expected depth of handling the subject, the number of students in each group and the extent of availability of teaching aids and assistants.

However, it is desirable to have three or four members in a team, each a specialist in one or the other aspect of the subject to be taught. For instance, there may be a teacher good in presenting the theoretical part of the subject in an interesting manner, another good in the use of technological teaching aids, another good in drawing diagrams and charts and yet another good in evaluating the impact of teaching through suitable testing. A combination of these teachers in a spirit of challenging cooperating would result in effective handling of the subject, more effective than what a single teacher can do, however talented he is. The team may also borrow the assistance from other teachers from the same department or sister departments who can supervise class room arrangements or operation of video tapes and projectors or display of maps and charts. Planning for team teaching consists of deciding and selecting what part of the syllabus/subject each teacher would handle.

Planning the lessons provides maximum utilisation of the special talents, skills and training each teacher possesses by pooling them together in an effort to achieve the most effective coverage of the teaching assignments. In planning the lessons and determining the role each teacher has to play in the implementation of the programme, the participating teacher have to show great flexibility and sense of adjustment. They should be accommodatitve enough to concede a point to their colleagues and avoid indiscretions like undermining the others' role or overlapping in the actual teaching process.

In team teaching a three-fold instructional method may be adopted. Firstly, large group instruction may be organised by combining several classes of the same level in a large room or theatre for presenting the general outline of the subject. The teacher specially talented in that subject element may present the lesson and the other team members may participate in promoting the understanding of the pupils and themselves assimilating the team experience. Secondly, small discussion groups are formed and teachers discuss the points which have been mentioned in the large group instruction classes. Here each teacher in the team gets an insight into each student's abilities and weaknesses. Thirdly, teacher-directed independent study groups are formed. There are directed towards creative and productive thinking.

Team teaching takes into account all the three phases of the teaching activity—the diagnostic, the perspective and the evaluative. In the first phase the team takes decision about the skills and knowledges the students need and analyses the topic in terms of concept formation, learning response and motivation. In the second phase the team plans the most economical and effective ways and strategies to impart the skill and knowledges it has decided upon. In the third phase the team tests the attainment of the students and its own teaching effectiveness. Suitable tests from time to time may be devised to evaluate the correlation between team teaching efforts and student achievement in terms of learning. Team teaching is still in its innovative and experimental stage in most developing countries. However, the advantages of a well-evolved system of team teaching are obvious.

Team teaching, for the first time, throws off the mantle of privacy and secrecy from the work of teachers. Each teacher is exposed to the members of his team even while engaged in actual teaching and is subject to the evaluation by them. Team teaching, thus, helps to bream down professional barriers and the sense of exclusiveness that inhibits all traditional class room teaching. Teachers are encouraged to be alert about their performance and the presence of other equally well-informed adults listening, observing and evaluating has a salary effect on the teachers' motivation to improve and excel. Team teaching is the most effective way of handling interdisciplinary subjects or topics.

Certain aspects of history, geography, economics and biology can be more effectively taught by enlisting the assistance of teachers belonging to these several departments into a teaching team. Students come to think of teaching-learning as a group activity and not as a quirk of individual teachers and students. The sense of participation in the immediate process of teaching and learning conceived as a cooperative activity that both teachers and students feel in team teaching makes learning an enjoyable and memorable experience, free from monotomy and dullness.

Internet technologies of teching

Development of Internet would lead to formation of information superhighway, where rapid access to information resources would be possible, irrespective of the place of initiation of search in the globe. In a sense all use of internet is educative involving access to information, because it contains huge quantities of data on numerous topics. However at present, there is no control over the relevant or irrelevant information being fed/ served through internet. Internet has information on most advanced research topics in highly technical or scientific areas to information on very petty topics. The use of Internet for education is left to the individual. The universities, colleges and schools have provided facilities to access Internet, but little has been done to systematically use it for teaching or Teleteaching. The use of the medium of internet could provide wider access to good quality education at low cost and to the wider population located in every nook and corner of the globe.

The internet use would remove the limitations of class-room size, fixed timings of imparting, education, restrictions on learner's pace of learning, learner's ability to afford quality education at the best possible university /college or school anywhere in the world. Internet may be considered as a tool to disseminate large quantities of information, to propel the masses forward on a path of prosperity, in the shortest possible time with minimum resources. The adversities of nature or the adversities faced by human beings because of their caste or creed can easily be removed with the help of education and training and certainly Internet technology is a great tool, which can be applied for this purpose.

All countries have been doing immense planning since time immemorial for educating its inhabitants. It has taken thousand years, but 100% education has not been made possible, due to various reasons. Now Internet technology offers the unique opportunity of providing education at a fast pace. Internet is the abbreviation of Inter-network Systems and is described as network of networks.

The Internet as defined in general sense is a global pool of information and services, accessible by means of locally executed interface software.' The Internet started out in 1969 as an experiment to build a national security computer network capable of surviving nuclear attack. Scientists accomplished this by connecting computers through networks. During 1970 the need for rapid communication and sharing the valuable data associated with military research projects was realised by American Government. The initial network prepared by Americans was called 'ARPANET' and 'MILNET', which allowed scientists, researchers and military persons located at diverse sites to communicate through electronic mail. The World Wide Web (WWW) allows systematic and wider access through service providers and has many user-friendly facilities, that makes it a very sophisticated and comprehensive tool developed so far, to access internet.

On World Wide Web 'pages represent the information. A page is stored on a particular host machine but can be made visible to web clients throughout the world. Pages have unique address and therefore can be retrieved explicitly, Web pages contain links to other pages and can be easily accessed with web browser. The page is not only visible on computer screen but can also be down loaded. Web pages can be constructed by anyone having the necessary tools. The electronic request for information navigates a long treacherous route through modem, over local and long distance phone lines, through routers that push it along, to the computer where the web page is stored. Then the information being retrieved flows through the same route to the requester. The information being sent is segmented in packets, which can be thought of as electronic envelopes containing part of a photograph or few pages of text. These packets, besides holding data are labelled with destination, a return address and an ID number. The routers read packet address and move it closer to the computer, where it is supposed to reach. Intranet is a descriptive term used for the implementation of the internet technologies within the corporate organisation. The objective here is to make information resources of an organisation available to each workstation in a standard format and at a fast rate.

The conventional model of imparting technical education comprises of class-room teaching, experimentation in laboratories, practice in workshops and vocational training in factories. During learning, the learner's have facility of utilising information resource centre, computer centre, learning resource utilization centre and also discuss the problems with peers and professors.

The teacher in this mode of imparting education uses variety of task specific and chapter oriented techniques for teaching like writing on black board display of audio-visual material, models, charts, slides or other techniques like group discussion question answer etc. The conventional model is a proven and time—tested model in every country and has served the purpose of providing technical education in an effective manner.

The internet can support different types of education

— Schooling

— Continuing education.

— Re-education or Re- Skilling.

— Task specific immediate education.

To provide Internet based education active supply of information is needed so as to enable the leaner based at home, to remain in contact with his teacher/ guide. This may involve computer based training or computer guided learning with a monitoring/ evaluation by a remotely located teacher guide. The student will get quality education at his doorsteps delivered by expert professors/ teachers and will be learning in virtual environment of the class. He/she shall also be in contact with his peers for any help or mutual discussions. On Internet students themselves can be encouraged to build their study material by utilising the already available material, books and magazines. In USA there are several programmes, which encourages students to use internet and create educational material that makes learning very simple, amusing and contagious. Though no system will be able to replace the real classroom teaching, teaching through Internet and multimedia creates virtual class-rooms and comes very close to the actual class room situations. The learning process on internet is interactive and interesting. The student has greater opportunity of creative thinking and putting the best of experiences gained from outside of classroom in their quest for learning.

Teleteaching

Different options of teleteaching include:

— World Wide Web.

— World Wide Web and Multimedia based self learning.

— Teleconferencing.

The first option is by utilising facility of World Wide Web (WWW). The NET University makes available sufficient courseware on Internet in the form of web pages. The learner after being enrolled in the NET University gets an Internet connection with a specific e-mail address. Students after surfing through the Internet can download the material relevant to their course. The problem with internet is downloading of graphic material from web pages requires enormous time and some times is frustrating. The problem will remain until high-speed Internet for real-time multimedia transfer becomes a reality.

Therefore the second option could be to supply learners with multimedia based self-learning material on CD-ROMs and utilise facility of Internet for on-line communication with the resource person, University and for generating extra reading material from the internet web pages. The learner goes through the contents of the module and thereafter attempts tutorials. Guidance/hints are given by computer to lead him/her to the right answer. If any queries persist, after this, it will be mailed to the resource person's address along with finished assignments through e-mail. The learner has freedom of discussing the problems with fellow learners, the addresses of whom will be provided by the university. This is the best way to teach a learner located remotely. The self-learning modules are prepared in such a way that it encourages students to discover learning. Where students attempts problems, certain hints are given in the beginning and if the students fail to find the right answer, they are guided to lead them to the right answer. This type of inquisitive self-learning makes much more impact on the students and has large retentivity in their minds. The advantage of this system is that learner is given more freedom to follow his pace of learning with respect to his or her own ability. The computer aided self-learning packages greatly reduces the interference of teacher particularly for mature learners. Packages can also be prepared to include performing of experiments and analysis of results. The interactive software prepared for this type of learning based on multimedia teaching gives students individual scores and also provides assistance in solving problems.

The last option of interactive learning is through teleconferencing, where the learner in a real-time audio and real-time video interacts with the resource person in a virtual classroom. Here the learner after listening to the lecture puts cross-questions directly to the Professor through video conferencing. He/she receives online replies to his/her questions. The classes in this mode are conducted at a predetermined schedule and learners are expected to be hooked to the Professor's electronic address at that particular time. The assignments etc. can be attempted by learners at their own pace and finished ones sent to the Professor through Internet. The Professor evaluates these and sends back the comments to individuals. The communication is fast but to complete the learning in a definite period, a fixed number of learners are attached to one Professor.

The scope for teleteaching in engineering is very wide and varies from imparting low level skills in basic trades like plumbing, draughtsmanship, measurement, inspection, quality control to the high level skills of creating building designs, or manufacturing products. With high degree of animation and simulation virtual labs can be created to facilitate experimentation. Packages for training of persons in trouble shooting of appliances and machines call be prepared, which interactively diagnose the problem and leads to the right fault tracing. To give learners actual feel of the things and sufficient hands on practice sessions, they shall be asked to visit institutions for practical demonstration at some intervals. Some visits to organisations/ factories can be made by learners themselves to acquaint them with the real life situations and working of machines and equipment. Later on learners prepare reports for submission to the resource person with their queries.

Knowledge sharing with fellow learners is an important part of the interactive learning. In fact some of the problems of industrial management which involves group discussion, group task or problem solving through teams can easily be taught to a group of learners with Internet, without learners actually making face to face contact. Computer guided packages would be particularly useful in imparting skills in technical areas. In teaching management, it could be case studies where the learner would be solving it through role playing situations. In training of industrial personnel, it could be training of the persons for skill upgradation *e.g.*, measuring or assembling operations where learners undertake instructions and with a set of guidelines prepares some assembly or measures some component. Each step is evaluated against predefined parameters and the performance level achieved by the learner is told to him as done in playing video games. The other use of teleteaching in technical education includes a very large and potentially profitable area of continuing education and in-service and pre-service training of teachers.

The major advantages of teleteaching include:

1) Promotes discovery learning.
2) Learning is learner oriented instead of teacher oriented.
3) Promotes knowledge sharing and problem solving in teams.
4) Learning is not confined to the walls of school/ college.
5) Keep distance learner motivated and in constant contact with the resource person.
6) It removes boredom or loneliness commonly associated with the learner of distance education programmes.
7) Low cost experimentation is possible in virtual labs.
8) Poor countries, which are short of resources and cannot create large infrastructure required for conventional teaching, can easily establish information structure with outside help for mass education programme.

In applying teleteaching, it would be much better and wiser if most of the educational material containing such type of graphics is delivered to the learner on CD-ROMs and Internet link is utilised for further reading and communicating with the resource person. In future with the coming of ISDN technology which delivers data five times as fast as regular modem, part of the problem of speedy transfer of data will be solved but this technology is expensive and difficult to install. The other solution could be that if a virtual university is having large number of its students located in specified geographical area it could create an Intranet, which shall provide faster access to its students.

Reformations in teacher profession

Recently, there has been a discernible trend in many parts of the world to restructure and deregulate state education. Central to these initiatives have been moves to disempower centralized educational bureaucracies and create in their place devolved systems of schooling, entailing significant degrees of institutional autonomy and a variety of forms of school-based management and administration. In many cases, these changes have been linked to an increased emphasis on parental choice and on competition between diversified and specialized forms of provision, thereby creating 'quasi-markets' in educational services.

Although such policies have received particular encouragement from New Right governments in Britain and the USA in the 1980s, and have subsequently been fostered by the IMF and the World Bank in Latin America and Eastern Europe, the political rhetoric of parties of the left has also begun to place increasing emphasis on diversity and choice in education. Even though these directions in education policy have not penetrated all countries, and they have been mediated differently by the traditions of different nation states and different political parties, the similarity between the broad trends in many parts of the world suggests that education policy may be witnessing something more significant than the passing political fashion that has come-in Britain and beyond-to be termed 'Thatcherism'. It is therefore sometimes suggested that these shifts in the ways in which education is organized reflect broader changes in the nature of advanced industrial societies, characterized by some commentators as post-Fordism and by others as post-modernity.

Thus, some observers suggest that the reforms can be understood in terms of the transportation of changing modes of regulation from the sphere of production into other arenas, such as schooling and welfare services. They point to a correspondence between the establishment of differentiated markets in welfare, and a shift in the economy away from Fordism towards a post-Fordist mode of accumulation which 'places a lower value on mass individual and collective consumption and creates pressures for a more differentiated production and distribution of health, education, transport and housing'.

Ball, for example, has claimed to see in new forms of schooling a move away from the 'Fordist' school towards a 'post-Fordist' one-the educational equivalent of flexible specialization driven by the imperatives of differentiated consumption replacing the old assembly-line world of mass production. These 'post-Fordist schools' are designed 'not only to produce the post-Fordist, multi-skilled, innovative worker but to behave in post-Fordist ways themselves; moving away from mass production and mass markets to niche markets and "flexible specialization"... a post-Fordist mind-set is thus having implications in schools for management styles, curriculum, pedagogy, and assessment'.

However, Kenway herself regards the rapid rise of the market form in education as something much more significant than post-Fordism; she therefore terms it a 'post-modern' phenomenon. In her own pessimistic version of post-modernity, 'transnational corporations and their myriad subsidiaries... shape and reshape our individual and collective identities as we plug in... to their cultural and economic communications networks'. Her picture is one in which notions of 'difference', far from being eradicated by the 'globalization of culture', are assembled, displayed, celebrated, commodified, and exploited. Such trends can be detected in the current emphasis on both tradition and diversity in education policy. In other accounts the rhetoric of 'new times' seems to offer more positive images of choice and diversity, reflecting the needs of communities and interest groups brought into prominence as a result of complex contemporary patterns of political, economic, and cultural differentiation, which intersect the traditional class divisions upon which common systems of mass education were predicated.

From this perspective, it is possible to contrast post-modernity to the oppressive uniformity of much modernist thinking-as 'a form of liberation, in which the fragmentation and plurality of cultures and social groups allow a hundred flowers to bloom'. Some feminists, for example, have seen attractions in the shift towards the pluralist models of society and culture associated with post-modernism. The possibilities for community-based rather than bureaucratically controlled welfare are also viewed positively by some minority ethnic groups, and many of the advocates of quasi-market systems of public education regard them as particularly beneficial for the urban poor. Part of the appeal of the recent education reforms thus lies in their declared intention to encourage the growth of different types of school, responsive to the needs of particular communities and interest groups. They also link to concepts of multiple identities and radical pluralism, and can thus seem more attractive than unidimensional notions of comprehensive schooling and, indeed, of citizenship.

Some aspects of the rhetoric of the new policies thus seem to connect to the aspirations of groups who have found little to identify with in the 'grand narratives' associated with class-based politics. In this sense, the reforms might be viewed as a rejection of all totalizing narratives and their replacement by 'a set of cultural projects united [only] by a self-proclaimed commitment to heterogeneity, fragmentation and difference'. In other words, support for schools run on a variety of principles reflect a broader shift from the assumptions of modernity to those of postmodernity. However, there are various problems with these 'new times' theses. They are not only notoriously vague' but also tend to exaggerate the extent to which we have moved to a new regime of accumulation.

Moreover, in the field of education, it is certainly difficult to establish a sharp distinction between mass and marketized systems. For example, the so-called 'common school' in the USA or the 'comprehensive system' in Britain were never as homogeneous as many commentators claim. Nor have there been decisive changes in the prevailing character of schools as institutions. In so far as recent changes in management practices represent an 'adjustment to the problems of Fordism' rather than signifying an entirely new direction, neo-Fordism may be a more appropriate term than post-Fordism. Although the changes may thus not be as momentous as Kenway and others suggest, her pessimistic analysis of what changes have taken place has rather more credibility than would an optimistic one. There does seem to have been an intensification of social differences, together with their celebration in a new rhetoric of legitimation.

However, as the new discourse of choice, specialization, and diversity replaces the previous one of common and comprehensive schooling, there is a growing body of empirical evidence that, rather than benefiting the disadvantaged, the emphasis on parental choice and school autonomy is further disadvantaging those least able to compete in the market. At the same time, it is increasing the differences between popular and less popular schools on a linear scale, reinforcing a vertical hierarchy of schooling types rather than producing the promised horizontal diversity.

For most members of disadvantaged groups, as opposed to the few individuals who escape from schools at the bottom of the status hierarchy, the new arrangements seem to be just a more sophisticated way of reproducing traditional distinctions between different types of school and between the people who attend them. To regard the current espousal of heterogeneity, pluralism, and local narratives as indicative of a new social order may be to mistake phenomenal forms for structural relations. Marxist critics of theories of postmodernism and postmodernity, such as Callinicos, who reassert the primacy of the class struggle, certainly take this view. Even Harvey, who does recognize significant changes, suggests that postmodernist cultural forms and more flexible modes of capital accumulation may be shifts in surface appearance, rather than signs of the emergence of some entirely new post-capitalist or even post-industrial society.

At most, current reforms would seem to relate to a version of post-modernity (PM1) that emphasizes 'distinction' and 'hierarchy' within a fragmented social order, rather than one (PM2) that positively celebrates 'difference' and 'heterogeneity' (Lash 1990). Thus, despite new forms of accumulation, together with some limited changes in patterns of social and cultural differentiation, the continuities seem as striking as the discontinuities. Nevertheless, new arrangements for managing education and other public services can be seen as new ways of resolving the problems of accumulation and legitimation facing the state, in a situation where the traditional Keynesian 'welfare state' is no longer deemed to be able to function effectively.

But even if current policies are new ways of dealing with old problems, there clearly have been changes in the state's mode of regulation. City Technology Colleges (CTCs), grantmaintained schools, and LEA schools with open enrolment and local management in England-and equivalent quasi-autonomous institutions in other parts of the world-are now operating alongside, and increasingly in place of, collective provision by elected bodies with a mandate to cater for the needs of the whole population. Similar reforms have been introduced into the health and housing fields. With the progressive removal of tiers of democratically elected government or administration between the central state and individual institutions, conventional political and bureaucratic control by public bodies is replaced by quasi-autonomous institutions with devolved budgets competing for clients in the marketplace-a system of market accountability sometimes assisted by a series of directly appointed agencies, trusts, and regulators.

Such quasi-autonomous institutions, state-funded but with considerable private and voluntary involvement in their operation, appear to make education less of a political issue. The political rhetoric accompanying the educational reforms in Britain certainly sought to suggest that education had been taken out of politics as normally understood. For Chubb and Moe in the USA, the removal of schools from the local political arena is a sine *qua non* of their success. So, although the extent of any underlying social changes can easily be exaggerated by various 'post-ist' forms of analysis, both the discourse, and the contexts of political struggles in and around education have been significantly altered by recent reforms. Not only have changes in the nature of the state influenced the reforms in education, but the reforms in education are themselves beginning to change the way we think about the role of the state and what we expect of it.

Green has pointed to the way in which education had not only been an important part of state activity in modern societies, but also played a significant role in the process of state formation itself in the eighteenth and nineteenth centuries. The current changes in education policy may similarly be linked to a redefinition of the nature of the state and a reworking of the relations between state and civil society. The new education policies foster the idea that responsibility for welfare, beyond the minimum required for public safety, is to be defined as a matter for individuals and families. As a result, not only is the scope of the state narrowed, but civil society becomes increasingly defined in market terms.

Although one of the many origins of the concept of civil society was the attempt by late eighteenth-century liberal economists to protect an autonomous economic sphere from the growing administrative power of the state, political radicals used it as a context for democratic debate and the fostering of active citizenship. However, Meehan suggests that, by the mid-twentieth century in Britain and some other countries, the establishment of political democracy and a concern that 'Private interests might overwhelm the public good' led to a view in many countries that state bureaucratic regulation itself might serve as 'a tool to improve the collective life of society'. This reliance on the state led to a decline in the autonomy and vitality of civil society.

As a result, education has increasingly been excluded from the public sphere. As many of the responsibilities adopted by the state during the postwar period begin to be devolved to an increasingly marketized version of civil society, consumer rights prevail over citizen rights. Some aspects of education have been 'privatized' not so much in the strictly economic sense as in that of transferring them to the private sphere; others have become a matter of state mandate rather than local democratic debate. This can be seen as part of that broader project to create a free economy and a strong state which, as far as democratic citizenship is concerned, seems to produce the worst of both worlds-reducing the opportunities for democratic debate and collective action about education within both the state and civil society. Meanwhile, in many countries certain aspects of state intervention have been maintained, indeed strengthened. Recent education reforms in England, notably the National Curriculum, are themselves actually as much to do with transferring power from the local to the central state as with giving autonomy to the schools.

While some of the extreme neo-liberals of the New Right would have liked to see the curriculum itself left to the market, the government seems to have been more persuaded on this score by the argument of neo-conservative pressure groups such as the Hillgate Group. This group argued that, even if market forces should ultimately be seen as the most desirable way of determining a school's curriculum, central-government imposition of a National Curriculum on all state schools was a necessary interim strategy to undermine the vested interests of a 'liberal educational establishment' which threatened educational standards and traditional values.

McKenzie claims that 'British governments have actually increased their claims to knowledge and authority over the education system whilst promoting a theoretical and superficial movement towards consumer sovereignty'. This is also the case, though to differing degrees, elsewhere. In terms of educational decision-making, the example of the National Curriculum suggests that the contemporary state has not merely devolved responsibility to a remarketized civil society. In the British case, it may have abdicated some responsibility for ensuring social justice by deregulating major aspects of education, but in increasing a limited number of state powers it has actually strengthened its capacity to foster particular interests while appearing to stand outside the frame.

To what extent, then, have these developments impacted upon the position of teachers? Are teachers, as Hargreaves suggests, caught in struggle between the forces of modernity and post-modernity in which the latter are winning out? And, even if we are sceptical about his postmodern thesis, is he right in suggesting that, despite the pressures currently being experienced by teachers in Canada and elsewhere, there is potentially much that could be positive in recent developments? Le Grand suggests that in England, during the so-called 'golden age of teacher control' from 1944 to the mid-1970s, parents of children in state schools were expected to trust the professionals and accept that teachers knew what was best for their children. This usually involved accepting a degree of uniformity in the system. He goes on to argue that the assumptions underlying what he calls the 'democratic socialist welfare state' have now been questioned, and that 'the notion that, for the sake of the collectivity, everyone would passively accept standardized, relatively low levels of services was challenged by studies showing that in key areas of welfare the middle classes extracted at least as much if not more than the poor in terms of both the quantity and quality of service'.

The belief that professionals are concerned only with the welfare of their clients has increasingly been challenged, with Public-Chóice theorists arguing that the behaviour of public servants and professionals could be better understood if they were assumed to be largely self-interested. The teachers of the 'swollen state' of postwar social democracy are thus now regarded as ill-adapted to be either agents of the narrowed state or entrepreneurial service-providers in a marketized civil society. In the light of this and the broader changes outlined above, there has now been something of a move away from the notion that the teaching profession should have a professional mandate to act on behalf of the state in the best interests of its citizens, to a view that teachers need to be subjected to the rigours of the market and/or greater control and surveillance on the part of the re-formed state.

As with the Hillgate Group's view of the purposes of the National Curriculum, the latter approach may be transitional, in that it is partly concerned with the reconstitution of teacher subjectivities to accord more closely with the demands of education in a society where the prevailing mode of regulation is changing. Even in countries like Britain and the USA, where professions have traditionally enjoyed considerable autonomy from the central state, there have been similar attempts to increase surveillance and supervision in earlier periods of transition and social upheaval.

In the current context, control strategies have taken a variety of forms. In many countries the power of the teaching unions has been challenged, both through the dismantling of former 'corporatist' styles of education decision-making and through the decentralization of education systems. In England, the reforms have been accompanied by swingeing attacks on the integrity of the teaching profession in general and the teachers' unions in particular. The unions' traditional involvement in policy-making, and even in negotiating teachers' pay, was systematically undermined by the Thatcher government during the 1980s, so that even some of the less militant unions expressed strong reservations about the government's reforms.

Research carried out by Sinclair et al., suggests that the atomization associated with school self-management has not yet entirely succeeded in breaking down the traditional power of teacher unions within the state education system. Many of the district-wide networks are still in place, and legal confusion about who is technically the employer in LEA schools operating under local management means that there are a number of issues which remain to be tested in the courts. However, in some grant-maintained schools and CTCs, where the legal issues are more clear-cut, unions are being forced to strengthen their plant bargaining capacity or are being marginalized by management. Only one grant-maintained school has so far derecognized teacher unions and withdrawn from national pay agreements, but some CTCs, which operate outside both national and local agreements, have established in-house staff associations within individual schools, or offered the less militant unions 'no-strike' agreements in return for recognition.

The notion that teachers are part of an 'education establishment', representing producer interests against those of the newly empowered consumer, has led to a questioning of both the altruism and the neutrality of teachers. Strategies for challenging the supposed self-interest of the profession are particularly evident in attempts to reform initial teacher education, especially in England. One strategy favoured by the neo-liberals is deregulation of the profession, to allow schools to go into the market, recruit graduates (or even non-graduates) without professional training, and prepare them on an apprenticeship basis in school. This also has some appeal to neo-conservative critics who have detected collectivist ideological bias among teacher educators in higher education.'

Thus, a recurring theme in the pamphlets of New Right pressure groups is the need to challenge the liberal educational establishment, which is seen to have been behind the 'progressive collapse' of the English educational system. This educational establishment is seen as prey to ideology and self-interest and no longer in touch with the public. It is therefore 'time to set aside... the professional educators and the majority of organised teacher unions... [who] are primarily responsible for the present state of Britain's schools'.. Neo-conservative concerns with 'enemies within', possibly combined with vocationalist concerns with international competitiveness, have meant that the British government has not pursued a policy of total deregulation.

Instead, it has introduced a common list of competences to be required of beginning teachers, regardless of the nature of the route by which they have achieved them. This has given rise to the suspicion that the government wants to 'deprofessionalize' teaching by ensuring that, wherever they are trained, teachers focus on the development of craft skills rather than professional understanding.

Just as basing training in particular schools can limit the development of broader perspectives on education, so might specifying particular competences encourage restricted rather than extended notions of professionalism and professionality.

It is also sometimes suggested that competence-based teacher education is undermining the dominant discourse of liberal humanism within the teaching profession and replacing it with one of technical rationality. Neither, though, involves the abandonment of notions of rationality associated with the Enlightenment project, which might be expected if these changes represented an abandonment of the dominant assumptions of modernity. Similar trends have been detected within schools. In New Zealand, Sullivan has suggested that lack of consultation with teachers over the reforms is in danger of creating a low-trust, hierarchical system rather than a high-trust, collegial one.

In England, Grace posits a shift from a social democratic to a market phase of school leadership, which Gewirtz: and Ball suggest is similar to the broader erosion of 'bureau-professional' regimes of institutional regulation in favour of 'new managerial' ones. Gewirtz and Ball themselves outline two 'ideal-type discourses of school headship', which they term 'welfarism' and 'new managerialism'. Welfarism denotes 'a primary ideological commitment to the material and emotional well-being of individuals and to the creation of a better and fairer society', though Fabian and Radical Welfarists differ about what this might involve.

New managerialism, on the other hand, is 'untainted' by the dominant welfarist values of the postwar era; the New Management discourse is essentially technicist in character, and good management involves 'the smooth and efficient implementation of aims set elsewhere within constraints also set elsewhere'. Although the real cases they discuss introduce 'some messiness into the neat polarization of these pristine binaries', they believe that they have identified a discursive shift of some significance. But here again, as Blackmore points out, the self-managing school retains 'strong modernist tendencies for a top-down, executive mode of decision-making... [alongside its] "weaker" post-modern claims to decentralise and encourage diversity, community ownership, local discretion, professional autonomy and flexible decision-making'.

Nevertheless, those changes that arc taking place in the nature of educational governance and in management practices in schools clearly impact upon the character of teachers' professional lives. To date, empirical evidence from various countries provides more support for Hargreaves' assertion that the reforms are leading to an intensification of teachers' work than for his claim that they have potential for developing more rewarding forms of teacher culture.

A survey conducted by Campbell and Neill on the effects of the National Curriculum on primary school teachers in England and Wales concluded that there had been no overall improvement in standards but that teachers had been driven to burnout. They found that a 54-hour week was now the norm for teachers of children aged 4 to 7, with one in ten working more than 60 hours, and respondents talked of tiredness, irritability, and depression, of sleeping badly, increased drinking, occasional crying in the staffroom, and a sense of guilt that they were neglecting their own families. Studies in New Zealand, where the National Curriculum loading is a less significant factor but school self-management has gone further, have produced similar figures. New Zealand teachers have reported high levels of stress, declining job satisfaction, and a desire to leave the profession, even where they felt the reforms had brought some benefits.

In another study of those schools with the greatest degree d autonomy, although principals still saw themselves as curriculum leaders, teachers stressed 'the current role as being more of a business manager'. Some of the small-scale ethnographic evidence from Britain and New Zealand chronicles in more detail the effects of the intensification of teachers' work and its consequences for industrial relations in schools.

In England, Bowe et al., point to real problems with both self-management and the National Curriculum as they are working out on the ground in secondary schools, and see them as contributing to a growing gulf between senior managers and teachers, and a clash between managerial and educational values. Laughlin et al; however, report evidence from other schools that the demands of LMS were (initially at any rate) absorbed by a core 'coping group' of senior managers whose efforts were able to leave the core educational values of the school relatively unscathed.

While headteachers themselves often claim that local management has increased the involvement of teaching staff in decision-making, a study of the effects of self-management on industrial relations in schools by Sinclair et al., suggests that the very logic of the reforms is that 'headteachers are no longer partners in the process of educating pupils-they become allocators of resources within the school, managers who are driven to ensure that the activities of employees are appropriate to the needs of the business, and givers of rewards to those whose contribution to the business is most highly regarded'. When schools were managed from a more distant bureaucracy, there was often a sense of headteacher and teachers being the professionals fighting a common cause against the distant bureaucracy.

With self-management, there has sometimes been a much sharper sense that the school governors and the senior management team are 'management' and teaching and other staff the 'workers'. Halpin et al., suggest that, in the case of grantmaintained schools, the very process of running a self-managing unit can result in an increase in the distance of headteachers from classroom teachers, although in some cases headteachers themselves are coming under pressure from governing bodies acting like Boards of Directors. Classroom teachers face a number of new pressures-increased workloads, attempts to use them more flexibly to counter the effects of budget restrictions, performance-related pay, and the substitution of full-time, permanent, qualified, and experienced staff by part-time, temporary, less-qualified and less-experienced (and therefore less-expensive) alternatives.

Women teachers, traditionally concentrated in the lower ranks of the teaching workforce, are particularly vulnerable to exploitation in these circumstances. A recent report by the National Foundation for Educational Research confirms that many of these trends have accelerated since the introduction of local management (Maychell 1994). This, of course, has potential implications for teachers' conditions of service and poses new challenges for the teacher unions. There have been suggestions, for example by Kerchner and Mitchell in the USA and Barber in the UK, that the teaching unions need to develop a new mode of operation, sometimes termed 'third generation' or "professional' unionism, in which they negotiate educational as well as industrial issues and potentially become partners with management in educational decision-making to serve the best interests of learners.

Self-management has been seen to pose a threat to traditional styles of trade unionism, but to provide real opportunities for this new-style version. It could also be a way of giving classroom teachers a voice in management without diverting them from their primary role. Barber, Rowe, and Whitty mounted a small research project, with funding from a national teachers' union, to see how far union representatives in England were actually involved in school-based decision making on the ground. Only about 15 per cent of school union representatives had ever been consulted about the budget, the curriculum, or the school development plan.

Subsequent fieldwork suggested that even these figures exaggerated the extent of genuine consultation, let alone formal involvement of unions in school management. We found little evidence of union representatives participating in issues other than those associated with 'second generational unionism', that is, giving advice to members, negotiating with management over grievances, and campaigning on issues related to pay and conditions of work. Many felt that there was a fine line to be drawn between third-generation trade unionism and the sort of collaboration that makes it difficult for unions to bargain for their members' interests.

Flexibility and claims of enhanced professionalism could sometimes become a cover for exploitation of teachers and worsening conditions of service. The rhetoric of reform in the USA has often made far more reference to school-based shared decision-making (SBDM) as a way of enhancing teacher professionalism than has hitherto been the case in England. Yet, although much of the rhetoric of the American reform movement has emphasized the importance of empowering teachers, this has often not come about in practice.

Wohlstetter et al., have suggested that site-based management will only have positive effects if it is implemented in accordance with what, drawing upon the literature of private-sector management, they term the 'high-involvement model'. This requires teacher involvement in decision-making, good information, knowledge and skills, and power and rewards. However, even the more participatory forms of teacher involvement in decision making can have unintended consequences. In Minnesota charter schools, for example, 'as much as teachers appreciated being board members and making administrative decisions, wearing two hats required a great deal of time and effort' from which they would eventually require some relief. Even in this context, it may therefore be important to take seriously the political insights of those teachers who resist attempts to engage them in management without addressing the broader meaning and consequences of the reforms. If, as much of the initial research evidence suggests (Whitty 1997), recent reforms are encouraging advantaged schools and advantaged families to maximize their advantage, then it is particularly important that there is an arena in which such broader issues can be considered not only by teachers but by other stakeholders in public education.

As Henig says of the USA, 'the sad irony of the current education-reform movement is that, through over-identification with school choice proposals rooted in market-based ideas, the healthy impulse to consider radical reforms to address social problems may be channeled into initiatives that further erode the potential for collective deliberation and collective response'. Yet, if social relations are increasingly accommodated in the notion of the strong state and the free economy, then neither the state nor civil society will be the context of active democratic citizenship through which such broader issues can be addressed and social justice pursued.

The reassertion of citizenship rights in education would seem to require the development of a new public sphere between the state and a marketized civil society, in which new forms of collective association can be developed. However, given what has been dismantled by New Right governments, creating a new public sphere in which educational matters can even be debated-let alone determined-poses considerable challenges. Foucault points out that what he called new forms of association, such as trade unions and political parties, arose in the nineteenth century as a counterbalance to the prerogative of the state, and that they acted as the seedbed of new ideas.

We need to consider what might be the modem versions of these collectivist forms of association to counterbalance not only the prerogative of the state, but also that of the market. Part of the challenge must be to move away from atomized decision-making to the reassertion of collective responsibility, without recreating the very bureaucratic systems whose shortcomings have helped to legitimate the current tendency to treat education as a private good rather than a public responsibility. We need to ask how can we use the positive aspects of choice and autonomy to facilitate community empowerment rather than exacerbating social differentiation.

In England, the increasingly centrist Labour Party seems to have adopted many rightist policies, while the Left has done little yet to develop a concept of public education which looks significantly different from the state education so often criticized in the past for its role in reproducing and legitimating social inequalities. And even if the social democratic era looks better in retrospect, and in comparison with current policies, than it did at the time, that does not remove the need to rethink what might be progressive policies for the next century. If new approaches are to be granted more legitimacy than previous ones, what new institutions might help to foster them-initially within a new public sphere in which ideas can be debated, but potentially as new forms of democratic governance themselves?

Clearly, such institutions could take various forms and they will certainly need to take different forms in different societies. They will no doubt be struggled over, and some will be more open to hegemonic incorporation than others. Some may actually be created by the state, as the realization dawns that a marketized civil society itself creates contradictions that need to be managed. Thus, there is likely to be both a bottom-up and a top-down pressure to create new institutions within which struggles over the control of education will take place. Careful consideration will need to be given to the composition, nature, and powers of new institutional forms if they are to prove an appropriate way of reasserting democratic citizenship-rights in education in the late twentieth century and beyond. They will also need to respond to critiques of the gender bias of conventional forms of political association in most modern societies.

Paradoxically, current forms of democracy in England may be even less appropriate than those associated with directly elected School Boards in the nineteenth century, which used 'an advanced form of proportional representation [which] ensured that all the major political and religious groupings could be represented on the School Boards, so that positive policies at this level achieved a genuine consensus'. Similar issues face the teaching profession. As Keith puts it, in calling on teachers to foster the emergence of hitherto,silenced voices', 'we need a new discourse that joins the themes of collaboration, care, commitment and community to those of difference, equity, rights, dialogue, and a wider sense of community'.

Hargreaves suggests that the conventional notion of professionalism is one 'which is grounded in notions of esoteric knowledge, specialist expertise and public status' and that this is being superseded by one which involves 'the exercise of discretionary judgement within conditions of unavoidable and perpetual uncertainty'. It is certainly the case that teachers will need to be responsive to changing demands, but it is also the case that there will be an expectation of accountability to constituencies that have tended to be ignored. Both state control and market forces imply a 'low trust' relationship between society and its teachers, of the sort which currently exists in England and which Sullivan suggests is developing in New Zealand.

Media characterizations of teacher unions often tend to encourage popular suspicion of teachers. Furthermore, the defence of the education service has too often been conducted within the assumptions of the 'old' politics of education, which involved consultation between government, employers, and unions but excluded whole constituencies-notably parents and business-to whom the New Right has subsequently successfully appealed.

We need to ask some fundamental questions about who has a legitimate right to be involved in defining teacher professionalism. It is perhaps indicative of the paucity of thinking on this that some of the left teacher educators who, 20 years ago, were criticizing the élitism of the professions, should now be amongst those suggesting that teachers should adopt the modes of self regulation traditionally associated with the conservative professions of medicine and the law. In the Australian case, Knight et al. argue for what they call 'democratic professionalism', which seeks to demystify professional work and facilitate 'the participation in decision-making by students, parents and others'.

They acknowledge a tension between the profession's claim to particular and specialist knowledge and expertise and a degree of relative autonomy, and a requirement that it be open to the needs and concerns of other groups in a democratic society. They also concede that 'the practice of open or democratic professionalism is largely lacking in formal teacher education' as it has traditionally been conducted. Interestingly, they go on to posit alternative forms of teacher education that stress flexibility and diversity for a 'post-Fordist future'. In a way, this takes us back to where we began. Whether or not the changes that are taking place in education do reflect fundamental changes in modes of accumulation and modes of social solidarity, signalled by terms such as post-Fordism and post-modernity, they do need to be confronted.

At the level of rhetoric, the recent reforms of the New Right have probably been more responsive than their critics usually concede to those limited, but none the less tangible, social and cultural shifts that have been taking place in modern societies. A straightforward return to the old order of things would be neither feasible nor sensible. Social democratic approaches to education which continue to favour the idea of a common school are faced with the need to respond to increasing specialization and social diversity.

However, this does not necessarily mean that the only future for public education lies with the particular marketized forms that are currently fashionable. If we are to avoid the atomization of educational decision-making, and associated tendencies towards fragmentation and polarization between schools and within schools, we need to create new contexts for determining appropriate institutional and curricular arrangements on behalf of the whole society. This will require new forms of association in the public sphere within which citizen rights in education policy-and indeed other areas of public policy—can be reasserted against current trends towards both a restricted version of the state and a marketized civil society.

7

Sociopolitical influences in Schooling

The school is the miniature society and a social institution to serve its purposes. It is entrusted with the responsibility of training and bringing up the students so that they may be able to take part effectively, efficiently and harmoniously in the community to which they belong. Prof K.G. Saiyidain has rightly remarked, "A people's school must obviously be based on the people's needs and problems. Its curriculum should be an epitome of their life. Its method of work must be approximate to theirs: It should reflect all that is significant and characteristic in the life of the community in his natural setting". Hence the schools as an epitome of people's life, must include all kinds of useful activities important problems and significant features of our day-to-day life.

Sociological influneces

Students should be given various learning experiences inside the school which they will face outside.

Otherwise, they will prove worthless, helpless and ineffective individuals. On the other hand, if they are properly trained in the schools, they will be able to occupy their rightful places in the community. The need for linking the school life with the life in the community cannot be overemphasized. The Secondary Education Commission, 1952 have stressed, "The starting point of educational reform must be the rethinking of the school to life and restoring of the intimate relationship between them which has broken down with the development of the formal tradition of education". Such intimate and living relationship between the school and the community can be established by introducing various kinds of active occupation, the desired values and behaviour patterns in the school.

The entire school life should be infused with the spirit of community life. Dewey held that the school be a child's habitat where he should learn "through direct living, instead of being only a place to learn lessons having an abstract and remote reference of some possible living to be done in future. It gets a chance to be a miniature community, an embryonic society". The relationship between the school and the community can be summed up in the following words of Ryburn, "There must be vital connection between the life of pupils in schools and the life of the community from which they come. There must be a vital connection between the school, which is the corporate life of pupils and teachers and the community.

Relationship between the school and the community can be strengthened and the former can be made a miniature community through close corporation and mutual give and take between them. In a democratic set up such relationship is not only essential, but also imperative. The community, even at the stage of its underdevelopment, possesses abundant resources like forms and forts, old and new constructions, temples and monuments, places of new social, economic, historical, cultural, technological, artistic and aesthetic importance. Besides, there are fairs and festivals, rich heritage and customs as well as rich human resources like artists and artisans, craftsmen and clergymen, doctors, teachers and so on. On the other hand, schools have buildings, equipment, furniture, play-ground, libraries and laboratories. They are not merely meant for children. The whole community must benefit from these resources.

Educational literature frequently makes reference to "family back-ground" as a summarizing variable that impacts on school achievement, IQ, level of aspiration, and other learners outcomes associated with the school experience. This practice has become so common as to create stereotyped expectations associated with family background, social class identity, and family structure. For example, when a teacher speaks of a child coming from a "good home," this is usually interpreted to mean that the child is the product of a two-parent, middle-class, white family of adequate economic means who are loving and supportive of the child. By implication, variations in this stereotype mean that the home is less "good." This generalization is, of course, often incorrect. A child can be the product of a middle-class family and have a psychologically and emotionally devastating family experience.

A child from a working-class family might have a family background that provides strong psychological and emotional support. A child from a one-parent family can be and often is secure, stable, well adjusted, and a high a achiever. The number of children coming fro one-parent families is so high today that it can no longer be considered in any sense unusual. The teaching profession would be well served by dropping the use of the expression "broken home" because of its pejorative and inaccurate connotations. The human family is a small *kinship system*, which means that it helps us identify who is related to whom by blood or by marriage. The smallest family unit is the conjugal family and includes only the husband and wife. If children are added to this basic unit, it is called a *nuclear family*. If, within the same household, there reside other relatives besides the father, mother, and children, we have an *extended family*. Extended families usually include parents, children, grandparents, aunts, uncles, cousins, and possibly great-grandparents.

In modern, urban-oriented societies, and especially in the United States, the nuclear family is the dominant arrangement. In the traditional societies of the world, some form of the extended family is the more common pattern. The family is what sociologists refer to as a "primary group," and it is the most significant instrument of socialization in lives of most persons. It is a "primary group" because there ia great deal of face-to-face, direct contact among members and because much of the individual's life is spent in such a group. It is from the family that the individual learns some of the most important things he or she needs to know in life.

The family teaches the individual the traditions, folkways, and mores of society—to speak a language, to develop a value system, and to form conscience. How the individual views himself or herself and the world is largely conditioned by family life. There is convincing research support for the idea that social class influence of the family is felt early in life. Kagan reports several studies conducted in recent years that document the early—as early as the first birthday—

and persistent influence of family social class identity. He reports studies indicating that "by 20 and 29 months of age, the class of the child's family had become a major predictor of attentiveness, volcanization, and smiling." One of the most emotionally relevant differences associated with family social class identity is in the area of language development and use. These differences have been consistently confirmed by studies that extend over a period of forty or more years.

The differences on whatever measures are taken uniformly favor the middle social class children over those from lower or working-class families. The middle-class child typically has learned both restricted and elaborated linguistic modes and is able to adjust to the appropriate mode as the social setting varies. The lower-class child has his or her communication limited to the restricted linguistic mode. Middle-class children have more extensive vocabularies, produce more mature sentence structures, and are more precise in their articulation and pronunciation than are lower-class children. These differences seem to be associated with early family upbringing in which mothers encourage cognitive development by talking to their young children, providing explanations, encouraging freedom of exploration, and avoiding unnecessary intrusions into the activities of the child.

The middle-class child's socialization provides more freedom, more self-involvement, more of an attitude of being able to control one's destiny. The environments of lower-class families are less conducive to this type of cognitive development, especially in language development. These differences are related directly to the child's performance in school. The sequence of achievement disability proceeds somewhat as follows: The child comes to school with limited linguistic facility and with restricted firsthand experience out of which concepts can be intellectualized. These deficiencies become immediately apparent when the child is confronted with the task of learning to read, usually in the first grade.

The school becomes largely a custodial center rather than an educational institution. Teachers have an incredibly difficult, stressful, and tension-ridden work environment. For many it is a challenge simply to survive in what is literally a dangerous place. Student absenteeism is high, and school officials make little effort to enforce truancy laws. Teachers usually breathe a sigh of relief when the troublemakers are absent. The school curriculum is based on values that have little meaning for children and teenagers who come from a world of strutting pimps, drug pushers, and apartment houses shared with rats and cockroaches. A child terrorized by a street gang can hardly be expected to be highly motivated to attend to what is being presented in the classroom. Teachers, school officials, political leaders, legislators, and citizens generally must realize once and for all that the problems associated with the underclass cannot be solved through educational efforts alone.

To suggest that public education can somehow provide solutions to a dangerous social condition of this magnitude is hopelessly naive. Indeed, public education by itself is no answer at all to this serious cluster of problems. If this society is to overcome the problems of the underclass, it will have to mount a major rehabilitation effort, of which education would necessarily be a part. But national priorities are not so arranged at the present time, and there is little to suggest that they will be in the near future. Meanwhile, the most prosperous and highly educated nation on earth continues to sit on a social time bomb that will one day surely explode and create a major upheaval in social relations in this country. What is being suggested should not be construed to mean that the school has no constructive role to play in helping children from the underclass. We are suggesting only that the school cannot do it along. Successful strategies for dealing with the problems of the underclass will need to extend across a broad spectrum of social and health services, including social, psychological, economic, political, educational, vocational, and allied health spheres.

Until society sees to fit to tackle this problem on a broad front, teachers must do the best they can in making a conscientious effort to teach these children to read, write, and perform basic arithmetic operations simply as survival skills. Beyond that teachers need to identify and help develop whatever talents these individual children have. Additionally, the school can contribute to finding solutions to the problems of the underclass by better educating the children of the middle and upper classes, who will one day be the policy-makers who set social priorities for the society.

Political influeneces

Today, school governance was thoroughly enmeshed in political activity at the local level. Corruption, graft, and less objectionable forms of political influence characterized hiring of teachers, purchase of textbooks, construction contracts, and the employment of noncertified personnel not only in the large urban areas but in smaller communities as well. The malaise that afflicted school administration was so pervasive that it became the object of a national reform movement, consistent with the progressive political ideology of the early part of this century.

Highly respected and powerful scholars and educational leaders gave support and leadership to the effort to remove school governance from the grip of local politics.

As a result, school districts came to be autonomous political units, independent of other local jurisdictions such as local country or city governments. The efforts to reform the administrative structure of schools also initiated the movement to consolidate and centralize schools, a process that continued well into the 1970s. The consolidation and centralization of schools appealed to business-minded Americans because it resembled a corporation structure. The efficient corporate model was obviously attractive as compared to the decentralized, unbusinesslike way in which schools conducted their affairs. Indeed, the term *businesslike* is considered to be synonymous with efficiency. A major cornerstone of the school district reorganization effort was to eliminate wherever possible those districts that were too small to operate efficiently.

At the end of World War II there were over 100,000 school districts in the United States. By 1960 that number had been reduced to 42,000; and by 1970, to about 18,000. Today there are approximately 16,000 school districts. The legal governing body of a school district is the school board, known as the board of directors or as the board trustees.

School boards are given the power by state law to establish local school policies, consistent with guidelines and laws of the state. Their responsibilities include such matters as hiring the superintendent, approving curriculum documents, setting the school calendar, negotiating contracts with employees, receiving and expanding funds, establishing a budget, a developing and maintaining facilities. The school superintendent is the chief executive officer of the board, and it is through the office of the superintendent that the board policies are actually implemented.

School board members have authority only when sitting as a board; that is, an individual school board member, on his or her own, has no more authority to direct the affairs of the school than any other citizen in the community has. This is often not understood, and, as a consequence, sometimes board members will attempt to usurp responsibilities that are more appropriately those of the superintendent, principal, teachers, budget director, curriculum director, or other professional staff. Many studies have been made of the nature and composition of school boards. Typically, boards consist of five to nine members who are elected for a period of from three to six years. Their level of education tends to be above average, which means that school policies in most places are being set by persons who have themselves succeeded in school.

Most board members are white makes who are proprietors, businessmen, executives, and professionals. Tradition and public policy hold that school board members should give their time and talent as a public service; that is, they should serve without salary or only at a token salary, they should be nonpartisan in their political affiliation, and they should be elected at large. These requirements are intended to reduce the more objectionable political aspects of board membership.

In recent years there have been renewed efforts to halt or even to reverse the trend toward centralization. This has been promoted by minority groups, especially blacks, living in the large urban areas. It would be a mistake, however, to associate this movement only with inner-city blacks. Other groups such as Indians and/or Native Americans,

Latinos, and Asians have also been active in working toward greater local control of schools. The disadvantaged minorities have not been satisfied with the way schools have served their children and feel that, if they had more to say about setting policies and making decisions, they would be better served.

As a consequence, there has been considerable pressure to get what is called "community control" of schools. The issues that are involved in centralization-decentralization represent value conflicts having to do with keeping decision making close to the grass roots while at the same time having an efficient administrative operation. Because it is essentially a question of values, there is no way that it can be resolved entirely on the basis of expertise. What is being sought is a system that will maximize both democratic control over decision making and also one that will maximize efficiency in governmental operations.

Most advocates of centralization would not go so far as to push for a nationally centralized system of education. Summarily, most advocates of decentralization would not want to return to the days of a school district at every crossroad in the land. Most feel that schools should accommodate the educational needs of local constituents. Two ways have been suggested to achieve school decentralization. One might be called *political* decentralization. Under this system, large consolidated school districts now operating under the direction of a single school board would be split into smaller districts. This, essentially, would reverse the consolidation trend that has been taking place for the better part of this century.

Each of these newly created administrative units would be autonomous, have its own school board, and be under local community control. As such, it would set its own policies, hire personnel, approve the curriculum, set its own budget, and so on. Although this type of political decentralization has a certain nostalgic attraction, it is really not a practical or feasible alternative to what is done today. Public services for today's communities require such complex and costly delivery systems that a metropolitan-wide effort is required to have them become a reality. This is true in the case of public transportation, water and electrical services, fire and police protection, sewer and garbage services, and, to some extent, health care. Increasingly, such service districts include all, or a good part, of the entire metropolitan region.

The move toward political decentralization of school districts would take communities in the opposite direction of metropolitanism, a very unlikely development. A more realistic approach to preserving or restoring some semblance of local control is to handle it through administrative decentralization. Under this arrangement, the large district boundaries are maintained, and there is a central governing board. An effort is made to separate functions in a way that will maximize both efficiency and democratic control. Thus, such activities as purchasing, budgeting, and personnel services are handled at the central administrative office level. This provides the district many advantages in terms of cost and efficiency.

For example, payrolls and bookkeeping can be computeralized for the entire district, thereby eliminating the need to duplicate the operation several times. The district can exercise economies by making purchases on bid and making them in such large quantities that suppliers are willing and able to offer them at a lower price. Whereas the district centralizes functions such as those just described, it decentralizes functions that involve curriculum and instruction. For instance, the district might be divided into several areas, each of which is headed by a regional administrator. Such areas might even have school councils that consist of local parents who advise the school authorities with respect to school policies. Although such school councils may not have any legal basis, they do, nonetheless, have credibility and can have considerable power. Parent and student involvement at the local level helps to ensure a meaningful curriculum for children attending local schools.

Because administrative decentralization preserves the advantages of both a centralized and decentralized system, it has been implemented in many large city school districts in recent years. In a decentralized administrative organization the authority and responsibility for education is dispersed. For example, in our system, authority and responsibility for education is shared by local communities, larger school districts, and states. The assumption is that when there is such dispersion of authority and responsibility, the system will more adequately take care of local needs. A further assumption is that this system will reduce the amount of arbitrariness in decision making because the farther away from the effects of a decision that the decision is made, the more likely it is to be arbitrary. Another assumption is that local involvement in decision making will result in greater interest in schools.

All of these assumptions and others like them that surrounded the complicated issue of local control are open to much question. They are partially true; perhaps in some instances, altogether true. In other cases, they may not be true at all. Certainly, local control of schools does not necessarily mean better quality of education.

Individuals usually favor local control of schools for some combination of the following reasons:

1) *Advocates of local control feel that the schools belong to the people*: This view argues that schools are literally owned and operated by the taxpayers of the local community. School administrators, teachers, and other personnel associated with the school district are employees of the local community. At such, these employees should be accountable to the citizens of the local community. Because the schools belong to the people of the local community, if follows that local citizens would inform the school as to the kind of educational program they want for their children and would supervise the work of the school to ensure that it was being carried out. Teachers who are unable or unwilling to perform in accordance with the mandates of local citizens would be dismissed. Naturally, organized teacher groups believe otherwise, namely, that they do not work well when they are under such close supervision and that are professionals they must be permitted a considerable amount of autonomy in the exercise of professional decision making.

2) *Local control reflects local needs*: Advocates of local control often state that they do not need bureaucrats in the central office many miles away or officials in the state education office to tell them what kind of education their children need. They insist that the persons who can best decide on local education needs are local citizens. Obviously, this point and the foregoing one are closely related.

3) *School management and curriculum will be more closely monitored when control is at the local level*: If this administrators and teachers are accountable to local constituents, parents will

more likely monitor school activities themselves rather than rely on representatives from the central office to do it for them. Who is the first to know if a teacher is not doing his or her job responsibility and adequately? Local control advocates say that it is the parents of the children with whom the teacher is working. Consequently, they are able to call such a situation to the attention of the school authorities can be made at the local level. Parents are not likely to be very effective if they have to register their concerns at some anonymous bureaucratic office many miles away. It follows, too, that the schools would be more responsive to such local criticism and suggestion. In order to get this type of representatives, local authorities must remain vigilant and alert to what is going on in the schools.

4) *People who are affected by decisions should be involved in making them*: Of course, those who support local control believe this is more likely to happen if decisions are made at the local level. The fact is that in representative governments we are more often than not involved only indirectly in decisions that affect us. Even though participatory democracy has become a popular concept in recent years, it is simply not possible for us to be involved in everything. Local control advocates would say that one is not asking to "be involved in everything"—only in the education of one's children. The education of one's children is an extension of parental responsibility and cannot and should not be relinquished to a state agency such as the public schools. Democratic decision making under a representative system is based on the concept of "consent of the governed," and in this case, the governed are not willing to give consent.

5) *People will be more interested in schools if they are controlled locally*: If local perceive schools as belonging to them, they are more likely to pride themselves on having good schools and will be more interested in supporting what they do. Schools are more than educational institutions; they ar symbols of the community. They contribute to community solidarity and unity. The high school football or basketball game is not only an athletic event; it is an expression of community loyalty and esprit de corps. Thus, the school has important socialization functions for a community beyond fulfilling educational needs that are served when the school is controlled and operated locally. Often communities are very upset about a school closure, not because this will do violence to the education of children locally but because such a closure says something about the community itself.

Individuals usually do not favor local control of schools for some combination of the following reasons:

1) *Localism promotes parochialism, narrowness of vision*: Opponents of local control do not deny many of the arguments made in its favor. Indeed, they would say that it is precisely what is wrong will be reflected in the school when schools are controlled locally. "If desegregation, for example, were left in the hands of local citizens, we would still be at the stage we were in the early 1950s," say opponents of local control. Opponents also say that children may get their early educations at the local neighbourbood school, but they do not usually spend a lifetime in that community. They grow up and move away. Therefore, they must have a familiarity not only with the local area but with the world beyond.

2) *School expenditures will work to the advantage of local elites and to the disadvantage of low socioeconomic status families:* It is further argued that the social class composition of the community has little to do with contradicting this principle. However the local community is constituted with respect to income, occupation, race, ethnic groups, or social class, *some* group can be identified as being most influential in decision making. That group of elites will see to it that school funds are expended in accordance with its views of what constitutes a good education. The net effect of this is a replication of social class structure at the local community level from one generation to the next. Local control ensures that the "haves" will continue to get in generous amounts and the "have-nots" will continue to be shortchanged by the schools. Opponents argue that if it is equity of education that is being sought, one does not get it through the mechanism of local control. They would say that policy formation has to take place beyond the local community—where local elites cannot dominate and control decision-making process.

3) *When education is controlled locally, it does not address itself to large societal needs*: The world of today's children does not begin and end at the boundary of the local community. People and places interact with each other. A community has many interlocking social, political, economic, and geographic links and bonds with other places. As a nation, we are heavily involved in international relations. "We cannot educate children only in terms of he needs of the local community," the opponents to local community control tell us. Every school in the country has to be concerned with those broad social issues that concern us as a nation. Today's children not only need a

community perspective but also need to see the world from the perspective of the region and the nation.

4) *Localism works contrary to the integration of neighborhoods into the larger community*: Too great an emphasis on the local community can promote separatism just at a time when society is stressing integration. If one community is black, another is Chicano, another all white, and so on, the local operation of schools in those communities accentuates the racial and ethnic variable. Very substantial efforts have been made in recent years to avoid such homogeneity of racial and ethnic composition of schools; indeed, they are required by law to be otherwise constituted.

5) *The improvement of education is too complex, too sophisticated, and too large to be handled adequately at the local level*: What is really being said here is that what is needed is not localism but metropolitanism. The concern should be spread over a wider rather than a narrower area because social and educational problems are usually pervasive to a large region, not limited to a neighborhood, according to the opponents of local control. To believe that local persons, who are often poorly educated themselves, have the wisdom and the expertise to make sound decisions about the education of their children approaches incredible heights of naivete. Such procedures might have been adequate in the day of the hoosier schoolmaster and his little rural school, but not for children who will spend most of their lives in the twenty-first century.

6) *Funds for special projects are often used poorly*: Guidelines for the funding of federal education projects have required that projects be governed

by local executive boards consisting of members of "the community," Modeled after self-improvement programs in Communist countries, such involvement is supposed to develop skills of participatory democracy and at the same time ensure the project's relevance to the group involved. Of course, it rarely works that way, according to opponents, because the money is squandered on worthless projects or otherwise misappropriated. Persons who have been totally unaccustomed to handling anything but trivial amount of money in their personal lives, now find themselves in charge of huge amounts of money, a responsibility for which they are totally unequipped either by personal experience or professional expertise.

7) *It is more difficult for professional personnel to engage in negotiated contracts*: It is obviously easier for a union to negotiate with a single school board of a large city than it is to deal with all units all the local level. But supporters of localism would take the opposite view. They would want to bargain with teachers at the local level. They would want to hire, fire, or reward teachers. This issue, therefore, is one that places the teachers' unions and local community advocates on opposite sides.

8) *Localism defeats high priority social goals such as integration, cultural pluralism, and metropolitan coordination*: Great strides have been made in the last quarter century in achieving these broad-based social goals. Localism seems to fly in the face of these trends. It is difficult to support school integration and desegregation, for example, and at the same time support the separation that is suggested by local control. The revitalization of communities cannot occur through efforts of the

> local community alone. The problems are too complex and their resolution too costly to be handled by such a limited effort. Good social policies are made by persons who are competent to make them. To suggest that people at the local level have such competence by themselves is probably expecting too much.

The issue of local control of schools is not one that can be resolved entirely on the basis of objective data and expertise. It is obvious that the problem is enmeshed in different and conflicting value orientations. This means that opponents as well as advocates are likely to overstate their particular point of view. For instance, let us take the matter of professional autonomy. Should teachers be accountable to, and supervised by, local laypersons? The answer to this question cannot be a clear-cut yes or no. The truth is that teachers *are* accountable to local citizens and parents, but this does not mean that teachers are or must be under the constant supervision of parents. Teachers *do* exercise a considerable amount of freedom is carrying out their duties and responsibilities, yet they are not completely autonomous in performing their professional roles. This same type of compromise position characterizes most of the specific points of conflict regarding local of schools.

Role of political power groups

These traditional views of politics are too narrow for our purposes. Instead, we will take a broad view of politics. The definition of Professor Harold Lasswell will suit our purpose: "The study of politics is the study of influence and the influential." Politics in education, therefore, may take many forms because individuals and groups are always trying to introduce the views of others. In we discussed critics of the schools and, in that setting, talked about various pressure groups. Such groups might also be considered political power groups that attempt to, and often do, influence school decision making.

Teachers and even administrators have held securely to the belief that schools somehow ar outside the realm of politics. Despite the fact that the most important decisions affecting schools, namely, how they are financed, are wholly political, school people insist on clinging to the naive belief that "schools are above politics." As a result, persons most closely associated with school decision making often have the least well-developed political skills. The time has come for those associated with school decision making to set aside the romantic notion that schools are not involved in politics. Schools are and always have been influenced by local, state, and federal political power groups. This is so because schools serve many constituent groups, each of which has its own set or priorities for the schools. They are not all mutually exclusive, of course, but neither are they wholly alike. The efforts to influence decisions in accordance with a group's own enlightened self-interests often involve the use of political power.

Teacher unions

In many states, the state teachers' union is one of the most powerful lobbys in the state legislature. Having the authority to negotiate contracts at the local level, as is the case everywhere today, puts the local teachers' union in a position of power that equals or even exceeds that of the school board, who are the elected representatives of the people of the community.

Student groups

Recently, students groups have not been a particularly potent political force in education in this country until relatively. Teachers taught, professors professed, administrators administered, boards of regents set standards for admission and completion, and students could pretty much take it or leave it. The adults made the rules and regulations; students were expected to comply with them. Students could involve themselves in so-called student councils and student governing bodies at the high school and college levels, but these were governing bodies at the high school and college levels, but these were frequently controlled by the institutional establishment.

The governance of institutions was rarely challenged seriously on any issue of substance. All of this began to change dramatically at the college and university levels with the return to the campus of the veterans of World War II. Attending under the GI Bill of Rights, these men and women invaded the campuses of the country by the hundreds of thousands. They had already had their career plans delayed because of the war, most were several years older than the conventional college student, and most were highly self-directed in terms of their career goals. Also, many were fed up with the bureaucracy and seemingly senseless regulation of military life and were not about to put up with it as civilians.

The students, then for the first time, began putting real pressure on colleges and universities to reform their procedures and to provide a sympathetic ear to the demands of the students. Institutions had little choice, really, for they could not survive without the income these potential students could provide. Thus the World War II veterans of the period between 1946 and 1956 paved the way for student involvement in educational decision making at the college and university levels. Institutions had been accommodating student demands for nearly two decades before the extreme student activism of the 1960s and, therefore, should have been able to cope with it. Nonetheless, when student activism reached its peak in the late 1960s, these institutions found themselves in complete disarray and, in some instances, became practically ungovernable.

These developments had the effect of dramatizing the political power of student groups in campus decision making. As a result, students have become active participants in the processes of decision making on college and university campuses. There is an awareness of the rights of students and a sensitivity to the need to involve students in decision making. Today we find student members on many committees that deal with the academic and institutional affairs not only on college and university campuses but in secondary schools as well.

Business and corporate groups

Business and corporate interests organize themselves around such organizations as the chamber of commerce, Kiwanis Club, the Rotary Club, and the local taxpayers' association. These men and women are likely to have many social contacts at local private clubs, at business luncheons, at community affairs, and even in each other's homes. The business and corporate interests have been stereotyped as bedrock political, economic, and social conservatism in this country. There is, however, growing evidence that there is not as solid agreement among leaders of these groups that there once was. Everett Ladd. Jr. sees these differences as essentially *generational* and refers to them as representing moderate" and "orthodox" conservatism. Moderate conservatives accept the service state and the governmental intervention that accompanies it. Even though they may inveigh against it at Rotary luncheons and convention banquets, back in the privacy of the boardroom they try to shape its uses, especially in promoting economic development and in advancing the immediate interests of the business middle class. Orthodox conservatives, in contrast, remain profoundly and genuinely uncomfortable with the New Deal state.

As practical politicians, such conservatives usually understand full well the limits on how far they may reasonably expect to cut back government. But still, their objective is to produce a situation where government taxes less, spends less, and regulates less." Business groups have often been represented as opposed to good education. This is simply not true. Increasingly, the business community is recognizing that schools are vitally important to the equality of life in a community.

Religious groups

Public education and religious groups often encounter value conflicts. The issues become political when pressure is brought to bear on the school to *do* something that it is not now doing or to *stop* doing something that it is doing. Examples of the first concern is to persuade schools to engage in prayer recitation and/or *Bible* reading or to teach the creation theory. Examples of the second concern are pressures to get schools to stop using inquiry procedures, and so refrain from including sex education or evolution in the curriculum.

The extent to which religious groups are powerful political agents depends largely on the community. In those places where the entire community is of a single religious persuasion, the religious influence can be, and usually is, very strong. If a community is heterogeneous in its religious composition, no one group is powerful enough to dominate the public school decision making.

Minority groups

By the late 1960s, hardly any school decision could be made without taking into account the effect it might have on the minority and ethnic component of the community. These groups gained considerable strength as a result of several favorable judicial decisions and because of federal and state legislation. Although these groups are not as powerful politically as they may have been a decade ago, they will wield formidable political power.

For instance, political analysts suggest that the black vote was responsible for the election of President Carter in 1976. The political and social climate of the period between 1960 and 1970 encouraged self-determination for minority and ethnic groups. Guidelines for federal projects not only encouraged the involvement of minorities and ethnics but required it. The Civil Right Act of 1964 opened many doors to opportunity for these groups and enhanced their political strength. The formation of human rights commissions in states, affirmative action programs, and a growing public awareness of discrimination also strengthened minority and ethnic groups politically.

Courts and legistratures

The courts have been heavily involved in educational decision making in this country. This, of course, changed with the landmark decision of *Brown v. The Board of Education of Topeka, Kansas.* The resolution of the Brown case in favor of the litigants not only outlawed the separate but equal principle, but it also ushered in a whole new era of the involvement of the courts in educational policy information. This came about, in part, because of changes in judicial procedure that made "class action" suits easier to file. a class action lawsuit means that the outcome of the case will affect not only the individual litigant but also all others who are similarly grieved or affected. Thus, a class action lawsuit has the effect of establishing policy.

David L. Kirp has noted that this relaxation of the procedures in filing class action lawsuits, along with the expansion of the substantative meaning of the Equal Protection Clause of the Fourteenth Amendment, were instrumental in the judicial system's becoming a vehicle for efforts to secure distributive justice.

As was explained in for a period of nearly twenty years following the Brown case, one case after another found its way into the counts. Clearly, this was done in order to achieve justice when local institutions were unable or unwilling to provide it. One might say that the unresponsiveness of traditional institutions to human needs encourages judicial involvement in policy formation for public education. But this development was greatly slowed by the U.S. Supreme Court decision in the Rodriguez case in 1973 and the Bakke decision in 1978. The judicial success in recent years has not been as predictable as it once was, making potential litigants are wary in becoming involved in a lengthy and costly lawsuit that might eventually have adverse class action consequences.

Changes in school funding practices, with a greater share of the costs of education being paid by the state, coupled with citizen concern over student achievement, have given ascendance to state legislatures as powerful political forces in educational decision making. Another reason for the growing potency of the state legislature is the increased strength of other politically influential groups. For example, the local school authorities can no longer deal effectively with the powerful teachers' unions, business groups, and taxpayers' associations.

These deal local authorities cry for help from the state legislatures in setting down policies having to do with contract negotiations, funding, student rights, tax rates, and many other complex issues. The same forces that have reduced the influence of the judicial system on educational policy formation have *increased* the role of the state legislatures. There is little doubt that the state legislature today is the most powerful political body affecting educational decisions.

Increasingly, political groups are recognizing this and are taking their problems directly to the state legislature. This applies no matter what the problem might be—curriculum, school finance, personnel, affirmative action, minority group education, and so on. Local political units are not able to deal with these complex problems, and the federal government either refuses to or cannot legally become involved. Consequently, it is the state legislature that has become the educational unit of first and last resort in resolving educational issues.

8

Need of Humanistic and Value-oriented Education

The purpose of all education was to create 'gentlemen' out of the rough and raw homosapiens. True knowledge was no more the acquirement of culture, particularly from books, but was the power to do the right thing in a given situation. The goal of liberal education was to free man from ignorance, superstition, meanness and servility so that his responses to several life situations would be human, generous and harmonious. A man educated in the liberal tradition has the power to rise above immediate circumstances, has the ability to subordinate personal or group interests to the general good and self-centredness to humanistic goals. Though we associate liberal education primarily with the study of humanities and arts, a liberally educated man is equally inquisitive about the other branches of knowledge also. He is frec from ignorance and superstition; he consciously rises above the vulgar, the mean and the servile.

Today the growth of utilitarian science, the spread of new economic and political ideas and the innovations in psychological and sociological studies have contributed to the materialisation of education and the dehumanisation of the educated. Utility and success in the world became the test of educational achievement. The worth of educational experience is measured today by the degree to which it helps to which it helps to provide the actual life-needs of the society and the individual. Educational institutions have become places to produce skillful labourers endowed with several efficiencies and trained to slog.

Education for culture and knowledge is being slowly replaced by education for living. Teaching has become a job and education a pursuit after training. Such a system is incapable of leading the youth towards humanistic actions or concerns. Aristotle said, "A task and also an art or a science must be deemed vulgar if it renders the body or soul or mind of free men useless for the employments and actions of virtue. Hence we entitle vulgar all such arts as deteriorate the condition of the body, and also the industries that earn wages; for they make the mind preoccupied and degraded".

Modern education makes the mind preoccupied with triflin concerns and degrades it by distorting the impulses. It may be termed vulgar from the Aristotelian point of view. Tagore lamented the dehumanisation of education and the consequent degeneration of human instincts in the learner. He ridiculed the education that is based on the collection of information and facts and aimed solely at the acceleration of material comfort. "The great use of education", wrote, "is not merely to collect facts but to know man and to make oneself known to man." Tagore insisted that schools are repulsive and anti-educational; love and action are the only mediums through which perfect knowledge could be attained. A sharper reaction to the evil of materialistic education came from Sri Aurobindo. He thought that the education given in our schools and universities had been 'bad in kind and in addition, denationalising, degrading and impoverishing to the national mind.' He argued that education should be based on the Indian conception and vision of man, nature and humanity.

Humanitstic education

Our cultural conception of humanity is based on the ancient vision of the universal manifesting in the human race, evolving through life and mind but with a high ultimate spiritual aim. So the goal of education should be to inspire the working of the spirit in the individual. Its central aim is the building of the powers of the human and spirit, it is the formation or the evoking of knowledge, character, culture,—that at least if no more". In the West the schooling system came under attack by the deschoolers and the humanists. The deschoolers condemned the school as a tool of oppression, as a 'manipulative institution'.

The humanists advocated a reorientation of the educational process towards human beings and human concerns rather than towards economy and work. The revolt has been against the institionalisation of education by the State and against the assumption that the only channel of learning is the school. The school began to arrogate as the only repository of all educational wisdom and subserve the intentions of the materialistic society. Liberal studies have been replaced by the sciences and later by technology. Even the study of social sciences has begun to assume the pattern of pure sciences. The system has lost its internal balance.

Carl Rogers, Philip H. Coombs, Weinstein and a host of others pioneered the humanistic revival. They pointed out that teaching and imparting knowledge in the way schools do now make no sense in a fast-changing world. Today the goal of education should be the facilitation of change and learning and not mere imparting of knowledge. The only man who is educated is the man who has learned how to learn and who has learned that all learning proceeds from and ends with man.

Humanistic education begins with the assumption that 'teaching is first and foremost a relationship between teacher and student which includes human behavior, human meanings and human understandings that grow out of uniquely human experiences.' Humanistic education places emphasis on the genuineness and realness of the relationship between the student and the teacher. They come into direct and effective personal contact with each other; they participate in a mutually affective activity of learning and establish a perfectly harmonious relationship between each other. The teacher cares for the learner, prizes his feelings, values his reactions and facilities his learning.

The initiation and success of such learning does not depend on the teacher's teaching skill or qualification or on the material facilities available in the campus but on the attitudinal qualities which exist in the personal relationship between the teacher and the learner. The most depressing feature of the present system is the absence of those attitudinal qualities that harmonise the teacher-learner relationship. No significant learning takes place in an atmosphere of confrontation between the teacher and the learner. The teacher should be able to transform even confrontationist situations and other frustrations into a part of his total experience. For this he should have a well-considered assurance of personal values.

No humanisation or even socialisation comes out of the uneasy and often suspicious relationship between the teacher and the learner. Even the acquisition of information that partially takes place in our schools today is effective only at the physical level whereas true education should transcend the physical and embrace the mental and the spiritual. Bertnard Russell speaks of four characteristics that form the basis of a good character to be acquired through education. They are vitality, courage, sensitiveness and intelligence. These can be instilled in children at the very early stages through a proper care of their emotional and physical needs. Children need knowledge but it should be imparted through love and care. The instincts and reflexes of a child are developed into diverse habits and reactions by the influence of the environment.

A good system of childhood education can define these early habits and reactions and direct them towards humanistic goals. "It is the business of early education", wrote Russell, "to train the instincts so that they may produce a harmonious character, constructive rather than destructive, affectionate rather than sullen, courageous, frank and intelligent", That is, in sort, humanistic education. The educational scene in India today represents the erosion of humanistic values and the define harmony.

The degeneration in humanistic values began with the resurgence of nationalism in the last decade of the nineteenth century. The spirit of nationalism and patriotism was a welcome feature of the Indian ethos as it was an expression of the desire for liberty, self-determination and growth. However, it unwittingly narrowed down our aspirations to the national level. While pleading for a new educational ideology suitable to our national aspirations, Sri Aurobindo, however, warned against the intrusion of a false and narrow patriotism into the field of education. "Mankind and its needs are the same everywhere", wrote Sri

Aurobindo, "and truth and knowledge are one and have no country; education too must be a thing universal and without nationality or borders." Education aims at the confluence of the affective and cognitive skills. 'Affective' refers to feeling or emotional aspects of experience while 'cognitive' refers to the activity of the mind.

Humanistic education lays stress on the confluence of these two elements with an edge for the 'affective' over the 'cognitive'. The ultimate condition is harmony between feeling and thought, emotion an intellect, intuition and intelligence. The great malady of the present system is the divorce between these confluent elements rendering the vast educational efforts in the country meaningless and harmful. The American poet Archibald MacLeish speaks about this predicament thus, "We do not feel our knowledge. Nothing could better illustrate the flaw at the heart of our civilisation...Knowledge without feeling if not knowledge and can lead only to public irresponsibility and indifference, and conceivably to ruin". In achieving the humanistic goals of education, the teachers have a creative role to play. By establishing a personal meaning in their relationship with students, the teacher has to help their self actualisation process. The teacher's role is not to indoctrinate or to dominate the students but to guide them to engage themselves in 'value clarifications' in the light of the knowledge they acquire from several sources.

The humanistic educational efforts are directed towards the decentralising activity of the learner in the direction of establishing reciprocal relationship with others. The teacher is the luminous centre of the creative process of education. He is in the flux of the ever-expanding horizon of learning and responsive to its several vicissitudes. "A most important truth", wrote Tagore, "which we are apt to forget is that a teacher can never truly teach unless he is still learning himself. A lamp can never light another lamp unless it continues to burn its own flame. The teacher who has come to the end of his subject, who has no living traffic with his knowledge, but merely repeats his lessons to his students can only load their minds; he cannot quicken them." In recent times there has been an increased sensitivity to the failures of our education system to live upto the idealistic hopes we entertain for it.

The disciplinary between the behaviour of even educated individuals in their everyday activities and what the have learnt at school is becoming increasingly shocking. As a result, the school system and the teachers have come under bitter attack and most of the ills of society are being attributed to the education system. True, our education system makes provision to impart a variety of knowledge and skills to its recipients. But it fails to produce any intimate personal meaning or awareness relating to social and individual life. In other words, our system has failed either to impart any value awareness at all or to enable us to approximate our life pattern to the value system we receive.

Value-oriented education

The ultimate goal of all education is to help unfold our consciousness through learning, discipline, devotion and value formation. As Piaget says, education should enable the child to move from 'egocentric centering' upon self to a decentring of activity leading to the formation of harmonious and reciprocal human relationship. It is to create persons capable of doing new things in a new way stead of repeating what other generations have done. The great danger today in dopy slogans and readymade trends of thought that intrude into our consciousness and distort it. To resist the onslaught of the virulent ethos that surrounds us, to distinguish what is true from what is specious and to help emanate an aura of harmony and peace in society, men and women have to acquire and sustain a virile value system through education.

The philosophy of value education and the methodology of its practice assume that great importance in a multi-religious society like ours passing through a disturbing phase of social transformation. A stable unchanging society would tend to call for fewer moral decisions from the individual beliefs and mode of life are called into question and the entire gamut of everyday life in flux, taking moral decisions and assuming moral responsibility for actions pose difficulties unless the individual's conduct is moulded by a creed of values.

So the problem of value education is closely linked with the problem of social transformation and personal fulfilment. Value education is not intended to create values in children but to awaken them to the rich tradition of values they have already in their bones and to regulate their intelligence, inclinations and imagination in consonance with those values. A society can survive even if beliefs are various but unless there is a common system of values it cannot cohere. Moreover, proliferation of beliefs in the absence of a unifying cord of common values will lead to total anarchy and societal disintegration. One of the promised programmes in the New Education Policy is the introduction of a value-based system of education in the country. The Policy document refers to the 'progressive erosion of values and the resultant pollution of public life' and makes a platitudinous statement that it is impossible to sustain an organised society without adhering to some norms of social, political and economic behaviour. It hopes that a viable value system would be inculcated through education based on rationality and a scientific and moral approach to life.

However, the National Policy on Education does not outline any viable plan of action or suggest a methodology for education. In fact, the policy mentions only social values like patriotism, secularism, peace and so on and is silent on the more fundamental spiritual and moral values without which social values themselves cannot be sustained. There are two kinds of values a good education system can instil in students. They are basic or spiritual values and social or life values. Basic values are the foundations on which life values are to be built.

Our failure to inculcate values through education has been the result of lopsided attempts to five priority to life values over basic values. The NCERT has formulated a set of 83 essential values that can be inculcated through a well-monitored system of early education. The Sri Sathya Sai Education Trust has adopted these values and reduced them into five basic values-sathya, sadacharn, santi, prema and ahimsa. However, these values may better be restated as truth, beauty, love, righteousness and courage. The endeavour of education should be to instil these fundamental values first and the proceed, as the child's consciousness develops, to others. Value education should begin with the preschool and by the time the child reaches the tenth class, it should be aware of value implications, right conduct and other related value norms. Once the basic values are effectively instilled, no further organised attempt is necessary to instil the life values. What are the practical ways in which value education can be undertaken during the first ten years of a child's educational career?

The most common practice adopted in the Indian schools is to teach 'moral education' for an hour or two a week. This is done with all the paraphernalia of syllabus, textbooks and examinations. This practice should be discouraged because spiritual and moral values cannot be taught with textbooks, blackboard and chalk pieces. Tagore wrote, "I consider moral instruction utter waste of time effort, and I am frightened that good people should be so keen on it. It is as futile as it is disagreeable and I cannot think of anything that does more harm to society". Values constitute an enduring psycho-physical disposition which inhibit instinctive impulses and regulate our desires and inclinations. As such they are not easily amenable to be taught in small doses like history or mathematics.

Value education should take pace as an integral part of general instruction without making it boaringly explicit or tauntingly oppressive to children. There is no curriculum, syllabus or examination for value education. It is based on a hidden curriculum as a part and extension of the normal curriculum and syllabus in other subjects. It is for the teacher to convert each small occasion available during instruction to the inculcation of values by drawing the attention of the students in a suggestive manner to the value content of each topic, incident or idea.

So value education is not different or separate from other teaching activity but a clever adaptation of a part of the normal teaching activity to help students internalise the values involved in what is being taught. This can be done by a resourceful teacher whether he teaches Wordsworth's 'Daffodils' or the fundamentals of physics. Teaching of religion is often mistaken for value education. Our denominational schools used to identify moral education with teaching of the scriptures. Article 28 of the Constitution prohibits religious instruction in educational institutions wholly maintained out of State funds and Section (3) of the same Article stipulates that no person attending an educational institution shall be required to attend religious instruction classes without his consent. Does it mean that children in their early stages of development should be isolated from the influence of religion?

Religious values comprise almost all human values. Religion is insight into reality and its ultimate expression is the service to humanity. Different religions are only different ways in which the truth is expressed and the test of a religion is not a belief but action. We have quarrels about religion because, as Dr. Radhakrishnan says. "We are religious with our spinal cord, not with our whole being". As such there is no harm if religious values are brought to the attention of children without presenting them as dogmas and rigid creeds. Teaching of religion should not degenerate into propaganda or imparting of supervision. In the hands of teachers with no religious or sectarian prejudices, instruction in religion can assume noble strength and can be an effective way of imparting values. What can be more rewarding for a child than learning the principles underlying the teachings of the Buddha or Christ? The best way of imparting value education is to make it a part of the general teaching and co-curricular activities.

However, we have, in our country, curriculum-syllabus-examination based system of education and so it would be unthinkable for most teachers to carry out value instruction without textbooks. Teaching of languages gives plenty of opportunities to emphasise the values of love, compassion, beauty, righteousness, friendship, loyalty and so on. Language textbooks are either good literary works or collections of good literary pieces. There is nothing more wholesome than a good work of literature. There was a time when teachers in primary and middle schools insisted on children learning the prescribed poems by heart. The regional language textbooks always contain a few poems selected from classics and even English textbooks have simple poems of Shakespeare, Milton or Wordsworth noted for their value content.

Today, 'learning by heart' is looked down upon as 'rote-learning' and both teachers and students are averse to it. We fail to recognise that 'learning by heart' has a sobering effect on the mental and emotional attitude of children and that the whole value-personality of the child is affected by it. The methodology of value-based language teaching consisting

1. assimilation of the text by the students,
2. pointing out the specific values involved in each lesson.
3. relating these values to our social and cultural life suggesting suitable examples,
4. relating values to student's cognitive, emotional and intellectual development,
5. suggesting to forsake contra-values.

The application of this methodology depends on the type of textbooks prescribed. Most language textbooks in the country today frighten the students and depress the teachers. So great care should be taken in the preparation of language textbooks. Similarly, teaching of sciences of social sciences can be used to present both basic life values like truth, courage, beauty, honesty, industry, integrity and so on. Science is an attempt to define man's relationship with the universe. It is the mystery of the universe that haunts the scientist. The learning of science should be related to man's perpetual quest for truth and illumination.

Social sciences are man's attempt to define his relationship with society. So the teacher of social sciences should not be merely content with enumerating principles but should delve deep into the inexorable law of social mechanism and its significance and bring out the coherent shape of values that govern social changes. Thus teaching of science should awaken the students to

1. the scientists devotion to truth and his perseverance and sacrifice,
2. the significant of scientific theories and inventions in eradicating superstition and irrational beliefs,
3. the essential unity and sanctity of life, and
4. the insignificance of the ego and the significance of humility before Nature's powers.

The teaching of social sciences should be oriented towards highlighting the following aspects:

1. The basic and life values implied in each social movement, incident, innovation and idea.
2. Relating these values to our cultural traditions and history.
3. Distinguishing social events, ideas, movements and laws from the point of view of their value implications.
4. Pointing out the social disharmony caused by contra-versus.
5. Relating the values to the personality development of the student.

Textbooks in sciences and social sciences cannot be rewritten according to the whim of the value-educators. It is not that we need a different set of textbooks but we need a different kind of interpretation of the contents in the already existing textbooks. If value education is introduced as a supplementary course, suitable textbooks have to be evolve. Such a course may consist of the principles of religion, Gandhism, rationalism, and philosophical ideas of great men. There are several groups, institutions and organisations in the country at present engaged in activities that contribute to value education.

Educational institutions should establish liaison with such organisations and persons so that 'interactive sessions' may be arranged. The funds at present wasted on politically inspired union activities in colleges and chaotic youth festivals and camps may be profitably spent on these. At least a few universities should undertake value education research on some sensitive areas. Such researches may help in identifying the areas that need value education support, in evolving curriculum and syllabus and in formulating an effective methodology of value education. Value instruction becomes meaningful and effective only if the teacher himself assimilates and practices the values he teaches. One of the distortions that menaces our education system today is the presence of teachers who by their living example confuse and distort the value formation of students.

The ideal teacher is one who guides his students to the sources of knowledge and learning that will substantiate or refute their own beliefs and values. The teacher's task is value clarification and this task can be effectively performed only by those who approximate their life styles and activities to the ideals they preach. The parents have a role in preserving and enhancing the values the children assimilate through education. The values taught in the classroom must find their reflection in the attitudes and life styles of parents.

Unless parents play this complementary role, whatever basic value signals children receive from schools would be wasted away and a paradoxical situation of 'what the schools do, the parents undo' will arise. In any value based system of instruction the affective and the cognitive elements must flow integrally together and form a confluent strain. A proper balance between the ingredients of emotion and those of intelligent in our thoughts, desires and actions should be ensured because both knowledge without right emotions and emotions unrestrained by right knowledge are dangerous. In a technological age fraught with possibilities of evil, value education becomes all the more relevant.

Index